Statistics for Economics, Accounting and Business Studies

For Patricia

Statistics for Economics, Accounting and Business Studies

Michael Barrow

Longman
London and New York

Longman Group Limited,
Longman House, Burnt Mill, Harlow,
Essex CM20 2JE, England
and Associated Companies throughout the world.

Published in the United States of America
by Longman Publishing, New York

© Longman Group UK Limited 1988

First published 1988
Fifth impression 1995

British Library Cataloguing in Publication Data
Barrow, Michael
    Statistics for economics, accounting and
    business studies.

    1. Economics — Statistical methods
    I. Title
    519.5′02433   HB137

ISBN 0-582-00359-8

Library of Congress Cataloging in Publication Data
Barrow, Michael
    Statistics for economic, accounting, and
    business studies/Michael Barrow
    000p. cm.

    ISBN 0–582–00359–8
    1. Economics — Statistical methods. 2. Commercial
    statistics.
    I. Title. II. Series.
    HB137.B37 1988
    330 — dc19   87–27959
                        CIP

Set in 10/11 Times
Produced through Longman Malaysia, PA

Contents

Preface

This text was written for what must be a fairly common reason: I found no text which adequately suited the needs of the course I was teaching. No doubt other tutors will say the same about this book, but I hope that it comes closer to their needs than other texts.

The text is aimed directly at students of economics and the closely related disciplines of accountancy and business, and tries to provide examples and problems relevant to those subjects, using real data where possible. This book is at an elementary level and requires no prior knowledge of statistics, nor advanced mathematics. However, it is not a cookbook of statistical recipes: it covers all the relevant concepts so than an understanding of why a particular statistical test should be used is gained. These concepts are introduced naturally in the course of the text as they are required, rather than having a section to themselves. The book can form the basis of a one- or two-term course, depending upon the intensity of the teaching.

As well as explaining statistical concepts and methods, the different schools of thought about statistical methodology are discussed, giving the reader some insight into some of the debates that have taken place in the subject. The book uses the methods of classical statistical analysis, for which some justification is given in Chapter 6, as well as presenting criticism which has been made of these methods.

An increasingly relevant question these days is the degree of integration of computing into teaching material for statistics. Most of the problems in this book are designed to be solved 'by hand', except for some of the questions on regression and time series analysis. There is no doubt, however, that the use of computers to teach statistics can make the subject much more interesting and takes the chore out of lengthy calculation. To this end the text emphasises understanding and use of statistical reasoning as much as, if not more than, calculation. The section on multiple regression, for example, does not give formulae for calculating coefficients, standard errors, etc. but discusses in some detail the interpretation of computer-generated results. Tutors will no doubt wish to introduce computing into their courses and will devise suitable exercises for themselves.

Finally I must thank Mike Sumner for encouragement and for checking the draft of this text. Any errors which remain are my responsibility. Typing of the text was carried out in varying proportions by Patricia Barrow, Liz Hinton, Simon Ogilvie and Teresa Weeks, to whom many thanks are due.

Acknowledgements

We are grateful to the following for permission to reproduce copyright material:

Biometrika Trustees for table A3, A4 & A5 from tables 8 and 12 in Vol. 1 and table 5 in Vol. 2 of *Biometrika Tables for Statisticians* (Third Edition, 1966); Harper and Row Publishers Inc. for table A2 from *Economic Statistics and Econometrics* by E.J. Kane Copyright © 1968 by Harper & Row Publishers Inc.; The Controller of Her Majesty's Stationery Office for tables 2.1, 2.4 & 2.8 (adapted) (*Digest of U.K. Energy Statistics* 1985), 2.11 (*Housing and Construction Statistics* 1975–85), 2.17 (*Annual Abstract of Statistics* 1986), 8.4 (*Key Data* 1986), 9.1 (*Transport Statistics GB* 1975–85), 9.9 (*Economic Trends* 1986), 10.1 (*Monthly Digest of Statistics* 1983, 1985); Institute of Mathematical Statistics for table A6 (*Annals of Statistics* Vols. 9 and 20, 1939, 1949).

Introduction

Statistics is a subject which can be (and is) applied to every aspect of our lives. A glance at the annual *Guide to Official Statistics*, for example, published by the UK Central Statistical Office gives some idea of the range of material available. Thus, under the letter 'S' one finds entries for such disparate subjects as salaries, schools, semolina(!), shipbuilding, short-time working, spoons, and social surveys. It seems clear that, whatever subject you wish to consider, there are data available to illuminate your study. However, it is a sad fact that many people do not understand the use of statistics, do not know how to draw proper inferences (conclusions) from them, or misrepresent them.

The subject may usefully be divided into two parts, descriptive statistics (Chs 1 and 2) and inferential statistics (Chs 5 – 10), which are based upon the theory of probability (Chs 3 and 4). Descriptive statistics are used to summarise information which would otherwise be too complex to take in, by use of such means as averages and graphs. The aim of this branch of statistics is to summarise the data in a way which does not distort the meaning that is contained within.

The subject of inferential statistics studies the relationship between a population (in the statistical sense) and a sample drawn from that population; in particular, the inferences which can be legitimately drawn about the population from the sample data. For example, the population might consist of all cars sold in the UK in the last decade, and it might be desired to know what proportion of them had been involved in an accident. It would be too expensive to collect information on all these cars, but some idea of the answer could be obtained from a sample drawn from the population. Data from the sample (e.g. the proportion of cars in the sample involved in an accident) can be used to make an estimate of a population parameter (e.g. the unknown proportion of all cars in the population involved in an accident) or to test particular hypotheses about the population (e.g. whether or not a majority of all cars have been involved in an accident). An important point to realise about this process is that there is still some uncertainty about the result obtained, because the sample may not properly represent the population under study. This can occur simply by chance or because of poor sampling technique. Chapters 5 and 6 (on estimation and hypothesis testing) discuss the issues involved in the chance element of sampling, and Chapter 7 (sampling methods) examines the sampling process to ensure good sample design.

The results of statistical analysis can be used in two ways: one is to aid decision making, the other is to inform one's belief in the truth of a hypothesis. In accountancy or business, statistics are more likely to be used in the first role (should the price of a product be reduced to increase sales and profitability?).

1

Due to the inevitable uncertainty involved in random sampling, it is possible that the wrong decision will be made, on the basis of the evidence available. It is important to be aware of the costs of incorrect decisions, and to interpret statistical evidence in this light. It should be remembered that there are limitations to all statistical analyses, and that the statistics themselves do not make decisions, but are one input into the decision-making process. One should not stop thinking about the problem at hand simply because some statistics are available

In economics statistical evidence is usually used in a different way. Rarely is one piece of statistical work 'decisive'; rather it is added to the body of evidence which researchers use to evaluate the worth of different economic theories. This is why there are so many statistical analyses of particular economic problems, such as the effects of unemployment benefits upon the level of unemployment.

These two purposes, decision making and degree of belief, may be related to different schools of thought in statistics, which approach the subject in slightly different ways. Classical statistics (which is the approach adopted in this book) emphasises the making of decisions and the costs of making incorrect decisions. Bayesian statistics emphasises the degree of belief approach, rejecting the dichotomous decision-based approach. However, the differences between the two approaches can be overemphasised, and in this author's view what is more important is to understand the principles underlying the approach adopted so as to be able to interpret statistical results correctly. The differences between classical and Bayesian approaches are further discussed in Chapter 6.

This raises the important question about the relationship between the role of theory (be it economic, business, or otherwise) and evidence. It is often felt that debates may be settled 'by appeal to the facts', without any prior idea of what facts one is looking for. Unfortunately, it is not possible to look at statistical data in a vacuum in the hope that they will 'tell you something'. It is notoriously easy to read into data facts that are simply not there. For example, random data often seem to have patterns in them, containing some message to be extracted (see Table A1 in the appendix (p.247) if you wish to try this out). It is essential to have some theoretical understanding of the problem in hand in order to successfully evaluate available data. A knowledge of the theory of probability and thus of how random data is generated, will help one to discriminate between meaningless (random) and meaningful data. This point is discussed in more detail throughout the text.

Finally it is worth adding a few words of general advice to the statistical beginner. Although it is important to gain a thorough understanding of the principles underlying statistical methods, one should not lose sight of common sense. Students are often over-impressed by sophisticated techniques, which they then apply inappropriately or unsuccessfully to a problem. A lot can be learned by a few simple techniques (carefully applied), such as drawing graphs, particularly in the preliminary stages of analysis. This can often give a useful overview of (or 'feel' for) the data which it is helpful to keep in mind when employing more sophisiticated techniques later on.

A point that is often ignored, or given low priority, is the quality of the data being used. Very often, complex techniques are applied to data that are of poor quality, with the consequence that results of dubious value are obtained. This is not to say that sophisticated techniques should not be used, but that the researcher's time could sometimes be used more productively checking on, and trying to improve, the quality of the data. This is unglamorous not to say tedious work, but it is essential to good statistical research. In a programme of research into a particular problem, perhaps a third of the time available should be devoted to the collection and checking of the data. There is little which is more annoying than to have to recalculate all the results because of an error discovered at a late stage in the data.

With these warnings in mind, it is to be hoped that by the time you finish this book you will have not only a knowledge of how to apply statistical techniques and why they should be applied, but also an idea of the limitations and pitfalls involved, as well as a notion of the debates which have taken place regarding the proper use of statistical methods.

1   Descriptive statistics

The aim of this branch of statistics is to present information, perhaps to oneself, in as clear, concise and accurate a form as possible. The difficulty in analysing many phenomena, be they economic, social or whatever, is that there is simply too much information available for the mind to assimilate. It may seem curious to suggest that one can have too much information, but there are limits to the processing power of the human brain and it is incapable of interpreting too much data. The task of descriptive statistics is therefore to summarise all of this information into a manageable form, while at the same time trying not to present a distorted picture of the subject matter.

Consider, for example, the problem of presenting information about the heights of all British citizens. This involves about 55 million individual measurements and to present the data in its raw form would not be particularly useful or informative (it would take up about 100,000 pages of this book, for example). It is significant that no one actually has all this information. It would be better if there were less information (data), but information which was still representative of the original data. Note that in doing this some of the information is deliberately discarded. Descriptive statistics might thus be described as the art of contructively throwing away most of the data!

There are many alternative ways in which data can be transformed into more useful forms, and there are few hard and fast rules about how this should be done. Newspapers and magazines often provide innovative (though not always successful) means of presenting data. There are, however, a number of techniques that are tried and tested, and these are the subject of this chapter.

There are essentially two methods of summarising raw data: graphical and numerical. The former relies on the adage that a picture is worth a thousand words (or rather, items of data) and provides a general overview of the data without being too precise. Numerical methods tend to give a less broad view, but are more precise and can therefore be used as input into more advanced techniques of statistical analysis, as explained in later chapters.

Graphical presentation

Frequency tables and distributions

We shall start off with an example relating to marks awarded to a group of students on a statistics course. The marks (out of ten) are presented in Table 1.1.

As it stands, the table is rather indigestible and difficult to interpret. Most of

Table 1.1 Marks of students on a statistics course

7	8	6	5	6	7	4
7	8	7	8	7	8	7
7	7	6	6	6	5	6
5	9	7	9	9	9	8
7	7	8	6	8	6	7
6	5	5	6	6	6	8
6	9	7	8	6	6	5
7	9	8	4	2	6	6

Table 1.2 Frequency table of students' marks

Mark	Frequency
x_i	f_i
2	1
3	0
4	2
5	6
6	17
7	14
8	10
9	6
10	0
	56

the marks seem to lie in the range six to eight out of ten, which gives a rough guide to the general ability of the group, but there are few much lower marks which can be observed if the data are examined closely. It would be preferable to have the data in a more presentable form and this may be done by constructing a *frequency table*, as is done in Table 1.2.

Associated with each mark (labelled x_i) is its frequency (labelled f_i), which is simply the number of times that particular mark occurs. The frequencies have been summed to ensure that all 56 observations have been included. This table is then presented graphically in Fig 1.1, where the different marks are placed on the horizontal axis and the frequencies on the vertical axis.

This is termed a *frequency distribution* or *histogram* (it is also referred to as a bar chart, for obvious reasons). The height of each bar represents the frequency with which that mark occurs. Note that both axes have been labelled and that the graph has been given a title. This may not seem to be important to you now, but it is infuriating to go back to some previous work, find a beautifully prepared graph, and have not the faintest idea of what it represents! Be warned therefore.

The frequency table and distribution give a much clearer presentation of the data than the original table. It is immediately obvious that the lowest mark is two and the highest nine. The majority of marks do lie in the range six to eight, and the average seems to be about seven. Presenting the information in this alternative manner is more helpful to the reader, because the frequency table has reduced 56 pieces of information (the number of marks given in Table 1.1) to 16 (the eight relevant marks and their associated frequencies).

Table 1.3 presents a different set of data, on the annual incomes (measured to the nearest £100) of 80 executives. Some new difficulties arise in constructing the frequency table and histogram.

Again, there is a clear need for the data to be represented in a more informative way. However, if a frequency table were to be constructed along

Figure 1.1 Frequency distribution of students' marks

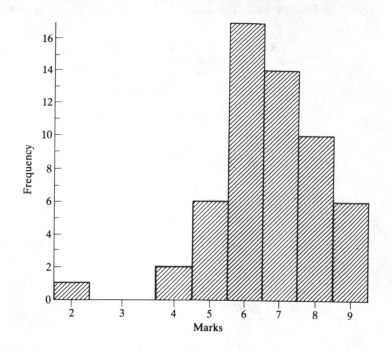

Table 1.3 The incomes of 80 executives (£ p.a.)

20,400	22,600	19,200	22,800	18,200	23,900	18,700	21,400
23,300	20,800	19,300	18,600	17,300	21,600	17,300	20,600
20,000	17,400	17,400	15,500	24,200	22,100	15,900	21,500
18,100	27,700	22,300	16,800	19,100	19,400	17,000	17,000
26,700	22,600	21,200	17,900	20,100	20,000	23,400	19,800
17,200	17,200	21,300	24,400	22,200	17,300	24,400	16,600
17,100	15,400	16,100	21,200	19,100	21,200	22,100	18,800
18,800	18,400	15,600	21,200	25,300	26,900	21,000	19,400
23,300	20,700	20,400	19,800	19,800	17,300	18,300	15,700
23,600	14,800	21,300	18,400	21,900	22,200	27,600	20,600

the lines set out above there would not be much of a gain in clarity. This is because each income only occurs once or, at most, very few times. The frequency table would consist of a long list of the incomes, and next to it a column of frequencies consisting mainly of ones, with the occasional two or three. This is not a great help.

7

A better approach is first to group the incomes into *class intervals*, such as incomes from £14,500 up to £15,500 per annum, and then to count the number of incomes which fall into each class interval. This *grouped data* is presented in Table 1.4.

Table 1.4: Frequency table of the data in Table 1.3

Income class (£ p.a.)	Frequency
14,500–	2
15,500–	5
16,500–	13
17,500–	6
18,500–	10
19,500–	8
20,500–	12
21,500–	8
22,500–	6
23,500–	5
24,500–	1
25,500–	0
26,500–	2
27,500–	2
28,500–	0

The table allocates the observations into *class intervals*. The first class interval, of incomes from £14,500 up to (but not including) £15,500, contains two observations, i.e. the individuals earning £14,800 and £15,400. The term 'frequency' is used for the number of observations in each class interval. The next class interval contains five observations, and so on up to the final class of incomes above £27,500. The major decision to be made in drawing up a frequency table is the width of the class intervals, here taken to be £1,000. The narrower the class interval (and thus the more classes), the greater the resemblance between the summary table and the original data. The wider the class interval, the more the data has been summarised and the easier it is to observe any message contained in the data, though more of the original information has been thrown away. There is therefore a trade-off; there is no unique, correct answer to how many classes there should be. It is a matter of judgement for the statistician to make, and depends upon the purposes towards which the data are being put and upon the total number of observations available. As a rule of thumb, most sets of data can be adequately summarised with ten to twenty classes, as in the example above.

The information in Table 1.4 can be presented in the form of a frequency distribution or histogram just as before, and this is done in Fig. 1.2.

Figure 1.2 Frequency distribution of 80 executives' incomes

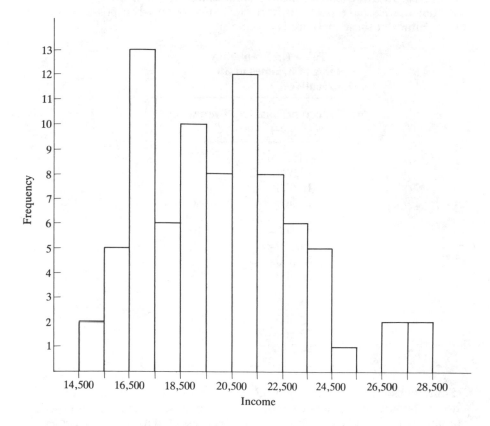

It is much easier and quicker to draw inferences from Fig. 1.2 than it is from the raw data, or even from the frequency table. It is easy to see that the observations range from about £15,000 up to £28,000; most incomes seem to be clustered around the lower end of this range, with only a few individuals earning above £25,000; and the average seems to lie around the £19,000 to £20,000 mark. Note that the finer detail of the data has been lost by using the frequency table and frequency distribution. Presented with the data in this form it is no longer possible to reconstruct the original values. However, it is fairly clear that these losses are worthwhile in terms of the clarity gained.

A slight problem arises in constructing the frequency table if some of the observations lie exactly on the class boundary. For example, there is one individual with an income of exactly £15,500. To which class should this person

9

be assigned? The normal convention is to assign him to the higher class, which is why the classes are defined as between £14,500 and *up to but not including* £15,500. An alternative would be to define the classes as £14,450 to £15,450, i.e. making the class intervals lie on a finer gradation than the observations themselves. In this example, income is measured to the nearest £100, so the class boundaries have been made to lie half-way between possible income levels. Either of these methods is acceptable.

Table 1.5 Frequency table of incomes of 80 executives

Income class (£ p.a.)	Frequency
<15,500	2
15,500–	5
16,500–	13
17,500–	6
18,500–	10
19,500–	8
20,500–	12
21,500–	8
22,500–	6
23,500–	6
25,500–	2
≥27,500	2

Sometimes grouped data might be pesented with unequal class widths and with the boundaries of the first and last class intervals unknown. Suppose, for example that instead of Table 1.4 the data is presented as shown in Table 1.5. Here the last five classes have been combined into three, and the outer boundaries of the first and last class intervals are unknown. How should the frequency distribution be drawn? It is apparent that it should end up looking similar to Fig. 1.2, though it cannot contain as much detail. Between £15,500 and £23,500 the tables are the same. Above £23,500 the class width doubles to £2,000, and there are six observations in the interval £23,500 to £25,500. Since it is no longer known how the six are distributed between the two sub-intervals (£23,500–£24,500 and £24,500–£25,500), the assumption is made that there are three observations in each, and so a bar of this height is drawn in the histogram (see Fig. 1.3). Note that it would be wrong to draw a bar of six units in height. Since the class width has doubled, the height of the bar is halved. Thus it is the *area* of the bar and not its height that is relevant when constructing a histogram. In the first example, the class intervals were all of equal width, so that it was immaterial whether the height or the area was referred to. The same principles applied to the next class interval (£25,500 up to £27,500) lead to a bar of height one unit.

The final class does not have a known upper boundary, so a value has to be assumed. This is a matter of judgement and there is no definitive answer. Fortunately the exact value chosen does not matter too much since it usually only affects a few observations in the tails of the distribution. A value of £29,500 is chosen, which means that the bar has a height of one unit. For the first class interval the value chosen as the lower limit is £13,500, so that the height of the bar is again one unit. It is evident that following these guidelines yields a frequency distribution which closely resembles Fig. 1.2 which was based on more detailed figures.

Figure 1.3 Frequency distribution of 80 executives' incomes

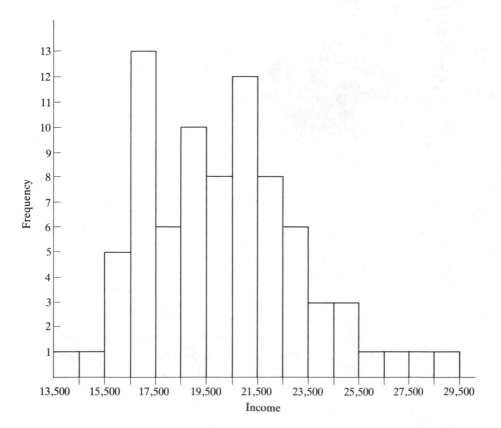

Cumulative frequency distributions

It is sometimes useful to present data in the form of a *cumulative frequency distribution*. The method for doing this is the same whether individual (students' marks) or grouped (executives' incomes) data are used. We shall therefore use the latter example in what follows. The cumulative frequencies show the number of executives with incomes below a particular level. These are obtained by adding successive frequencies together, as is done in Table 1.6. It should be noted that the final figure in the cumulative frequency column is the same as the total frequency. This must always be so, and serves as a useful check on calculations.

Table 1.6 Table of cumulative frequencies

Income class (x)	Frequency (f)	Cumulative frequency (F)
14,500–	2	2
15,500–	5	7
16,500–	13	20
17,500–	6	26
18,500–	10	36
19,500–	8	44
20,500–	12	56
21,500–	8	64
22,500–	6	70
23,500–	5	75
24,500–	1	76
25,500–	0	76
26,500–	2	78
27,500–	2	80

The cumulative frequency (F) column is obtained by summing the successive frequencies. Thus 2 + 5 = 7, 2 + 5 + 13 = 20, and so on.

The cumulative frequency distribution is shown in Fig. 1.4 and is obtained directly from the table of cumulative frequencies. From it, it is possible to read off the number of individuals whose income lies below any desired figure. For example, 44 individuals have incomes below £20,500.

It should be obvious that the frequency distribution and cumulative frequency distribution present exactly the same information, only in different forms, and that either one of them can be derived from the other. Note, for example, that

Figure 1.4 Cumulative frequency distribution of 80 executives' incomes

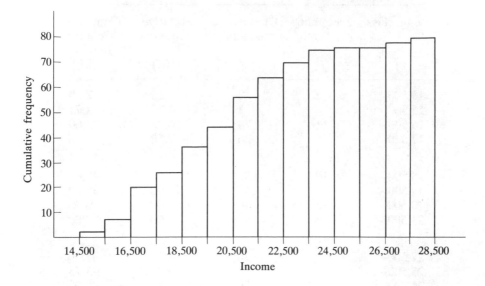

the cumulative frequency distribution is at its steepest where the frequency distribution is at its maximum. The cumulative frequency distribution is sometimes called an *ogive*.

Relative frequency and cumulative relative frequency distributions

A *relative frequency distribution* shows the proportion of observations which lie in each class interval, rather than the actual number. The proportion is obtained by dividing the frequency in each class interval by the sum of the frequencies, then multiply by 100 to obtain a percentage figure. *Cumulative relative frequencies* may then be obtained by summing successive relative frequencies. The results of these calculations are presented in Table 1.7. Thus the first figure in the relative frequency column, 2.50, is 2/80, expressed as a percentage. Table 1.7 shows, for example, that 10% of executives have incomes between £19,500 and £20,500 and that 55% of them have incomes below £20,500 p.a. It is also simple to calculate that 45% (100% − 55%) of executives have incomes of £20,500 and above. Note again that the final figure in the cumulative relative frequency column must be 100: if not, an error has been made somewhere.

Figures showing the relative frequency distribution and the cumulative relative frequency distribution are not shown since they have exactly the same shapes as the frequency distribution and the cumulative frequency distribution, except that the scales on the axes are changed. This should be obvious, since they are illustrating exactly the same underlying data.

Relative frequency distributions are most useful for comparing two or more

13

Table 1.7 Relative and cumulative relative frequencies

Income class	Frequency	Cumulative frequency	Relative frequency	Cumulative relative frequency
(x)	(f)	(F)	$(\%f)$	$(\%F)$
14,500–	2	2	2.50	2.50
15,500–	5	7	6.25	8.75
16,500–	13	20	16.25	25.00
17,500–	6	26	7.50	32.50
18,500–	10	36	12.50	45.00
19,500–	8	44	10.00	55.00
20,500–	12	56	15.00	70.00
21,500–	8	64	10.00	80.00
22,500–	6	70	7.50	87.50
23,500–	5	75	6.25	93.75
24,500–	1	76	1.25	95.00
25,500–	0	76	0.00	95.00
26,500–	2	78	2.50	97.50
27,500–	2	80	2.50	100.00

different distributions, when there might be large differences between the actual frequencies but little between the relative frequencies. For example, a second group of 240 executives might contain 30 with incomes between £18,500 and £19,500, as against only ten in the first group. However, the relative frequencies are the same, at 12.5% which is the more relevant comparison.

Numerical presentation

There are several numerical measures which serve to summarise a distribution. The most common are measures of location and measures of dispersion. As in graphical presentation of data there is a choice of techniques available. However, one is not so free to employ non-standard methods, since the calculations performed are often used in further analyses of the data, which rely upon the calculations having been performed correctly. Furthermore, it would not be so obvious to the reader that non-standard methods have been used, so the wrong conclusions might be drawn.

Measures of location

The mean

Measures of location give an idea of where the data are centred. The best known of these is the mean, something loosely referred to as the average. Since this is not the only definition of the average, the term mean will be used. Strictly it should be referred to as the arithmetic mean since there are other forms of mean, such as the geometric mean. If $x_1, x_2, \ldots x_n$ represent the first, second, etc. of n observations of a variable x, then the mean, $\bar{x}$, of the variable is defined as

$$\bar{x} = \frac{x_1 + x_2 + \ldots + x_n}{n} \qquad [1.1]$$

i.e. the sum of the observations divided by n, the number of observations. A more compact way of writing this is

$$\bar{x} = \frac{\Sigma x_i}{n}$$

(The appendix to this chapter explains the use of Σ notation.)
As a simple example, given the following five values:

5 7 6 8 9

then their mean is

$$x = \frac{5 + 7 + 6 + 8 + 9}{5} = 7$$

For the example of the students' marks the sum of the 56 marks is 374, so the mean mark is

$$x = \frac{\Sigma x_i}{n} = \frac{374}{56} = 6.68 \quad \text{(to two decimal places)}$$

The students's marks are an example of a *discrete* variable, the value 7.2 gives an idea of where the centre of the distribution lies. Notice that none of the children actually achieves the mean mark, nor could they if only integer marks were awarded.

The children's marks are an example of a *discrete* variable, i.e. a variable which can only take on a finite number of values in a particular range, in this case the integers between 0 and 10. It is impossible for a child to get (say) 6.09 questions right. This may be contrasted with a *continuous* variable, such as height, which can take any value (such as 173.06753 cm) within some range. Just because height cannot be measured to this degree of accuracy, and is therefore expressed to the nearest centimetre or so, does not mean that it is a discrete variable.

A similar calculation for the 80 executives yields a mean income of £20,162

15

(using the raw data). The calculation is tedious, but no new principles are involved.

The mean may also be thought of as the balancing point of the distribution, since if a fulcrum were placed under the graph of the frequency distribution at this point it would just balance (in theory at least!).

If the data are presented with frequencies attached to each value of x_i, then the mean is found by use of the formula

$$\bar{x} = \frac{\Sigma f_i x_i}{\Sigma f_i} \tag{1.2}$$

(note that Σf_i is equivalent to n, and f_i is the frequency with which x_i occurs.)

The calculation of the mean of children's marks using this formula is set out in Table 1.8. The total of the frequencies, Σf_i, is found at the foot of the 'f_i' column, and the sum of all the marks, $\Sigma f_i x_i$, is at the foot of the '$f_i x_i$' column. The calculation obviously gives the same answer as using eqn [1.1]

Table 1.8 Calculation of the mean from a frequency table

x_i	f_i	$f_i x_i$
2	1	2
3	0	0
4	2	8
5	6	30
6	17	102
7	14	98
8	10	80
9	6	54
10	0	0
	56	374

$$\bar{x} = \frac{\Sigma f_i x_i}{\Sigma f_i} = \frac{374}{56} = 6.68$$

When data is presented as a frequency table with grouped data, then the mid-point of the class interval is used to represent the individual values of x_i in eqn [1.2] above. To illustrate these points we calculate in Table 1.9 the mean income of the executives, using the data presented in Table 1.4 (ignore column (5) for the moment; it will be used later).

Note that the 'mid-point' column has been divided by 1,000 for ease of calculation. Column (4), labelled $(f_i x_i)$, is the result of multiplying together the values in columns (2) and (3). The sum of this column, 1,610, is $\Sigma f_i x_i$. The sum of the frequencies, Σf_i, is 80, so that the mean is

Table 1.9 Calculation of the mean income of 80 executives from grouped data

Income class (1)	Mid-point (2) (x_i)	Frequency (3) (f_i)	(4) $(f_i x_i)$	(5) $(f_i x_i^2)$
14,500–	15	2	30	450
15,500–	16	5	80	1,280
16,500–	17	13	221	3,757
17,500–	18	6	108	1,944
18,500–	19	10	190	3,610
19,500–	20	8	160	3,200
20,500–	21	12	252	5,292
21,500–	22	8	176	3,872
22,500–	23	6	138	3,174
23,500–	24	5	120	2,880
24,500–	25	1	25	25
25,500–	26	0	0	0
26,500–	27	2	54	1,458
27,500–	28	2	56	1,568
		80	1,610	33,110

$$\bar{x} = \frac{\Sigma f_i x_i}{\Sigma f_i} = \frac{1,610}{80} = 20.125$$

The mean income of the executives is therefore £20,125 (the calculated value is multiplied by 1,000 again at the end to restore the original units of measurement).

The final class width is assumed to be £1,000, giving a mid-point of £28,000. The assumption made will of course affect the value of the mean calculated, so it is important to make a reasonable estimate. A different answer has been found from that using the raw data, and the reason is of course that some of the information contained in the original data has been lost (but remember that even that was already measured to the nearest £100). The difference is unlikely to be very large, however, and can reasonably be ignored. The answer obtained could be below or above the 'true' value, and the error is likely to be smaller the greater the number of class intervals.

Drawbacks of the mean: The mean is not the only or ideal measure of location. It aims to be representative of the data, yet there are circumstances in which it fails in this objective. It can be significantly affected by a few extreme, atypical observations (termed 'outliers'), which pull it away from the more numerous, typical observations. An example might be a very poor country with a very rich

17

king. The mean income in such circumstances would not give a genuine idea of how the mass of the population lived. Another instance where the mean might not be appropriate is measuring the 'typical' family size. The mean family size might turn out to be 4.27 persons, yet it would be difficult to find an example of this 'typical' family!

The geometric mean

The geometric mean is less often used than the arithmetic mean, but is useful when calculating average rates of growth, for example. Consider the data in Table 1.10 for the growth of nominal Gross Domestic Product (GDP) in the UK for 1982–4. What is the average rate of growth for the period?

Table 1.10

Year	1982	1983	1984
Growth rate(%)	9.1	8.6	6.3

Table 1.11

Year	1982	1983	1984
Factor	1.091	1.086	1.063

First, it is useful to transform the data into factors, as shown in Table 1.11. Thus 1982 GDP is higher than 1981 GDP by the factor 1.091, 1983 is higher than 1982 by the factor 1.086, and so on. Multiplying 1982 GDP by 1.086 would yield the 1983 figure. The advantage of this form of presentation is that it is easy to calculate growth over a series of years, simply by multiplying together the factors. Thus from 1981 to 1984, GDP grew by a factor of

$$1.091 \times 1.086 \times 1.063 = 1.259$$

Therefore GDP was 25.9% higher in 1984 than in 1981.

To find the average growth rate over the three-year period, the cube root of 1.259 must be taken. This yields

$$\sqrt[3]{1.259} = 1.080$$

or an average growth rate of 8.0% per annum. This is the *geometric mean* of the figures in Table 1.10. For a period of n years, the geometric mean is the nth root of the product of the factors for those years. A further example illustrates this.

Nominal GDP in the UK was £51,465m. in 1970, £319,354 m. in 1984. What was the average rate of growth of GDP over the period? First one takes the ratio of the figures to obtain the growth rate for the period as a whole:

$$\frac{319{,}354}{51{,}465} = 6.205$$

Thus the growth rate was 620.5% for the period of 14 years. The average annual growth rate for the period is found by taking the 14th root of 6.205 (a scientific calculator or logarithms may be used for this task). This gives

$$\sqrt[14]{6.205} = 1.139$$

which indicates an annual average growth rate of 13.9%.

Geometric and arithmetic means compared

The geometric mean is appropriately applied when the observations form part of a multiplicative process, as with the growth rate examples above. In a situation concerning growth, such as interest rates (where capital grows over time), the geometric mean should be used in preference to the arithmetic mean. Using the arithmetic mean will lead to similar answers over short time periods, but to larger errors as the time period expands. For example, the arithmetic mean of the figures in Table 1.10 is 8.0, the same as the geometric mean applied to Table 1.11 (the figures do differ in the second place of decimals). For the period 1970–84, the method of the arithmetic mean gives an average growth rate of 14.1%, higher than the correct figure of 13.9%.

Alternative measures of location

The median: A measure of location which suffers less from the problems mentioned above is the median. Referring back to the by now familiar executives, the median income is defined as the income of the individual in the 'middle' of the distribution. That is, if the executives were lined up in order of income, the poorest at the front, the richest at the back, then the person half-way along the income distribution would have the median income. As there is an even number of individuals, we have to interpolate between the incomes of the 40th and 41st individuals. We shall refer to the 40.5th person for convenience, even though it is not a very elegant expression. Fortunately, the 40th and 41st individuals both have an income of £20,000, so this is the median (if the values had been different the mean of them would have been calculated).

The major advantage of the median is that it is little affected by outliers. Suppose that one of the executives had an income of £250,000 instead of £20,600. The mean would now be £23,030, a significant change, whereas the median would not alter at all. The median would only change if the identity of the person with the median income changed; for example if the observation £19,200 (below the original median) were replaced by £250,000. Even so, the median would only change to £20,050 (the mean of £20,000 and £20,100, the incomes of the new 40th and 41st individuals).

If the median has to be calculated from grouped data, it is more difficult to know where the middle observation is located. It is simple enough to work out the class interval into which the middle observation falls, most easily done by

19

using the table of cumulative, or cumulative relative, frequencies (Tables 1.6 and 1.7). This can be seen to be the interval £19,500–£20,500. There are 36 individuals in the intervals preceding, and eight in this one, so the median income lies between the incomes of the fourth and fifth individuals in the interval (i.e. between the 40th and 41st individuals). To get a more precise estimate an assumption has to be made about how the executives are distributed through the interval. In the absence of further information it is best to assume that they are evenly spread, so the median income lies half-way through the interval, i.e. at £20,000. It is fortuitous that exactly the same answer is obtained as with the original data; this will not always be the case.

Calculating the median within a class interval can become quite tricky, so the following formula may be used

$$\text{median} = x_L + (x_U - x_L) \left[\frac{N/2 - F}{f} \right]$$

where

x_L = lower limit of class interval (£19,500 in this case)
x_U = upper limit of class interval (£20,500)
N = total frequency (80)
F = cumulative frequency up to class interval (36)
f = frequency within class interval (8)

The mode: The final measure of location is the mode. This is defined as the observation which occurs with the greatest frequency. Some care is needed when calculating the mode since it is quite sensitive to how the data are grouped. The raw data on executive salaries reveals that the figures £17,300 and £21,200 both occur four times, so the distribution is bi-modal; that is, if the frequency distribution were drawn, two peaks would be observed.

Once the data are grouped, however, only the class interval with the highest frequency can be found. From Table 1.2 this can be seen to be the interval £16,500 to £17,500 with 13 observations. This therefore is the modal group. A different grouping of the data, however, might give a different result. The calculation is not shown here, but if the data are grouped into classes with width £1,500, beginning at £14,250, then the modal group becomes £20,250–£21,750, a substantial shift. Care is therefore needed, and one should look out for two intervals with similar frequencies, where a slight regrouping might shift the mode. One should also look out for unequal class widths, since combining classes is bound to increase the associated frequency. One could shift the mode almost anywhere by combining sufficient class intervals! The best advice in this case is to calculate the frequencies as if the class widths were equal and then choose the modal group, as the following simple example demonstrates.

Class interval	Frequency
1–	7
10–	8
30–	4

The modal group is 1–10 since the frequency of 8 is associated with a class interval of double the width, so the 'real' frequency is only 4 (this 'real' frequency is referred to as the *frequency density*).

It is possible to find the modal value within a class interval but, given all the problems mentioned above, it is probably better to leave it as a modal group. There is the danger of presenting results with a spurious air of accuracy, so that presenting only the modal group again has advantages.

Choice of mean, median or mode

None of the measures of the location is uniquely best for all purposes. Choose the one appropriate for the task in hand. For example, if one wished to know how much income could potentially be given to each individual if incomes were redistributed, then the mean is appropriate (assuming there were no disincentive effects of redistributive taxation). If one wanted to know what the average lifestyle of executives was like, then the median or mode would be better, especially if there were outlying values.

One great advantage of the mean over the others is that it has a precise statistical formula and therefore its statistical properties can be investigated (this will be done in later chapters). This makes it very suitable for use in more advanced statistical analysis and it is therefore the most commonly used of all the measures of location.

Under certain circumstances the relationship between the mean, median and mode takes a particular form. Consider the frequency distribution as shown in Fig. 1.5, which is drawn as a smooth, continuous distribution for

Figure 1.5 The mean, median and mode for a skewed frequency distribution

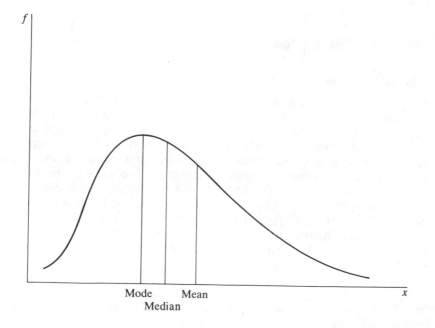

Figure 1.6 Two frequency distributions with the same mean

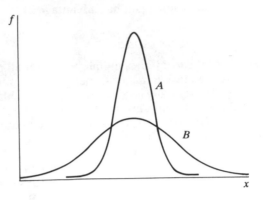

convenience. It is unimodal and skewed to the right, i.e. the longer tail is to the right.

In this case the mean is always greater than the median which is always greater than the mode. If the distribution were skewed to the left, then the order would obviously be reversed. A symmetric distribution (i.e. skewed neither to right nor left) would have the mean, median and mode at the same position.

Measures of dispersion

The variance and standard deviation

So far, distributions have been distinguished only on the basis of their means. However, two distributions with the same mean could still be very different, as shown in Fig. 1.6. Distribution B is clearly much more spread out than distribution A. If these represented the income distributions of two countries, then country B would have relatively more rich and poor people, even though both countries have the same average income. It would be useful to have a numerical measure which summarised the different degrees of dispersion of the distributions. It is most convenient, from a mathematical point of view, to measure the degree of dispersion around the mean, $\bar{x}$, of the distribution. One might consider, therefore, as a measure of dispersion, the mean deviation around the mean. The greater this value, the more spread out would be the distribution. Define

$$d_i = x_i - \bar{x}$$

as the deviation of observation x_i from the mean. The mean deviation from the mean would then be the mean of the d_i values, i.e.

$$\frac{\Sigma d_i}{n}$$

Substituting $d_i = x_i - \bar{x}$ gives

$$\frac{\Sigma(x_i - \bar{x})}{n}$$

The problem with this measure is that it is equal to zero whatever the shape of the distribution, so it is unable to discriminate between them. Simple manipulation of the formula shows this:

$$\frac{\Sigma(x_i - \bar{x})}{n} = \frac{\Sigma x_i - n\bar{x}}{n}$$

$$= \bar{x} - \bar{x} = 0$$

The reason for this is that some of the deviations are positive, some negative, and they cancel each other out (the definition of the mean ensures this). To remedy this problem the deviations can be squared (thus making them all positive) before being summed. One final alteration: this sum is divided by $n - 1$ rather than n. This measure is called the *variance* and is denoted by the symbol s^2.

$$s^2 = \frac{\Sigma(x_i - \bar{x})^2}{n - 1} \qquad [1.3]$$

The reason for using $n - 1$ rather than n as the divisor is that a sample of data (i.e. the 80 executives) is being used to obtain estimates of the mean and variance of the incomes of all executives. It turns out that dividing through by $n - 1$ gives a better estimate of the variance than using n. Exactly what is meant by a better estimate is explained in later chapters. If one had all the observations rather than just a sample of the data, then it would be correct to divide through by n rather than $n - 1$.

With grouped data, the variance is calculated by the formula

$$s^2 = \frac{\Sigma f_i(x_i - \bar{x})^2}{n - 1} \qquad [1.4]$$

For purposes of calculation it is easier to use the equivalent formula

$$s^2 = \frac{\Sigma f_i x_i^2 - n\bar{x}^2}{n - 1} \qquad [1.5]$$

To illustrate these points the variance of the executives' incomes will be calculated, using the data as set out in Table 1.9. Column (5) there, headed $f_i x_i^2$, is the result of multiplying columns (2) and (4) together and its sum is $\Sigma f_i x_i^2$. This provides all the information necessary to calculate the variance:

$$\Sigma f_i x_i = 1,610 \qquad \Sigma f_i x_i^2 = 33,110 \qquad \bar{x} = 20.125 \qquad n = 80$$

23

Substituting these values into the formula gives

$$s^2 = \frac{33{,}110 - 80 \times 20.125^2}{79} = 8.972$$

as the variance.

The question arises as to what units the variance is measured in. Since the deviations were squared in the course of the calculation, the answer must be that these are now in squared £s! This is a somewhat difficult concept to grapple with, so we shall return to ordinary £s by taking the square root of the variance, to obtain the *standard deviation*, denoted by s for obvious reasons. Thus

$$s = \sqrt{8.972}$$
$$= 2.995$$

The standard deviation is therefore £2,995. Note that the answer is multiplied by 1,000 to get the standard deviation of the original data. To get the variance of the original data one has to multiply by $1{,}000^2$, i.e. by 1,000,000. The variance of the original data is therefore 8,972,000 which is the square of 2,995.

If the raw data had been used to calculate the standard deviation, a value of £2,967 would have been obtained, which again demonstrates the effect of losing some of the original information. Unlike the case of the mean, calculating the standard deviation from grouped data will tend to overestimate the true value, as in this case, because it is assumed that all the values in a class interval lie at the mid-point of the interval when in fact they are likely to lie closer to the class boundary nearest the mean. In general the size of this error does not make it worthwhile trying to correct it.

We now have two useful measures, or statistics, with which to summarise a distribution and to compare different distributions, the mean and the standard deviation (or variance). Suppose a comparison is to be made between the remuneration of UK and US executives, using the following data (measured in £000)

$$\bar{x}_{UK} = 20.125 \qquad s_{UK} = 2.995$$
$$\bar{x}_{US} = 40.928 \qquad s_{US} = 7.490$$

US salaries are higher on average than those for the UK, and are also more dispersed. However, one might argue that US salaries are only more dispersed because the mean is higher and that, for example, the ratio of top to bottom salaries is about 2:1 in both countries, so that the degree of dispersion is approximately the same in both countries. One way of taking account of this argument is to measure the standard deviation relative to the mean. This gives the *coefficient of variation* and is denoted cv

$$cv = \frac{s}{\bar{x}}$$

Calculating this for each country yields the following results

$$cv_{US} = \frac{7.490}{40.928} = 0.183 \qquad cv_{UK} = \frac{2.995}{20.125} = 0.149$$

So the coefficient of variation for the US, at 18.3%, is still greater than that for the UK, 14.9%. This reinforces the view that US salaries are in fact more spread out. One should beware of drawing firm conclusions about the degree of inequality in the two countries, however. There are many ways of defining and measuring inequality, of which the standard deviation and cv are just two. Chapter 2 will look at this question in more detail.

The standard deviation might be further used to compare individual observations from two distributions in the following manner. Suppose there are two groups of pupils who have taken two separate exams; call them groups A and B. There is one prize to award to the best pupil overall. Should it be awarded to the best pupil of group A or of group B? It would be unfair simply to take the student with the highest mark, since one exam might have been more difficult than the other, the marking itself may have been more severe, or different marking scales may have been used. One solution would be to give the prize to the pupil who has done best relative to his own group. This could be measured by the number of standard deviations each pupil's mark is above or below the mean of his group. Only the marks of the best pupils in each group would have to be calculated, so the calculation is fairly straightforward. Suppose the data is as follows

Group A	Group B
$\bar{x}_A = 55$	$\bar{x}_B = 35$
$s_A = 20$	$s_B = 15$
Best mark $= 85$	Best mark $= 55$

The calculation is

Group A	Group B
$\dfrac{85 - 55}{20} = 1.50$	$\dfrac{55 - 35}{15} = 1.33$

Thus the prize is awarded to the pupil from group A, since to obtain a score of 1.50 standard deviations above the mean is considered to be a greater achievement than the 1.33 achieved by the best in group B. The implicit assumption behind this method is that the pupils in the two groups are in general of similar ability. If this is not considered to be the case, then the method is invalid.

The values calculated above are called *z-scores* and they play an important role in statistics. They will be encountered again in subsequent chapters. The *z*-score is therefore defined as

$$z = \frac{x_i - \bar{x}}{s}$$

(where x_i is an individual observation on the variable x).

Other measures of dispersion

The variance is the most widely used measure of dispersion because, like the mean, its statistical properties can be established. There are other measures, however, which also have their uses. The *range* is simply the difference between the largest and the smallest observations. It is easy to calculate once the data have been ranked, but it has little else in its favour. It makes use of only a small amount of the information available in the sample and is obviously very sensitive to outlying values. For the data on executive salaries the range is 27,700 = 14,800 = 12,900.

Quartiles are calculated in a similar manner to the median. The first quartile is the observation that occurs one-quarter of the way through the distribution, the third quartile occurs three-quarters of the way through, and the second quartile is the median itself. The first quartile is therefore 17,525 (one-quarter of the way between the 20th and 21st observations), and the third is 22,100 (three-quarters of the way between the 59th and 60th observations).

The *interquartile range* is the third quartile minus the first, i.e. 4,575 in the example. The *semi-interquartile range* is sometimes encountered and is defined as half the interquartile range. These are better measures of dispersion than the range since they ignore extreme values.

The idea behind quartiles can be generalised to *quintiles* (dividing the distribution into five equal parts), *deciles* (ten) and even *percentiles* (one hundred). Obviously a fairly large number of observations is required for the last to make much sense. Deciles are often encountered in discussing the distribution of income, such as in the statement that the top decile of the income distribution earns one-quarter of all the national income in the UK.

The major advantage of these alternative measures is that they are quick to calculate, at least once the data have been ranked. Nowadays, most statistical analysis is done by computer so that the argument that a particular measure is easy to calculate is no longer a very powerful one. However, they might be useful in preliminary analysis of a subject, in order to try to obtain a quick overview of the data.

A note on rounding

It is important to round answers to the appropriate degree, though it is not so easy to define what is appropriate. The arguments in favour of rounding are that it makes the answer clearer and it avoids giving a false impression of accuracy. Clearly it would be wrong to present the mean executive salary to two decimal places when the original data are only accurate to the nearest £100. If it were being presented in a report, it might be appropriate to round it to £20,100 since this would be clearer and possibly easier to remember. However, if the answer were being input into further analysis, it should *never* be rounded, since this could seriously affect subsequent calculations. One should never round intermediate calculations since rounding errors can accumulate: what is a small degree of rounding at an intermediate stage of calculation can become a large rounding error at the end.

Using secondary data sources

Most statistical work involves the use of secondary data, i.e. data collected and published by public or private sector agencies. This means that the researcher does not have to worry about carrying out a survey to obtain the information (see Chapter 7). Using published data would seem to be straightforward, but there are a number of problems that can arise and affect the results of the research.

The first point is to check that the data being collected are appropriate for the task in hand. It is often possible to measure a variable in several different ways, so a choice has to be made. For example, if measuring a firm's labour costs, should wage rates or earnings be used? Earnings are affected by the number of hours worked, bonus payments, etc. If extra hours of work produce extra output, then earnings might be a poor measure of labour costs per unit output, which determine a firm's competitiveness. The wage rate (per hour or per standard working week) would be better, but even the weekly wage needs to be used with caution if a long data series is used, since the length of the working week has fallen over time.

It is therefore important to check the definitions of the variables, which might require consulting a handbook or statistical guide. The UK National Accounts, for example, are fully described in *United Kingdom National Accounts Statistics, Sources and Methods* (HMSO). Another cause of difficulty is that the definition or measurement of a variable might change over time. The method of measuring UK unemployment has been revised 18 times since 1979, which makes comparison over time very difficult. Sometimes, it is possible to compensate for these changes, particularly if both methods of measurement are used for some time periods. It is impossible to give general advice on how this might be done since it depends on particular circumstances, but it usually involves painstaking and detailed analysis of the figures. Although this sort of work can be tedious, it is important as a precursor to proper statistical enquiry.

As well as definitions changing, figures may be revised as better information becomes available. As an example, the UK balance of payments (current balance) for 1970 is presented below, as published in successive years.

United Kingdom current balance, 1970 (£m.), as reported in:

1971	1972	1973	1974	1975	1976	1977	1978	...	1986
579	681	692	707	735	733	695	731	...	795

The difference between the largest and smallest figures is of the order of 37%. These figures should obviously, therefore, be used with caution. The balance of payments is particularly difficult to measure because it is the small difference between two large numbers, exports and imports. A 5% increase in measured exports and a 5% decrease in measured imports could thus change the measured balance of payments by 100% or more. Measuring imports is relatively straightforward, since they all have to be declared for customs purposes, but information regarding exports arrives more slowly. Government statisticians try to estimate the level of exports, therefore, but this is evidently a difficult task. The lesson from this is that it is best always to use the latest published information. To find the balance of payments in 1970, first consult 1987 publications, not those for 1970 or 1971.

On a more practical level, another piece of advice is always to take careful note of the data being collected, including the source. There is a very high probability that you will need to consult the source material again, and it is unlikely that you will remember the exact source (including volume and page numbers) in the distant future. The more comprehensive the notes the better. As well as the source of the data, the variable definitions should be noted. Is investment measured gross or net of depreciation, are profits before or after dividends, is expenditure at current or constant prices (see Chapter 2), is the data seasonally adjusted or not (see Chapter 10), etc? Questions such as these need to be considered when collecting the data. For these reasons it is usually better to take a photocopy of the data (beware of the copyright law, however). This will also rule out transcription errors.

Conclusion

It should now be clear that there are few hard and fast rules in descriptive statistics: the judgement of the statistician plays an important part. There is rarely a unique, right answer (though there are always plenty of wrong ones!) so it is important to be clear and present results honestly (thus countering Disraeli's dictum that there are three types of lies – lies, damned lies and statistics). It is also important to be able to interpret correctly the results obtained by other researchers and to be aware of any shortcomings that may be present. A swift perusal of the newspapers should provide you with some good practice at this (see also question 1.7). The skills necessary are best acquired by practice.

It is also important to keep in mind the purpose of any statistical analysis. It is not enough to work mechanically, simply substituting numbers into formulae and writing down the answers. The danger here is that if a mistake is made it will probably go unnoticed, whereas a moment's thought would show that the answer simply cannot be right (for example if a negative variance is calculated). It is often useful to try to guess the answer in advance, even if it is only a very rough guess. If the calculated answer turns out to be very different from that anticipated, it is quite possible that an error has been made, so the calculation should be checked. In the long run this should save time and effort, and help to eliminate many errors.

Problems

1.1 Use the data below to:

(a) Construct tables of frequencies, relative frequencies, cumulative frequencies and cumulative relative frequencies, using 20 as the lower boundary of the first class interval and a class width of 10.
(b) Draw a histogram and cumulative frequency distribution of the data.
(c) Calculate the mean and variance of the data, using the table you have constructed.
(d) What percentage of the observations lie: (i) above 49; (ii) more than one standard deviation above the mean?

22 35 46 43 53 64 24 33 39 53 61 29 36 38 43 47 72 69 58 53 51 42 48 46 40 49 41 37 39 33 26 22 21

1.2 The following data give the number of deaths in Britain in each age group in different years. Draw a histogram of the data and calculate the average age at death using any measure of the average that you think appropriate. Discuss the merits of each type of average in this case. Has the average changed very much over time? Does this encourage you about your life expectancy?

Age group:	<1	1–4	5–9	10–14	15–19	20–24	25–34
Deaths (1900–02):	87,242	37,834	8,429	4,696	7,047	8,766	19,154
(1980–2):	4,829	774	527	652	1,999	1,943	3,736

Age group:	35–44	45–54	55–64	65–74	75–84	>85
Deaths (1900–02):	24,739	30,488	37,610	39,765	28,320	6,563
(1980–2):	6,568	19,728	54,159	105,155	98,488	31,936

1.3 The following data give the duration of unemployment by age group for all males unemployed in July 1986

Age	Duration of unemployment (weeks)						Total
	≤2	2–8	8–26	26–52	52–104	>104	(000s)
			percentage figures				
16–19	9.2	18.0	29.8	24.0	14.3	4.7	273.4
20–24	10.2	14.0	20.7	18.3	15.8	21.0	442.5
25–34	5.0	9.8	18.8	17.2	16.9	32.3	531.4
35–49	4.0	8.2	16.6	15.1	15.9	40.3	521.2
50–59	3.0	5.9	14.4	15.6	16.3	44.9	388.1
≥60	6.7	11.8	29.7	30.7	10.0	11.4	74.8

Source: *Social Trends, 1987*, Table 4.25

(a) For the age groups 16–19, 25–34 and over 60, draw histograms showing the proportion unemployed in each duration category.
(b) Calculate the average duration of unemployment for each of these three categories.
(c) What appear to be the main differences between age groups in the experience of unemployment? Can you think of plausible reasons to account for these differences?
(d) Draw a histogram of the number of males in each age group unemployed for over one year.

1.4 A sample of ten students' marks on a test gave a mean of 64 and a standard deviation of 10. A second set of 15 marks gave a mean of 60 and a standard deviation of 15. If all 25 marks were amalgamated, what would be the mean and standard deviation?

1.5 Twelve pupils' scores in an exam were:

74 64 34 86 45 44 76 77 55 62 36 49

Another 15 pupils' scores on a different exam were:

55 33 43 49 48 59 22 37 51 29 42 50 43 51 31

If there are three prizes to award, who should they be given to, and why?

1.6 The incomes of 50 people in the USA were found to have a mean of $14,000 and a variance of 9,000,000. If the incomes were translated into £s at an exchange rate of £1 = $1.40, what would be the mean and variance of the data?

1.7 Criticise the following statistical reasoning: the average price of a dwelling in the fourth quarter of 1978 was £18,050. The average mortgage advance was £10,920. So purchasers had to find £7,130, that is, about 40% of the purchase price. On any basis that is an enormous outlay which young couples, in particular, who were buying a house for the first time would find incredibly difficult, if not impossible, to raise.

1.8 Rates of interest on bank deposit accounts for the years 1981 to 1984 were as follows

1981	1982	1983	1984
15.5%	10%	9%	9%

Assuming £5,000 invested at the beginning of 1981, what sum would this yield at the end of 1984, assuming all interest were reinvested? What is the average rate of interest for the period?

Appendix: Sigma notation

The Greek letter Σ (capital sigma) simply means 'add up', and is a shorthand way of writing what would otherwise be long algebraic expressions. Given the following observations on a variable x

x_1	x_2	x_3	x_4	x_5
3	5	6	4	8

then

$$\sum_{i=1}^{5} x_i = x_1 + x_2 + x_3 + x_4 + x_5$$
$$= 3 + 5 + 6 + 4 + 8$$
$$= 26$$

To expand the sigma expression, the subscript i is replaced by successive values, beginning with the value given below the sigma sign and ending with the one above it. Thus

$$\sum_{i=2}^{4} x_i = x_2 + x_3 + x_4$$
$$= 5 + 6 + 4$$
$$= 15$$

When it is clear what range of values i takes, the formula can be simplified to

$\sum\limits_{i} x_i$ or

$\sum x_i$ (this is the form used in this chapter).

Both of these expressions mean the sum of all the x_i values. When it is obvious which variable is being summed, then the i subscript may be dropped as well, leaving just $\sum x$.

When frequencies are associated with each of the observations, as in the data below,

i	1	2	3	4	5
x_i	3	5	6	4	8
f_i	2	2	4	3	1

then we may define

$$\begin{aligned}
\sum f_i x_i &= f_1 x_1 + f_2 x_2 + f_3 x_3 + f_4 x_4 + f_5 x_5 \\
&= 2 \times 3 + 2 \times 5 + 4 \times 6 + 3 \times 4 + 1 \times 8 \\
&= 60
\end{aligned}$$

Also

$$\sum f_i = 2 + 2 + 4 + 3 + 1 = 12$$

Thus the sum of all 12 observations is 60 and the mean is

$$\frac{\sum f_i x_i}{\sum f_i} = \frac{60}{12} = 5$$

Further examples of sigma notation are set out below, and evaluated using the data above.

$$\begin{aligned}
\sum x_i^2 &= x_1^2 + x_2^2 + x_3^2 + x_4^2 + x_5^2 = 150 \\
(\sum x_i)^2 &= (x_1 + x_2 + x_3 + x_4 + x_5)^2 = 676 \\
\sum k x_i &= k x_1 + k x_2 + k x_3 + k x_4 + k x_5 = k \sum x_i
\end{aligned}$$

where k is any constant. For $k = 2$, $\sum k x_i = 52$

$$\begin{aligned}
\sum (x_i - k) &= (x_1 - k) + \ldots + (x_5 - k) \\
&= \sum x_i - nk \\
&= 26 - 10 = 16 \\
\sum f_i x_i^2 &= f_1 x_1^2 + f_2 x_2^2 + f_3 x_3^2 + f_4 x_4^2 + f_5 x_5^2 \\
&= 324 \\
\sum f_i (x_i - k) &= f_1 (x_1 - k) + \ldots + f_5 (x_5 - k) \\
&= f_1 x_1 + \ldots + f_5 x_5 - k f_1 - \ldots - k f_5 \\
&= \sum f_i x_i - k \sum f_i \\
&- 60 - 2 \times 12 \\
&= 36
\end{aligned}$$

Sigma notation is used extensively in this book so it is worth spending some time mastering it. The following problems are thus worth tackling.

1. For the following data on the variable x,

$$4, \ 6, \ 3, \ 2, \ 5$$

evaluate Σx_i, Σx_i^2, $(\Sigma x_i)^2$, $\Sigma(x_i - 3)$, $\Sigma x_i - 3$.

2. Given the frequencies f_i associated with the above x values,

$$5, \ 3, \ 3, \ 8, \ 5$$

evaluate $\Sigma f_i x_i$, $\Sigma f_i x_i^2$, $\Sigma f_i(x_i - 3)$, $\Sigma f_i x_i - 3$.

3. Show, by manipulation of the formulae,

$$\frac{\Sigma f_i(x_i - k)}{\Sigma f_i} = \frac{\Sigma f_i x_i}{\Sigma f_i} - k$$

Answers

1. 20, 90, 400, 5, 17.
2. 88, 372, 16, 85.
3. $\dfrac{\Sigma f(x-k)}{\Sigma f} = \dfrac{\Sigma fx - k\Sigma f}{\Sigma f}$

$$= \frac{\Sigma fx}{\Sigma f} - \frac{k\Sigma f}{\Sigma f} = \frac{\Sigma fx}{\Sigma f} - k$$

2   Index numbers

Introduction

On 17 January 1987, *The Times* reported that the retail price index for December was 393.0 (January 1974=100). This was 0.3 per cent above the November figure, which was 391.7. The retail price index (RPI) referred to is an example of an *index number*, which summarises a whole mass of information about the prices of different goods and services. An index number is thus similar in purpose to other summary statistics such as the mean, and shares their advantages and disadvantages; it provides a useful overview of the data but misses out the finer detail.

Index numbers are most commonly used for following trends in data over time, such as the RPI measuring the price level or the index of industrial production (IIP) measuring the output of industry. The RPI also allows calculation of the rate of inflation, which is simply the rate of change of the price index; and from the IIP it is easy to measure the rate of growth of output. Index numbers are also used with cross-section data, for example an index of regional house prices would summarise information about the different levels of house prices in different regions of the country at a particular point in time. There are many other examples of index numbers in use, common ones being the *Financial Times* All Share index, the trade weighted exchange rate index, and the index of the value of retail sales.

This chapter will explain how index numbers are constructed from original data and the problems that arise in doing this. There is also a brief discussion of the RPI to illustrate some of these problems and to show how they are resolved in practice. Finally, a different set of index numbers is examined, which are used to measure inequality; such as inequality in the distribution of income, or in the market shares held by different firms competing in a market.

A simple index number

Consider the data in Table 2.1, relating to the price of coal bought by industry in the years 1980–84 (taken from the *Digest of UK Energy Statistics, 1985*). We assume that the product itself has not changed from year to year, so that the price index to be constructed can be said to be a faithful measure of the price of coal. This means, for example, that the quality of coal has not changed during the period.

Table 2.1 The price of coal to industry

	1980	1981	1982	1983	1984
Price (£/tonne)	35.0	39.9	47.9	49.6	49.6

Source: Adapted from *Digest of UK Energy Statistics, 1985*

Table 2.2. The price index for coal: 1980=100

1980: $\dfrac{35.0}{35.0} \times 100 = 100.0$

1981: $\dfrac{39.9}{35.0} \times 100 = 114.0$

1982: $\dfrac{47.9}{35.0} \times 100 = 136.9$

1983: $\dfrac{49.6}{35.0} \times 100 = 141.7$

1984: $\dfrac{49.6}{35.0} \times 100 = 141.7$

To construct a price index from this data we choose one year as the *reference year* (1980 is chosen) and set the price in that year at 100. The prices in the other years are then measured relative to the reference year figure of 100. The index, and its construction, are presented in Table 2.2.

The price index in Table 2.2 presents the same information as Table 2.1 but in a slightly different form. We have (perhaps) gained some degree of clarity, but we have lost the original information about the actual level of prices. Since it is almost always *relative* prices that are of interest, this loss of information about the actual price level is not serious, and information about relative prices is retained by the price index. For example, using either the index or actual prices, we can see that the price of coal was 41.7% higher in 1984 than in 1980.

The choice of reference year is arbitrary and we can easily change it for a different year. If we choose 1982 to be the reference year, then we set the price in that year equal to 100 and again measure all other prices relative to it. This is shown in Table 2.3 which can be derived from Table 2.2 or directly from the original data on prices. You should choose whichever reference year is most convenient for your purposes. Whichever year is chosen, the informational content is the same.

Table 2.3 The price index for coal: 1982=100

$$1980: \quad \frac{35.0}{47.9} \times 100 = 73.1$$

$$1981: \quad \frac{39.9}{47.9} \times 100 = 83.3$$

$$1982: \quad \frac{47.9}{47.9} \times 100 = 100$$

$$1983: \quad \frac{49.6}{47.9} \times 100 = 103.5$$

$$1984: \quad \frac{49.6}{47.9} \times 100 = 103.5$$

More than one commodity

In practice, of course, industry uses other sources of energy as well as coal, such as gas, petroleum and electricity. Suppose that an index of the cost of all fuels used by industry is wanted, rather than just for coal. This is the more common requirement in reality, rather than the simple index number series calculated above. If the price of each fuel were rising at the same rate, say at 5% per year, then it is straightforward to say that the price of energy to industry is rising at 5% per year also. But supposing, as is likely, that the prices are all rising at different rates, as shown in Table 2.4. Is it now possible to say how fast the price of energy is increasing? Several different prices now have to be combined in order to construct an index number, a more complex process than the simple index number calculated above.

From the data presented in Table 2.4 we can calculate that the price of coal has risen by 41.7% over the four-year period, petrol by 65.8%, gas by 49.9% and electricity by 22.1%. Which of these, if any, measures 'the' rising price of energy?

Table 2.4: Prices of energy sources used by industry

Year	Coal £/tonne	Petroleum £/tonne	Gas £/therm	Electricity £/MWh
1980	35.0	90.3	0.1757	23.66
1981	39.9	108.2	0.2159	27.06
1982	47.9	114.3	0.2324	29.39
1983	49.6	125.9	0.2406	29.04
1984	49.6	149.7	0.2634	28.89

Source: Adapted from *Digest of UK Statistics, 1985*

The Laspeyres index

We shall tackle this problem by taking a weighted average of the price rises of the individual fuels, the weights being derived from the quantities of each fuel used by the industry. Thus if industry uses relatively more coal than petrol we give more weight to the rise in the price of coal in the calculation.

We put this principle into effect by constructing a hypothetical 'shopping basket' of the fuels used by industry, and measure how the cost of this basket has risen (or fallen) over time. Table 2.5 gives the quantities of each fuel consumed by industry in 1980 (again from the *Digest of UK Energy Statistics, 1985*) and it is this which will constitute the shopping basket. 1980 is referred to as the *base year* since it is the quantities consumed in this year which are used to make up the shopping basket.

Table 2.5 Quantities of energy consumed by industry in 1980

	Coal	Petroleum	Gas	Electricity
Units	m. tonnes	m. tonnes	m. therms	m. MWh
Quantity	12.96	16.10	6317	79.73

The cost of the basket at 1980 prices therefore works out at (using Tables 2.4 and 2.5):

$$
\begin{array}{ll}
35.0 \times 12.96 & \text{(expenditure on coal, in £m.)} \\
+\ 90.3 \times 16.10 & \text{(expenditure on petroleum)} \\
+\ 0.1757 \times 6317 & \text{(expenditure on gas)} \\
+\ 23.66 \times 79.73 & \text{(expenditure on electricity)} \\
=\ £4{,}903.74\ \text{m.} & \text{(total expenditure on energy)}
\end{array}
$$

This may be written as $\Sigma p_{0i}q_{0i}$ where the summation is calculated over all the four fuels. p refers to prices, q to quantities. The first subscript (0) refers to the year, the second (i) to each energy source in turn. We refer to 1980 as year 0, 1981 as year 1, etc. for brevity of notation. Thus for example, p_{01} means the price of coal in 1980, q_{01} the consumption of coal by industry in 1980. Similarly, the cost of the basket in each of the following years is as shown in Table 2.6 (in £m.):

Table 2.6 The cost of a basket of energy 1980–84

Year	1980	1981	1982	1983	1984
Cost	4,903.74	5,780.46	6,272.35	6,505.04	7,020.28
Formula	$\Sigma p_{0i}q_{0i}$	$\Sigma p_{1i}q_{0i}$	$\Sigma p_{2i}q_{0i}$	$\Sigma p_{3i}q_{0i}$	$\Sigma p_{4i}q_{0i}$

To obtain the energy price index from this data we divide the cost of the basket in each successive year by $\Sigma p_{0i}q_{0i}$ (the cost of the basket in 1980) and multiply by 100. Hence the index is given by Table 2.7. The is called the *Laspeyres* price index after its inventor, and we say that it uses *base year weights* (i.e. consumption in the base year 1980 as the weights in the basket).

Table 2.7 Laspeyres price index for energy

Year	Cost of basket (1)	1980 Cost of basket (2)	Index (3)
1980	4,903.74	4,903.74	100.0
1981	5,780.46	4,903.74	117.9
1982	6,272.35	4,903.74	127.9
1983	6,505.04	4,903.74	132.7
1984	7,020.28	4,903.74	143.2

Column (3) is column (1) divided by column (2) and multiplied by 100.

Laspeyres index: an index number using base year quantities as weights.

We have also set the value of the index to 100 in 1980, i.e. the reference year and the base year coincide, though this is not essential.

The Laspeyres index for year n with the base year as year 0 is given by the formula

$$P_L^n = \frac{\Sigma p_{ni}q_{0i}}{\Sigma p_{0i}q_{0i}} \qquad [2.1]$$

(Henceforth we shall omit the i subscript on prices and quantities in the formulae for index numbers.)

37

Statistics for Economics, Accounting and Business Studies*

The Paasche index

The Laspeyres is not the only index which it is possible to construct. As we shall see, it is impossible to construct the 'perfect' index number, but we can get an approximation to it. The Laspeyres index is one such approximation. We have seen that this uses base year weights throughout the time period studied, effectively assuming that the same basket of commodities is purchased year after year. This might be thought an unlikely occurrence, especially as relative prices change over time (our example has electricity getting cheaper relative to other fuels). Table 2.8 gives the quantities consumed in the years after 1980.

Table 2.8 Quantities of energy consumed by industry 1980–1984

Energy source	Units	1980	1981	1982	1983	1984
Coal	m. tonnes	12.96	13.99	13.43	13.84	12.70
Petroleum	m. tonnes	16.10	14.00	12.82	11.34	10.23
Gas	m. therms	6,317	6,021	6,034	6,027	6,208
Electricity	m. MWh	79.73	77.03	73.91	74.17	77.66

Source: Adapted from *Digest of UK Energy Statistics, 1985*

Any of the years could have been chosen as the base year to be used in the construction of a Laspeyres price index. Each would have given a slightly different index number series because consumption is different in each year. We note, for example, that there has been a large reduction in consumption of petroleum, which might be expected since its price has increased most rapidly (there was a sharp rise in the price of oil in 1979). There is therefore a different basket of commodities for each year, and there is no more reason to take one year's basket as the basis of calculation than another year's. Whichever year is chosen, there remains the problem that the shopping basket remains unchanged over time and thus after a while becomes unrepresentative of what firms are using.

The Paasche index (denoted P_P) overcomes this problem by using *current year weights* to construct the index.

Paasche index: an index number using current year quantities as weights.

Suppose 1980 is to be the reference year, so $P_P^0 = 100$. To construct the Paasche index for 1981 we use the 1981 weights, for the 1982 value of the index we use the 1982 weights, and so on. An example will clarify matters.

The Paasche index for 1981 will be the cost of the 1981 basket at 1981 prices relative to its cost at 1980 prices, i.e.

$$P_P^1 = \frac{\Sigma p_1 q_1}{\Sigma p_0 q_1} \times 100 \qquad [2.2]$$

Now

38

$$\Sigma p_1 q_1 = (39.9 \times 13.99) + (108.2 \times 14.00) +$$
$$(0.2159 \times 6021) + (27.06 \times 77.03)$$
$$= 5,457.37$$

$$\Sigma p_0 q_1 = (35.0 \times 13.99) + (90.3 \times 14.00) +$$
$$(0.1757 \times 6021) + (23.66 \times 77.03)$$
$$= 4,634.27$$

So

$$P_P^1 = 5,457.37/4,634.27 \times 100 = 117.76$$

Note that this is slightly less than the value of the Laspeyres index for 1981. This will usually be so, the reason being that the Paasche index gives greater weight to those goods which have risen least rapidly in price, since people and firms tend to increase their purchases of those goods whose relative price has fallen. This assumes of course that people's tastes or the technology used by firms have not changed.

Is one of the indices more 'correct' than the other? Neither is definitely correct. It can be shown that the 'true' value lies somewhere between the two, but it is impossible to say exactly where. If all the items which make up the index increase in price at the same rate, then the Laspeyres and Paasche indices would give the same answer, so it is the change in *relative* prices and the resultant change in consumption patterns which causes problems.

The general formula for the Paasche index in year n is

$$P_P^n = \frac{\Sigma p_n q_n}{\Sigma p_0 q_n} \times 100 \qquad [2.3]$$

and this may be contrasted with eqn [2.1] for the Laspeyres index.

Calculation of the Paasche index yields the result shown in Table 2.9. The Paasche index in column (3) is calculated as the ratio of column (1) to column (2), multiplied by 100.

Table 2.9 Paasche index of cost of energy to industry 1980−84

Year	Cost of year's basket at current prices (1) $\Sigma p_n q_n$	Cost of year's basket at 1980 prices (2) $\Sigma p_0 q_n$	Index (3)
1980	4,903.74	4,903.74	100.0
1981	5,457.37	4,634.27	117.8
1982	5,683.14	4,436.58	128.1
1983	5,718.16	4,322.21	132.3
1984	6,040.14	4,296.45	140.6

Units of measurement

It is important that the units of measurement in the price and quantity tables be consistent. Note that in the example the price of coal was measured in £ per tonne and the consumption was measured in millions of tonnes. The other fuels were similarly treated (in the case of electricity, one MWh equals one million watt-hours). But suppose we had measured electricity consumption in kWh instead of MWh (1 MWh = 1000 kWh), but still measured its price in £ per MWh? We would then have data of 23.66 for price as before, but 79,730 for quantity. It is as if electricity consumption has been boosted a thousand-fold, and this would seriously distort the results. The (Laspeyres) energy price index would be (by a similiar calculation to the one above)

1980	1981	1982	1983	1984
100.00	114.38	124.23	122.77	122.16

This is therefore incorrect, and shows a lower value than the proper Laspeyres index (because electricity is now given too much weight in the calculation, and electricity prices were rising relatively slowly). In fact, the index as a whole shows a fall in the last two years due to the fall in electricity prices in those two years and the huge weight which is now attached to that energy source.

It is possible to make some manipulations of the units of measurement (usually to make calculation easier) as long as all items are treated alike. If, for example, all prices were measured in pence rather than pounds (so all prices in Table 2.4 were multiplied by 100), then this would have no effect on the resultant index, as you would expect. Similarly, if all quantity figures were measured in thousands of tonnes, thousands of therms and thousands of MWh, there would be no effects on the Laspeyres index, even if prices remained in £ per tonne, etc. But if electricity were measured in pence per MWh, while all other fuels were in £ per tonne, a wrong answer would again be obtained. Quantities consumed should also be measured over the same time period, e.g. millions of therms per annum. It does not matter what the time period is (days, weeks, months or years) as long as all the items are treated similarly.

Using expenditures as weights

On occasion the quantities of each commodity consumed are not available, but expenditures are, and a price index can still be constructed using slightly modified formulae. It is often easier to find the expenditure on a good than to know the actual quantity consumed (think of housing as an example). We shall illustrate the method with a simplified example, using the data on energy prices and consumption for the years 1980 and 1981 only. The data are repeated in Table 2.10. The data for consumption is assumed to be no longer available, only the expenditure on each energy source as a percentage of total expenditure. Expenditure is derived as the product of price and quantity consumed.

The formula for the Laspeyres index can easily be manipulated to accord with the data as presented in Table 2.10.

Table 2.10 Prices and expenditure shares

Year	Coal £/tonne	Petroleum £/tonne	Gas £/therm	Electricity £/MWh	Total
1980	35.0	90.3	0.1757	23.66	
1981	39.9	108.2	0.2159	27.06	
Expenditure share 1980	0.0925	0.2963	0.2263	0.3847	1.000

The expenditure share is calculated as the expenditure on each fuel in 1980, divided by total expenditure. These are obtained from Tables 2.4 and 2.5. Thus $0.0925 = 35.0 \times 12.96/4903.74$.)

$$P_L^n = \frac{\Sigma p_n q_0}{\Sigma p_0 q_0} \times 100$$

$$= \frac{\Sigma \dfrac{p_n}{p_0} p_0 q_0}{\Sigma \dfrac{p_0}{p_0} p_0 q_0} \times 100$$

$$= \frac{\Sigma \dfrac{p_n}{p_0} \dfrac{p_0 q_0}{\Sigma p_0 q_0}}{\Sigma \dfrac{p_0}{p_0} \dfrac{p_0 q_0}{\Sigma p_0 q_0}} \times 100$$

$$= \Sigma \frac{p_n}{p_0} \frac{p_0 q_0}{\Sigma p_0 q_0} \times 100 \qquad\qquad [2.4]$$

Equation [2.4] is made up of two component parts. The first, p_n/p_0, is simply the price in year n relative to the base year price for each energy source. The second component, $p_0 q_0 / \Sigma p_0 q_0$. is the proportion of total expenditure spent on each energy source in the base year, the data for which are in Table 2.10.

We shall calculate the value of the Laspeyres index for 1981 using 1980 as the base year. The calculation is therefore as follows

$$\frac{39.9}{35.0} \times 0.0925 + \frac{108.2}{90.3} \times 0.2963 + \frac{0.2159}{0.1757} \times 0.2263 + \frac{27.06}{23.66} \times 0.3847$$

$$= 1.1785$$

This gives the value of the index as 117.9, the same value as derived earlier using the more usual methods. Values of the index for subsequent years are calculated by appropriate application of eqn [2.4] above. This is left as an exercise for the reader, who may use Table 2.7 to verify the answers (see also problem 2.3 at the end of the chapter).

The Paasche index may similarly be calculated from data on prices and expenditure shares, as long as these are available for each year for which the index is required. The formula for the Paasche index is

$$P_P^n = \cfrac{1}{\Sigma \cfrac{p_0}{p_n} \cfrac{p_n q_n}{\Sigma p_n q_n}} \times 100 \qquad [2.5]$$

The calculation of the Paasche index is also left as an exercise (see problem 2.4).

Comparison of the Laspeyres and Paasche indices

The advantages of the Laspeyres index are that it is easy to calculate and that it has a fairly clear intuitive meaning, i.e. the cost each year of a particular basket of goods. The Paasche index involves more computation, and it is less easy to envisage what it refers to. As an example of this point, consider the following simple case. The Laspeyres index values for 1982 and 1983 are 127.9 and 132.7, respectively. The ratio of these two numbers, 1.0375, would suggest that prices rose by 3.75% between these years. What does this figure actually represent? The Laspeyres index for 1983 has been divided by the same index for 1982, i.e.

$$\frac{P_L^3}{P_L^2} = \frac{\Sigma p_3 q_0}{\Sigma p_0 q_0} \bigg/ \frac{\Sigma p_2 q_0}{\Sigma p_0 q_0} = \frac{\Sigma p_3 q_0}{\Sigma p_2 q_0}$$

which is the ratio of the cost of the 1980 basket at 1983 prices to its cost at 1982 prices. This makes some intuitive sense. Note that it is not the same as the Laspeyres index for 1983 with 1982 as base year. That would require using q_2 in the calculation.

If the same is done with the Paasche index numbers, an increase of 3.28% is obtained between 1982 and 1983. But the meaning of this is not so clear, for

$$\frac{P_P^3}{P_P^2} = \frac{\Sigma p_3 q_3}{\Sigma p_0 q_3} \bigg/ \frac{\Sigma p_2 q_2}{\Sigma p_0 q_2}$$

which does not simplify any further. This is a curious mixture of 1982 and 1983 quantities, and 1980, 1982 and 1983 prices!

The major advantage of the Paasche index is that the weights are continuously updated, so that the basket of goods never becomes out of date. In the case of the Laspeyres index the basket remains unchanged over a period, becoming less and less representative of what is being bought by consumers. When revision is finally made, there is therefore a large change in the weighting scheme. The extra complexity of calculations involved in the Paasche index is also less important now that computers do most of the work.

Quantity and value indices

Just as one can calculate price indices, it is also possible to calculate quantity and value indices. We first concentrate on quantity indices, which provide a measure of the total quantity of energy consumed by industry each year. The problem again is that we cannot easily aggregate the different sources of energy. It makes no sense to add together tonnes of coal and petroleum, therms of gas and megawatts of electricity. Some means has to be found to put these different fuels on a comparable basis. We shall proceed by way of an example but for expository purposes we shall use a different example in this section and examine the output of the construction industry. The reason for this change will become clear later. Suppose we wish to measure the output of the house-building industry over a period of years, where the performance of the industry over the period 1980–1984 is as given in Table 2.11.

Table 2.11 Dwellings built 1980–1984 (thousands)

	1980	1981	1982	1983	1984
Houses	128	102	93	105	120
Flats	46	40	37	36	28
Bungalows	40	38	38	42	46

Source: *Housing and Construction Statistics, 1975–85*

The data for the three types of dwelling have to be aggregated in some way to provide a measure of the total output of the industry. A simple method would be to add up the number of units of each type of dwelling produced each year. Thus in 1980 there were 214,000 dwelling units constructed, in 1981 there were 180,000 and so on. The problem with this is that one is not comparing like with like. A house is not the same as a flat, nor a bungalow. More resources are required to build a house than a flat, so a given number of houses built means greater output by the industry than if the same number of flats were built. As with the price indices, we need to weight the output of each of the dwelling types according to some measure of their importance to the economy. The usual way of assessing the importance to the economy is to use the price of each dwelling type, for this measures the valuation consumers put upon each type of dwelling. The prices of each type in 1980 (in £000), are as in Table 2.12.

Table 2.12 Prices of dwellings in 1980 (£000)

House	Flat	Bungalow
16.60	14.60	14.60

Just as quantities were used as weights in constructing price indices, so prices are used as weights in constructing quantity indices. Thus the Laspeyres quantity index for year n relative to year 0 is

$$Q_L^n = \frac{\Sigma p_0 q_n}{\Sigma p_0 q_0} \times 100 \qquad [2.6]$$

This is just the Laspeyres price index formula, but with the roles of p and q interchanged. We use the symbol Q to distinguish it from a price index. Calculation of the index is set out below

1980	1981	1982	1983	1984
$\Sigma p_0 q_0$	$\Sigma p_0 q_1$	$\Sigma p_0 q_2$	$\Sigma p_0 q_3$	$\Sigma p_0 q_4$
3,380.4	2,832.0	2,638.8	2,881.8	3,072.4

This gives the value of output in each year, valued at 1980 prices. The Laspeyres quantity index is calculated in Table 2.13. The index reveals that output fell between 1980 and 1982 before recovering somewhat. The overall fall during the period was of the order of 9%.

Table 2.13 Laspeyres index for output of the construction industry, 1980–84 (1980=100)

1980	3,380.4 / 3,380.4 × 100 =	100.00
1981	2,832.0 / 3,380.4 × 100 =	83.78
1982	2,638.8 / 3,380.4 × 100 =	78.06
1983	2,881.8 / 3,380.4 × 100 =	85.25
1984	3,072.4 / 3,380.4 × 100 =	90.89

A Paasche quantity index can also be constructed, analogous to a Paasche price index. The formula is

$$Q_P^n = \frac{\Sigma p_n q_n}{\Sigma p_n q_0} \times 100 \qquad [2.7]$$

The price of each type of dwelling in the subsequent years is given below (in £000)

	1981	1982	1983	1984
House	17.7	17.3	19.6	20.7
Flat	17.0	19.2	18.4	20.5
Bungalow	14.7	15.3	16.7	17.6

Using these figures and eqn [2.7] we obtain the values of the Paasche quantity index as (calculation not shown)

1980	100.00
1981	83.73
1982	78.19
1983	85.05
1984	90.02

The two indices give different results as in the case of the prices indices, though the differences are small in this case since there has not been much movement of relative prices.

It might be objected that the above index does not truly measure the output of the construction industry *per se*, because the prices, used as weights, measure not just the output of the industry but also the value of its inputs. Perhaps a quarter of the value of a house may be due to the land upon which it sits. The proportion is likely to be higher in the case of a bungalow and lower for a flat, especially a high-rise flat. This counts towards the price of a dwelling but is not truly part of the output of the construction industry. We shall therefore divide up the price into the construction cost and land cost.*

By way of example, the following figures are used (in £000).

	Price (1980)	Land value	Construction cost
House	16.6	3.6	13.0
Bungalow	14.6	3.9	10.7
Flat	14.6	1.7	12.9

If builders built 500 flats instead of 500 bungalows, output would appear to remain constant according to the Laspeyres quantity index calculated earlier because they both sell at the same price. But in fact there would have been an increase in output because the construction cost of flats is greater than it is for bungalows. Note that this error only occurs if value added by the construction industry constitutes a *different* proportion of the total price for each dwelling type. Unfortunately this is quite likely to be the case, as is readily apparent if one thinks of high-rise flats, for example.

To circumvent the problem, we use as weights *value added* in the construction industry, i.e. construction cost, rather than price. The calculation of the Laspeyres index with these different weights is given below. We shall use the symbol v to signify value added, which will replace price in the calculation.

1980	1981	1982	1983	1984
$\Sigma v_0 q_0$	$\Sigma v_0 q_1$	$\Sigma v_0 q_2$	$\Sigma v_0 q_3$	$\Sigma v_0 q_4$
2,672.2	2,244.2	2,095.1	2,292.0	2,453.0

This gives rise to the following index, which is the Laspeyres index using value added as weights rather than prices.

1980	1981	1982	1983	1984
100.00	83.98	78.40	85.77	91.80

This is not very different from the Laspeyres index calculated using price rather than value added, but shows that the former gave a slight underestimate of the true output of the construction industry in 1984. Obviously the slight difference in the quantity of land used in the construction of each type of dwelling has only a small effect upon the calculated index.

Calculation of the Paasche index requires knowledge of value added in each year. It is not calculated here but the method follows the principles outlined in earlier examples.

* It should now be clear why this example was chosen.

In practice, the calculation of value added for each item could be more complicated, since land is not the only input which is purchased. The costs of other materials could also be subtracted from the price to arrive at value added. Once the value added has been arrived at, however, calculation of the index is quite straightforward. The choice of whether to use value added or output prices as weights depends on the use which is made of the index. To measure the output of the construction industry, value added is appropriate, as we have seen. If, however, one wants some idea of the total activity in the industry, then output prices would be the better option.

Value indices

The value index for year n is

$$I_v^n = \frac{\Sigma p_n q_n}{\Sigma p_0 q_0} \times 100 \qquad [2.8]$$

and is simply a comparison of the year n basket at year n prices with the year 0 basket at year 0 prices. This measures how total expenditure has changed over time, which is made up of changes in prices and changes in quantities. There is obviously only one value index and one need not distinguish between Laspeyres and Paasche formulations. We have exhausted the usefulness of the construction industry example in deriving its value added, so we shall return to energy prices and consumption. The value index can be easily derived from Table 2.9.

1980	1981	1982	1983	1984
$\Sigma p_0 q_0$	$\Sigma p_1 q_1$	$\Sigma p_2 q_2$	$\Sigma p_3 q_3$	$\Sigma p_4 q_4$
4,903.74	5,457.37	5,683.14	5,718.16	6,040.14

Hence the value index is as shown in Table 2.14. The value index shows how industry's *expenditure* on energy is changing over time. Thus expenditure in 1984 was 23.17% higher than in 1980. What the value index does not tell us is how that increased expenditure may be divided up into (a) increases in the quantity of energy purchased, and (b) increases in the price of energy. It is to this that we now turn.

Table 2.14 Index of the value of energy consumed 1980–84

1980	1981	1982	1983	1984
100.00	111.29	115.89	116.60	123.17

Relationships between price, quantity and value indices

Just as multiplying a price by a quantity gives total value, or expenditure, the same is true of index numbers. The value index can be decomposed as the product of a price index and a quantity index. In particular, it is the product of a Paasche quantity index and Laspeyres price index, *or* the product of a Paasche price index and Laspeyres quantity index. This can be very simply demonstrated using sigma notation.

$$I_v^n = \frac{\Sigma p_n q_n}{\Sigma p_0 q_0} = \frac{\Sigma p_n q_n}{\Sigma p_n q_0} \times \frac{\Sigma p_n q_0}{\Sigma p_0 q_0} = Q_P^n \times P_L^n$$

or [2.9]

$$I_v^n = \frac{\Sigma p_n q_n}{\Sigma p_0 q_0} = \frac{\Sigma p_n q_n}{\Sigma p_0 q_n} \times \frac{\Sigma p_0 q_n}{\Sigma p_0 q_0} = P_P^n \times Q_L^n$$

Thus increases in value or expenditure can be decomposed into price and quantity effects. Two decompositions are possible and give slightly different answers.

It is also evident that a quantity index can be constructed by dividing a value index by a price index, since by manipulation of eqn [2.9]

$$Q_P^n = I_v^n \, / \, P_L^n \text{ or }$$

$$Q_L^n = I_v^n \, / \, P_P^n$$

[2.10]

Note that dividing a value index by a Laspeyres price index gives a Paasche quantity index, and dividing a value index by a Paasche price index gives a Laspeyres quantity index. This is known as *deflating* a time series and is a widely used and very useful technique. It changes a time series measured in *current* prices to one measured in *constant* prices. We shall reconsider our earlier data in the light of this. Firms' expenditure on energy in each year at current prices (i.e. the prices prevailing in that year) is (from Table 2.9)

£m. (current prices)

	$p_n q_n$
1980	4,903.74
1981	5,457.37
1982	5,683.14
1983	5,718.16
1984	6,040.14

We can use the Laspeyres price index already calculated to deflate the data. First of all we shall deflate it to constant 1980 prices, meaning that the 1980 figure will be unchanged but the others will be adjusted. This is done in Table 2.15.

Column (1) gives expenditure on energy at current prices. In column (2) is given the Laspeyres price index repeated from Table 2.7, and column (3) is derived by dividing column (1) by column (2) and multiplying by 100, giving expenditure on energy at constant 1980 prices. This is equivalent to a Paasche quantity index, as illustrated by eqn [2.7]. This is then turned into a proper index number series in column (4), and shows how industry has reduced its usage of energy over the period in response to rising prices. In fact, energy consumption has dropped by about 14% during the time that energy prices

47

Table 2.15 Deflating a value series by a price index to give a quantity index

	Expenditure at current prices £m. (1)	Laspeyres price index 1980 = 100 (2)	Expenditure at constant 1980 prices (3)	Paasche quantity index (4)
1980	4,903.74	100.0	4,903.74	100.00
1981	5,457.37	117.9	4,628.81	94.39
1982	5,683.14	127.9	4,443.43	90.61
1983	5,718.16	132.7	4,309.09	87.87
1984	6,040.14	143.2	4,217.98	86.02

have risen by 43%. It would be wrong, however, to say that the fall in consumption is due to the rise in price alone; there are many other factors, such as the demand for industry's output, which would also affect consumption.

Chain indices

Whenever an index number series over a long period of time is wanted, it is usually necessary to link together a number of separate indices, resulting in a *chain index*. Without access to the original raw data it is impossible to construct a proper Laspeyres or Paasche index, so the result will be a mixture of different types of index number but it is the best that can be done in the circumstances.

Suppose that the following two index number series are available. Access to the original data is assumed to be impossible.

Laspeyres index of energy prices 1980–84 (from Table 2.7)

1980	1981	1982	1983	1984
100	117.9	127.9	132.7	143.2

Laspeyres index of energy prices 1976–80 (1976=100)

1976	1977	1978	1979	1980
100	102.3	106.7	143.6	158.3

The two series have different reference years and use different shopping baskets of consumption. The first index measures the cost of the 1980 basket in each of the subsequent years. The second measures the price of the 1976 basket in subsequent years. There is an 'overlap' year which is 1980. How do we combine these into one continuous index covering the whole period?

The obvious calculation is to use the ratio of the costs of the two baskets in 1980, 158.3 / 100 = 1.583, to alter one of the series. To base the continuous series on 1976 = 100 means multiplying each of the post-1980 figures by 1.583 as is demonstrated in Table 2.16.

The continuous series could just as easily be based on 1980 = 100 by a

Table 2.16 A chain index of energy prices 1976–1984 (1976 = 100)

Year	'Old' index	'New' index	Continuous index	
1976	100		100	
1977	102.3		102.3	
1978	106.7		106.7	
1979	143.6		143.6	
1980	158.3	100	158.3	
1981		117.9	186.6	(117.9 × 1.583)
1982		127.9	202.5	(127.9 × 1.583)
1983		132.7	210.1	(132.7 × 1.583)
1984		143.2	236.7	(143.2 × 1.583)

simple rescaling, which would be equivalent to dividing the 'old' series by 1.583 and leaving the 'new' series unchanged.

The continuous series is not a proper Laspeyres index number as can be seen if we examine the formulae used. We shall examine the 1984 figure, 236.7, by way of example. This figure is calculated as $236.7 = 143.2 \times 158.3 / 100$ which in terms of our formulae is

$$\frac{\Sigma p_4 q_0}{\Sigma p_0 q_0} \times \frac{\Sigma p_9 q_6}{\Sigma p_6 q_6} / 100 \qquad [2.11]$$

(P_9 means the price in 1979.)

The proper Laspeyres index for 1984 using 1976 weights would be

$$\frac{\Sigma p_4 q_6}{\Sigma p_6 q_6} \times 100$$

There is no way that this can be derived from eqn [2.11], proving that the former is not a properly constructed Laspeyres index number. Although it is not a proper index number series, it does have the advantage of the weights being revised and therefore more up to date.

Similar problems arise when deriving a chain index from two Paasche index number series. Investigation of this is left to the reader; the method follows that outlined above for the Laspeyres case.

The retail price index

The UK retail price index is one of the most sophisticated of index numbers, involving the recording of the prices of 350 items each month, and weighting them on the basis of households' expenditure patterns as revealed by the annual Family Expenditure Survey (the FES is explained in more detail in Chapter 7 on sampling methods). The principles involved in the calculation are the same as set out above, but they are not strictly adhered to for a variety of reasons.

The RPI is something of a compromise between a Laspeyres and a Paasche index. It is calculated monthly, and within each calendar year the weights used remain constant so that it takes the form of a Laspeyres index. Each January, however, the weights are updated on the basis of evidence from the FES so that the index is in fact a set of chain-linked Laspeyres indices, the chaining taking place in January each year. Despite the formal appearance as a Laspeyres index, the RPI measured over a period of years has the characteristics of a Paasche index, due to the annual change in the weights.

Another departure from principle is the fact that about 14% of households are left out when expenditure weights are calculated. These consist of most pensioner households (10%) and the very rich (4%), because they tend to have significantly different spending patterns from those of the rest of the population and their inclusion would make the index too unrepresentative. A separate RPI is calculated for pensioners, and the very rich have to do without one.

A change in the quality of goods purchased can also be problematic, as alluded to earlier. If a manufacturer improves the quality of a product and charges more, is it fair to say that the price has gone up? Sometimes it is possible to measure improvement (if the power of a vacuum cleaner is increased, for example), but other cases are more difficult, such as if the punctuality of a train service is improved. By how much has quality improved? In many circumstances the statistician has to make a judgement about the best procedure to adopt.

Inequality indices

A separate set of index numbers relate to the measurement of inequality, such as inequality in the distribution of income. Inequality could of course be summarised by a measure of dispersion such as the variance, but a particular set of indices has been developed and is commonly used to represent inequality. This section examines three of these methods of measuring inequality: the Lorenz curve, the Gini coefficient and the concentration ratio. The first two are illustrated by an example relating to the distribution of income, the last by examining the market shares of firms in a particular market.

The Lorenz curve

Table 2.17 gives data for the distribution of income in the UK in 1982–83 (the data is from the *Annual Abstract of Statistics, 1986*, Table 15.2).

Looking at the table it is obvious that there is a substantial degree of inequality. For example, the poorest 9.17% (2,014 out of 21,970) of households have between zero and £2,500 each in annual income, while the richest 0.84% (185 out of 21,970) each earn in excess of £30,000. Although these figures give some idea of inequality, they only relate to a small proportion of the population. One could illustrate the data using a frequency distribution and associated statistics, but a better method is to draw a Lorenz curve of the distribution. This is a way of presenting the data with special emphasis placed upon the degree of inequality, and so is an improvement over the frequency

Table 2.17 The distribution of income in the UK, 1982/3

Income before tax (£)	Mid-point of interval	Number of households (thousands)
	1,250	2,014
2,500–	3,750	6,140
5,000–	6,500	6,220
8,000–	11,500	6,080
15,000–	22,500	1,331
30,000–	40,000	185
		21,970

Source: *Annual Abstract of Statistics, 1986*

distribution for this type of problem. The Lorenz curve shows the proportion of total income going to the poorest group of households, the proportion going to the next poorest group and so on all the way up the income distribution. An illustrative Lorenz curve is presented in Fig. 2.1. Along the horizontal axis is

Figure 2.1 A Lorenz curve

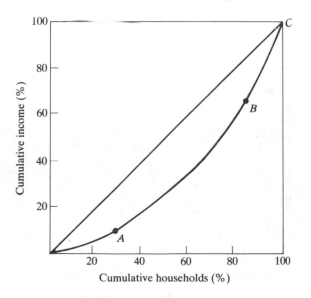

51

measured the cumulative percentage of households, going from 0 to 100%. Households are ranked from poorest to richest, so that the 20% mark, for example, represents the poorest 20% of the population. On the vertical axis is measured the cumulative percentage income of households, again running from 0 to 100%. A point such as A on the diagram shows that the poorest 30% of households obtained only 15% of total income. Further up the curve, point B shows that the poorest 85% of the population earned 65% of total income, implying that the richest 15% earned 35% of all income. In this manner the Lorenz curve presents a picture of the whole of the income distribution. Since households are ranked from poorest to richest, the cumulative percentage income obtained must always be less than the cumulative percentage of households, and so the data points must lie below the 45° line. The Lorenz curve is simply the line traced out by all points such as A and B for a particular distribution.

A few things should be immediately obvious about the Lorenz curve:

(a) Since 0% of households earn 0% of income and 100% of households earn 100% of income, the curve must run from the origin, point O to point C.
(b) As already explained, the curve must lie everywhere below the 45° line.
(c) The curve must be concave from above since as we move to the right we are adding successively richer and richer households. The curve in Fig. 2.2 is therefore an impossibility.
(d) If all households had identical incomes, then the poorest 20% would earn 20% of all income, the poorest 50% would earn 50% and so on. The

Figure 2.2 An inadmissible Lorenz curve

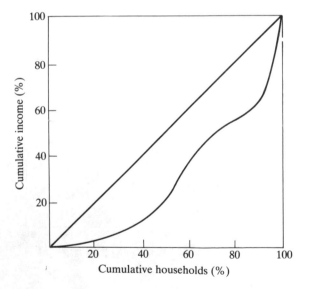

Lorenz curve would then be coincident with the 45° line, which therefore represents the line of complete equality. Furthermore, the further is the Lorenz curve from the 45° line, the greater the degree of inequality.

Before discussing the Lorenz curve further we shall derive it for the data in Table 2.17. This is done in Table 2.18.

Table 2.18 Calculation of a Lorenz curve

Income before tax (1)	x (2)	f (3)	fx (£000) (4)	%fx (5)	%fx cumulative (6)	%f (7)	%f cumulative (8)
0–	1,250	2,014	2,517.5	1.45	1.45	9.17	9.17
2,500–	3,750	6,140	23,025.0	13.29	14.74	27.95	37.11
5,000–	6,500	6,220	40,430.0	23.34	38.08	28.31	65.43
8,000–	11,500	6,080	69,920.0	40.36	78.44	27.67	93.10
15,000–	22,500	1,331	29,947.5	17.29	95.73	6.06	99.16
30,000–	40,000	185	7,400.0	4.27	100.00	0.84	100.00

We have to derive the cumulative percentage of households, taking the poorest first, and the percentage of total income earned by those households. These are given in columns (6) and (8) respectively of Table 2.18. They are derived as follows. Columns (2) and (3) are repeated from Table 2.17. Column (4) is the product of columns (2) and (3) and therefore gives the total income accruing to that class. In column (5) is measured the *percentage* of total income accruing to each class and is simply each row of column (4) as a percentage of the column total (e.g. 2,517.5 is 1.46% of 172,550). Thus the poorest income group gets 1.46% of total income. Column (6) just cumulates column (5) and shows, for example, that the four poorest income groups obtain 78.36% of total income. Column (7) is derived from column (3) and gives the percentage of households in each income group; thus there are 9.17% of all households in the poorest group. Column (8) simply cumulates column (7).

From columns (6) and (8) can be read off the results of the calculation. The poorest 37.11% of households obtained only 14.80% of total income, for example. Figure 2.3 presents the Lorenz curve of the data. The data from columns (6) and (8) of Table 2.18 have been plotted and joined by a smooth curve to give the Lorenz curve. Obviously we have had to interpolate between the observations. If we had a finer breakdown of income classes, we could obtain the Lorenz curve more accurately, but even with only half a dozen or so classes a reasonably accurate result can be obtained.

The Lorenz curve gives a quickly assimilated picture of the income distribution, but its most useful purpose is for comparison of different distributions (e.g. of different countries) or of the change in the distribution over time in one country. This is not always a straightforward task, as Fig. 2.4 illustrates.

In (a) it is clear that the income distribution labelled A is more unequal than

53

Figure 2.3 Lorenz curve of UK pre-tax incomes, 1982–83

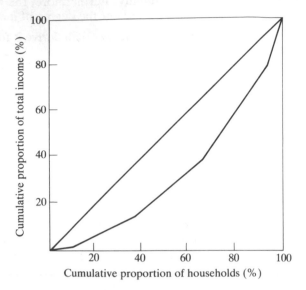

Figure 2.4 Comparing Lorenz curves

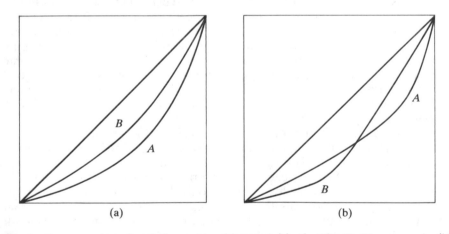

B; the Lorenz curve for A lies everywhere outside that for B. However, in (b) things are not so clear cut since the Lorenz curves cross, a perfectly feasible outcome. In B those at the very bottom of the income distribution are very badly off and have a lesser share of total income than in A, but on the other hand A exhibits greater inequality at the top of the distribution: there are a few extremely rich households. Which distribution is to be preferred is a matter of personal taste: some people are averse to extreme poverty while others have a greater moral objection to extreme wealth. The preference might also depend on the average level of income in the two cases. Inequality may not be very objectionable if the average level of income is quite high. The Lorenz curve illustrates the differences between distributions but does not say that one is to be preferred to the other.

The Gini coefficient

The Gini coefficient is a numerical representation of the degree of inequality in a distribution and can be derived directly from the Lorenz curve. In the Lorenz curve illustrated in Fig. 2.5 the Gini coefficient is the ratio of area A to the sum of areas A and B.

Figure 2.5 Calculating the Gini coefficient

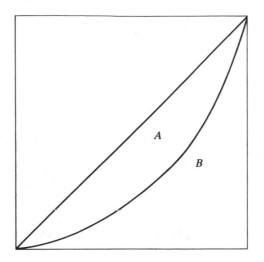

The Gini coefficient therefore goes from extreme values of 0, indicating complete equality, to 1 representing complete inequality (one individual having all the income). Values of the Gini coefficient nearer unity are associated with greater inequality, though the association is not always straightforward. The problem is that a low Gini coefficient could still mean extreme poverty at the bottom of the income distribution but reasonable equality further up. Thus it might be wrong to say that one country has a 'fairer' distribution of income than another on the basis of a lower Gini coefficient. It is the same problem as comparing two distributions whose Lorenz curves cross.

The calculation of the Gini coefficient is a somewhat tedious affair since it is not easy to measure areas A and B. The simplest method is often to overlay the Lorenz curve with gridded paper and count squares (and parts of them) to establish the sizes of A and B. This method is illustrated in Fig. 2.6. Area A is 4.4 squares in size, Area A + B is 12.50 squares, so the Gini coefficient is 4.4 / 12.50 = 0.35 or approximately 35%. It is interesting to compare this figure with results for earlier times (these figures come from Soltow (1968), and

Figure 2.6 Lorenz curve of UK pre-tax incomes, 1982–83

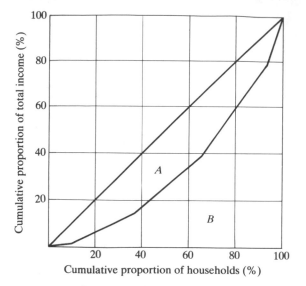

may not be strictly comparable with the figure above because of slightly different data sets).

1688	1801–3	1867	1913	1962
0.55	0.56	0.52	0.43–0.63	0.34

These figures indicate a general reduction in inequality over time, though there would seem to have been little reduction over the last two decades or so. These figures are before taxes so ignore any redistribution through the tax system.

Concentration ratios

The concentration ratio is commonly used to examine the distribution of market shares among firms competing in a market. Of course it would be possible to measure this using the Lorenz curve and Gini coefficient but the concentration ratio has the advantage that it can be calculated on the basis of less information and tends to focus attention on the largest firms in the industry. The concentration ratio is often used as a measure of the competitiveness of a particular market but, as with all statistics, it requires careful interpretation.

A market is said to be concentrated if most of the demand is met by a small number of suppliers. The limiting case is monopoly where the whole of the market is supplied by a single firm. We shall measure the degree of concentration by the *five firm concentration ratio*, which is the proportion of the market held by the largest five firms, and it is denoted C_5. The larger is this proportion, the greater the degree of concentration and potentially the less competitive is the market. Table 2.19 gives the sales figures of the ten firms in a particular

Table 2.19 Data on sales volume by firm

Firm	Sales volume (millions of units)
A	180
B	115
C	90
D	62
E	35
F	25
G	19
H	18
I	15
J	10

industry. For convenience the firms have already been ranked by size from A (the largest) to J (the smallest). The output of the five largest firms is 482, out of a total of 569, so the five firm concentration ratio is $C_5 = 84.7\%$, i.e. 84.7% of the market is supplied by the five largest firms.

Without supporting evidence it is hard to interpret this figure. Does it mean that the market is not competitive and the consumer is being exploited? Some industries, such as the computer industry, have a very high concentration ratio yet it is hard to deny that they are very competitive. On the other hand, some industries with no large firms have restrictive practices, entry barriers, etc., which mean that they are not very competitive (lawyers might be one example). A further point is that there may be a *threat* of competition from outside the industry which keeps the few firms acting competitively.

Concentration ratios can be calculated for different numbers of largest firms, e.g. the three firm or four firm concentration ratios. Straightforward calculation reveals them to be 67.7% and 78.6% respectively for the data given in Table 2.19, There is little reason in general to prefer one measure to the others, and they may give different pictures of the degree of concentration in an industry.

The concentration ratio calculated above relates to the quantity of output produced by each firm, but it is possible to do the same with sales revenue, employment, investment or any other variable for which data are available. The interpretation of the results will be different in each case. For example, the largest firms in an industry, while producing the majority of output, might not provide the greater part of employment if they use more capital – intensive methods of production. Concentration ratios obviously have to be treated with caution therefore, and are probably best combined with case studies of the particular industry before conclusions are reached about the degree of competition.

Problems

2.1 The following figures show UK exports and imports in £m., at constant prices) for 1980–85. Construct an index number series for each with 1980=100, then rescale the series to 1983=100.

Year	1980	1981	1982	1983	1984	1985
Exports	47,364	50,698	55,558	60,684	70,488	78,331
Imports	49,773	51,169	56,978	66,101	78,967	84,790

Is it possible, using only the index numbers, to construct an index number series for the balance of trade? If not, what is the minimum amount of additional information required?

2.2 The following data show telephone charges and numbers of calls made in different categories for 1981–85. Construct a Laspeyres price index, based on 1981 = 100, for the price of telephone calls.

Price (in pence) per five-minute call:

Year	Local	Type of call Long distance	International
1981	4.50	33	144
1982	4.75	35	156
1983	4.90	37	168
1984	5.25	38	170
1985	6.00	40	178

Number of calls per day (millions):

Local	Long distance	International
7.86	3.50	0.45

If the telephone company were regulated, so that the index of its prices could not rise by more than a certain percentage over a period of time, would the company prefer this to be calculated using a Laspeyres or Paasche index?

2.3 Use the data on energy prices in Table 2.4 and the expenditure shares given in Table 2.10 to construct the Laspeyres price index for 1982 onwards, using 1980 = 100. Check that these results are the same as those given in Table 2.7.

2.4 Expenditure shares on energy are given below for the years 1981–84 (figures in percentages).

Year	Coal	Petroleum	Gas	Electricity
1981	10.23	27.76	23.82	38.19
1982	11.32	25.78	24.67	38.22
1983	12.00	24.97	25.36	37.67
1984	10.43	25.35	27.07	37.14

Use this data together with the price data from Table 2.4 to calculate a Paasche index of energy prices. Verify that your answers correspond with those in Table 2.9.

2.5 Derive the Paasche price index formula using expenditure share weights (eqn [2.5]) from the formula using quantity weights (eqn [2.3]). The derivation is similar to that for the Laspeyres index given in the text.

2.6 A family's consumption pattern and the prices it faces are set out in the table that follows (the example is simplified to keep down the burden of calculation).

Quantities consumed:

	1981	1982	1983	1984
Food	7	8	8	9
Housing	10	10	11	11
Transport	5	6	8	8

Prices:

	1981	1982	1983	1984
Food	5	6	8	9
Housing	4	6	8	10
Transport	5	6	5	6

(a) Derive the value index of the family's expenditure for the years 1981–84, setting 1981 = 100.
(b) The (Paasche) retail price index for the same period is

1981	1982	1983	1984
75	100	130	160

Deflate the value index by this price index, setting the resulting index at 1981 = 100. What does this new index represent?
(c) Do you think the family is becoming better or worse off? If the weights used in the retail price index were 6,12 and 3 for food, housing and transport, respectively, do you think your index over – or underestimates the true change in the family's living standards?

2.7 The following data (adapted from *Inland Revenue Statistics 1986*, HMSO, Table 4.7) gives details of the distribution of marketable wealth in the UK in 1976 and 1984.

Range of wealth (£000)	Mid-point	Number of adults 1976	Number of adults 1984
0–	2.5	27,950	18,345
5–	10	9,315	8,960
15–	32.5	2,750	12,370
50–	75	365	2,050
100–	150	160	725

(a) Draw the Lorenz curves and calculate the Gini coefficients for this data.
(b) Has the inequality of wealth increased or decreased during the period?
(c) Does it matter that wealth is not adjusted for inflation between the two years? Is the comparison still valid?
(d) Why is there greater inequality in the distribution of wealth than in that of income (as established in the text)?
(e) How might the definition of 'wealth' be widened, and how might this affect the figures? (See Table 4.8 of the Inland Revenue statistics.)

Reference

L. Soltow (1968) 'Long run changes in British income inequality', *Economic History Review*, pp. 17–29.

3 Probability

Introduction

In October 1985 Mrs Evelyn Adams of New Jersey, USA, won $3.9 million in the State lottery at odds of 1 in 3,200,000. In February 1986 she again won, though this time only (!) $1.4 million at odds of 1 in 5,200,000. The odds against both these wins were calculated at about 1 in 17,300 billion. she is quoted as saying 'They say good things come in threes, so . . .'.

The above story illustrates the principles of probability at work. These same principles underlie the theory of statistical inference, the process of drawing conclusions (inferences) from a set of sample data. A simple example will illustrate this point. Suppose that a company selling tea believes that there is a connection between sales of tea and the price charged for it. To test this supposition a sample of data on tea sales and prices charged is collected, which turns out to show a connection between the two. There are two possibilities:

(a) There is a connection between tea sales and prices, which the sample data reflect; or
(b) There is not a connection but, *by chance*, the sample data show a connection. A different sample would very likely not show a connection. The sample data do not reflect the true state of affairs.

The task is to decide which of (a) or (b) is true and which false. The methodology which is commonly followed in statistics is the following. First, it is *assumed* that (b) is true, that there is in fact no connection. On the basis of this assumption, the probability of getting the sample data is calculated, using the principles of probability theory. If this probability turns out to be very low, say one in a hundred, then the initial assumption of the truth of (b) is rejected in favour of the alternative (a), that there is some connection. For example, if tea sales rose *every time* that the price fell, it would be concluded that there is some connection between the two, rather than this just being due to chance.

A numerical example will help make this clear. Suppose we wish to know if a coin is fair, i.e. is equally likely to fall heads or tails. The coin is tossed ten times and ten heads are recorded. This constitutes the sample data. *If* the coin were fair, the chances of this happening are one in 1,024, so a fairly unlikely event seems to have occurred. It is therefore concluded that the coin is not fair on the basis of the sample evidence.

The theory of probability is used to calculate the probability of the same data occurring (one in 1,024 above) and so is central to a study of statistical inference. This chapter will introduce the basic concepts of probability theory and the rules which allow the probabilities of quite complex events to be calculated. This will lead on to the idea of a probability distribution and then on to statistical inference itself.

The probability of an event

The first task is to define precisely what is meant by probability. This is not a straightforward matter and there are a number of different schools of thought. It should by now be clear that statistics is not the precise subject it is usually believed to be!

Suppose a coin is tossed. What is the probability that it will come down heads? Most people would reply 'one–half', but how is this figure arrived at, and what is its meaning? The most popular view is that of the frequentist school.

The frequentist school

This school of thought is also known as the 'objective' school. It asserts that the probability of getting a head is given by the proportion of heads one would get in the long run, i.e. if the coin were tossed many times. Thus the first results of tossing the coin might be as follows:

Toss	1	2	3	4	5	6	7
Result	H	H	T	H	T	H	T
Proportion of heads	1	1	2/3	3/4	3/5	4/6	4/7

This is illustrated in Fig. 3.1.

Figure 3.1

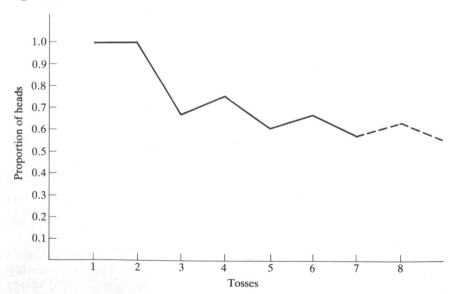

After a while the proportion of heads will settle at some particular fraction and subsequent tosses will individually have an insignificant impact upon that value. This proportion is the desired probability, according to the frequentist school. Strictly, it is the proportion of heads observed as the number of tosses approaches infinity.

$$\text{Probability} = \frac{\text{Number of heads}}{\text{Number of tosses}} \text{ as the number of tosses approaches infinity.}$$

Although this approach appears attractive, it does have its problems. It seems to be practical and objective, but it is not, for one couldn't actually toss the coin an infinite number of times. One could perhaps toss it a large, but finite, number of times but one then has to decide how large is 'large'. Furthermore, one would have to conduct the test every time one took a new coin. The result hardly seems to justify the effort.

Another approach is the 'principle of insufficient reason'. This suggests that since there is no reason to favour heads or tails they should be thought equally likely, the probability of each being one-half. But what if the coin landed on its edge? This is unlikely but not *totally* impossible. Does the principle of insufficient reason require assigning probabilities of one-third to each of heads, tails and edge? This is clearly absurd. But what probability should be given to the edge? The principle gives no guidance.

A more serious problem with the frequentist approach is that it is inapplicable to many problems. If we ask 'what is the probability of IBM going bankrupt within the next year?', it is clear that the frequentist school has no answer. To find the answer one would have to rerun history an infinite number of times and calculate in what proportion of them IBM went bankrupt next year! This makes the coin tossing experiment seem straightforward . . . Yet the IBM problem is clearly an important one which requires an answer. (Firms are anxious to know the credit-worthiness of their customers, which involves this probability.)

The frequentist approach clearly has its shortcomings, so we turn to the other main school of thought to see what it has to offer.

The subjective approach

This is the school of thought that Mrs Adams appears to belong to. This school rejects the frequentist approach because of the difficulties outlined above. It concludes that there is no objective way to measure probability, and therefore probability is really the *degree of belief* held by an individual that an event will occur. It is inevitably subjective, and therefore some members of this school would argue that the probability of an event is the degree of belief it is *rational* to hold. But this then shifts the argument to what is meant by 'rational'. Others would say that any degree of belief can be held, but that one should alter that degree of belief in certain ways in the light of evidence. It is this latter criterion that prevents the whole theory being totally subjective, in which 'anything goes'. Thus one can believe that the probability of heads is 1/100, but not after observing ten heads in a row. The belief must be updated. It does however, leave the problem, of how the initial (usually termed 'prior') beliefs are arrived at. This updating of beliefs is associated in particular with the Bayesian approach to statistical inference. The Bayesian approach is discussed in more detail below.

There is therefore no agreement as to the precise definition of the probability of an event. There is insufficient space here to explore these issues in more detail so the problem will be solved by ignoring it! The probability of an event occurring will be defined as a certain value, without worrying overmuch about its exact meaning. Fortunately, despite the differences noted above, in many practical instances the same answer is arrived at so it does not matter too much which view is held. Most people, of whatever persuasion, would agree that the probability of heads is one-half. If they think it one-quarter, offer then an even bet on heads until they change their mind. You're almost certain to win money, in the long run. . . .

These arguments will be taken up again later on, when statistical inference, and the different approaches to it, are discussed. This book will use what are known as classical methods of analysis, which are based on the frequentist approach to probability, and may be contrasted with the Bayesian approach.

Probability theory: the building blocks

We start off with the idea of an *experiment* (such as tossing a coin) which has a number of possible *outcomes* (heads or tails for the toss of a coin). These outcomes are *mutually exclusive*, which means that only one of them can occur when an experiment is conducted. It is obviously impossible for both heads and tails to occur simultaneously, for example. These outcomes constitute the *sample space* of the experiment, which is therefore just a list of all the possible outcomes of the experiment.

Sample space: all the possible outcomes of an experiment.

The sample space may be represented in a variety of ways. For the tossing of a coin the sample space is:

heads, tails   (the edge will be excluded!)

If a card is drawn at random from a pack of cards, the sample space may be presented as follows:

	A	K	Q	J	10	9	8	7	6	5	4	3	2
S	.	.	.	.	.	.	.	.	.	.	.	.	.
H	.	.	.	.	.	.	.	.	.	.	.	.	.
D	.	.	.	.	.	.	.	.	.	.	.	.	.
C	.	.	.	.	.	.	.	.	.	.	.	.	.

Each point represents one of the cards in the pack and there are 52 points represented. This is probably a better way of presenting the sample space then writing down all 52 cards in turn, since it is more compact. When tackling problems of probability it often helps clarify matters if the sample space is written out. There are usually several ways in which it may be presented, so the one most convenient for the problem at hand should be chosen.

Associated with each outcome in the sample space is a probability, which is the chance of that outcome occurring in a single experiment. A single performance of an experiment is known as a *trial*. For example, the probability of heads or tails in one trial is one-half; the probability of any particular card being picked is 1/52. These probabilities are not calculated in any way but are based on the principles set out in the previous section. It would be quite in order therefore to associate different values with each of the outcomes in the sample space. If the coin was believed to be biased towards heads, then values of three-quarters and one-quarter might be assigned to heads and tails, respectively. However, one is not entitled to assign *any* values to the outcomes in the sample space; there are rules which must be followed, essentially to ensure that contradictions cannot arise. These rules put restrictions on the values which may be assigned to the different outcomes, and are as follows.

Let the probability that the outcome A occurs be written $P(A)$. Thus P(heads) is the probability of heads in a single toss of a coin and we assert that

P(heads) $=$ 1/2

The probability of an outcome occurring must always satisfy certain conditions:

(a) If an outcome is certain to occur, then the probability of its occurrence is defined to be one (i.e. it occurs in 100% of all trials).

$P(A) = 1$ A is certain to occur.

(b) If an outcome is certain not to occur, then the probability of its occurrence is defined as zero (it occurs in 0% of all trials).

$P(A) = 0$ A is certain not to occur.

Since one cannot be more certain than certain, probabilities of more than one or less than zero can *never* occur.

(c) Therefore the probability that an outcome occurs must lie between zero and one, inclusive. Thus

$0 \leq P(A) \leq 1$

(d) Since the sample space lists all possible outcomes and they are mutually exclusive, one of the outcomes is certain to occur. This means that if the probabilities of all outcomes in the sample space are added together, the result must be one.

$\Sigma P = 1$ where the summation is over all outcomes in the sample space.

This is an important property of probabilities, and serves as a useful check on calculations (if the probabilities of all outcomes in the sample space are calculated and do not sum to one, a mistake *must* have been made).

(e) The *complement* of an outcome is defined as all the elements of the sample space apart from that outcome. Thus the complement of heads is tails. The complement of the outcome A is written $\sim A$ and

65

$P(\sim A) = 1 - P(A)$.

This is an example of the use of rule (d) above; A and $\sim A$ together make up the whole of the sample space so the sum of their probabilities is one.

Probabilities of compound events

Most practical problems require the calculation of the probability of a set of outcomes rather than just a single outcome in the sample space. For example, the probability of drawing a spade at random from a pack of cards encompasses thirteen points in the sample space, not just one. This probability is 13/52, or one-quarter, which is fairly obvious; but for more complex problems the answer is not immediately evident. We shall refer to a set of outcomes in the sample space as a *compound event* (an outcome is sometimes termed a simple event).

Compound event: a set of outcomes in the sample space.

Examples of compound events are:

(i) getting a five or a six on single throw of the die
(ii) picking up an ace and a queen to complete a 'straight' in a game of poker

It is sometimes possible to calculate the probability of a compound event occurring by examining the sample space, such as in the above case of drawing a spade. However, in many cases this is not so, for the sample space is too complex, or even impossible, to write down. For example, the sample space for three draws of a card from a pack consists of over 140,000 points! An alternative method has to be found, and this is to derive the probability of the compound event from the probabilities of the outcomes of which it is made up.

If the two above examples of compound events are examined closely, it can be seen that outcomes, or simple events, are being compounded by 'and' and 'or' into compound events. In the first case 'or' is used to compound the outcomes 'getting a five on a throw of the die' and 'getting a six on a throw of a die'. In the second example, 'and' compounds the outcomes 'picking up an ace' and 'picking up a queen'. The words 'and' and 'or' used in this way are known as *operators*, and all compound events are made up of simple events compounded by these two operators. The rules set out in the sections below show how the probabilities of compound events can be calculated from simple event probabilities, based upon use of the 'and' and 'or' operators.

The addition rule

This rule is associated with the 'or' operator. Take example (i) above, the probability of getting a five or a six in a single throw of the die. The symbol 'v' will be used to represent the operator 'or', so the desired probability is written $P(5 \vee 6)$. The rule for deriving this from the probabilities of the simple events is

$$P(5 \vee 6) = P(5) + P(6)$$
$$= 1/6 + 1/6$$
$$= 1/3$$

Or, more generally, if there are two simple events, A and B, then

$$P(A \vee B) = P(A) + P(B). \qquad [3.1]$$

This answer can be verified by drawing the sample space, as follows

1   2   3   4   5   6

.   .   .   .   .   .

Each dot represents a simple event. The compound event makes up two out of the six points, so the probability is 2/6 or 1/3. This is obviously the sum of the simple probabilities $P(5)$ and $P(6)$, each represented by a single dot.

Consider now a second example, which requires a slight extension of the rule. What is the probability of obtaining a queen or a spade in a single draw from a deck of cards? The simple probabilities are

P(queen) = 4/52   (there are four queens in a pack)
P(spade) = 13/52   (thirteen spades in a pack)

The rule gives the following answer (which will subsequently be shown to be incorrect):

$$P(Q \vee S) = P(Q) + P(S)$$
$$= 4/52 + 13/52$$
$$= 17/52$$

But if the sample space is examined, the correct answer is found to be 16/52.

What went wrong with the rule? The problem is that one point in the sample space was double counted, the one representing the queen of spades. It was counted once as representing a spade, and again as representing a queen. The problem is that the event 'drawing a queen *and* a spade' (i.e. the queen of spades) is possible, and gets double counted. Therefore the rule has to be modified by subtracting the probability of getting a queen *and* a spade. The symbol '∧' is used to represent 'and'. Thus

$$P(Q \vee S) = P(Q) + P(S) - P(Q \wedge S)$$
$$= 4/52 + 13/52 - 1/52$$
$$= 16/52$$

which is the right answer.

The general rule is

$$P(A \lor B) = P(A) + P(B) - P(A \land B) \tag{3.2}$$

Why, then, did the first example work, where $P(5 \land 6)$ was ignored? In that case $P(5 \land 6) = 0$, since it is impossible for both a five and a six to appear in a single throw of a die. Therefore it makes no difference to the result. When two events cannot simultaneously occur, they are said to be *mutually exclusive*, and $P(A \land B) = 0$.

Mutually exclusive events: Two events, A and B, are mutually exclusive if $P(A \land B) = 0$.

Thus the addition rule can be summarised as

$$P(A \lor B) = P(A) + P(B) - P(A \land B)$$

and, if A and B are mutually exclusive, $P(A \land B) = 0$ and the rule reduces to

$$P(A \lor B) = P(A) + P(B).$$

The multiplication rule

This is the rule associated with the 'and' operator. The example considered here will be the sex of children born to a mother. If she has two children, what is the probability that they are both boys? This is really the compound event of a boy on the first birth *and* a boy on the second birth. Assume that in a single birth a boy or a girl is equally likely to be born. Hence

$$P(\text{boy}) = P(\text{girl}) = 1/2$$

Denote by $P(B1)$ the probability of a boy being born in the first birth, and by $P(B2)$ the probability of a boy on the second birth. Thus the probability $P(B1 \land B2)$ is required, and this is given by the formula:

$$P(B1 \land B2) = P(B1) \times P(B2) \tag{3.3}$$

Thus

$$\begin{aligned} P(B1 \land B2) &= 1/2 \times 1/2 \\ &= 1/4 \end{aligned}$$

Intuitively, the multiplication rule can be understood as follows. One-half of all mothers will have a boy on their first birth, and of this half, half again will have boys on the second birth, making one-quarter of all mothers having two boys.

Like the addition rule, the multiplication rule requires slight modification before it can be applied more generally. The above example assumed first and second births to be *independent* events, i.e. that having a boy on the first birth does not affect the probability of a boy on the second birth. This might not be the case (twins, for example, are very often the same sex). The expression

$$P(B2 \mid B1)$$

is used to indicate the probability of the event *B*2 *given* that the event *B*1 has occurred. Independent events can then be defined as follows.

Independent events: Two events, A and B, are independent if the probability of one occurring is not affected by the fact of the other having occurred. Thus

$P(B \mid A) = P(B)$, and $P(A \mid B) = P(A)$.

It is also the case that, for independent events

$P(B \mid A) = P(B \mid \sim A)$ and $P(A \mid B) = P(A \mid \sim B)$.

Because *B*1 and *B*2 are assumed to be independent events

$P(B2 \mid B1) = P(B2) = 1/2$

It should also be clear that

$P(B2 \mid G1) = 1 - P(B2 \mid B1) = 1/2$

since *G*1 (the first born being a girl) is the complement of *B*1.

To see the effect of the assumption of independence, it will now be dropped and instead it will be assumed that the first birth being a boy (girl) makes it *more* likely that the second is a boy (girl). Let this probability be 0.6 (instead of 0.5 as before). The first child is still equally likely to be a boy or a girl. This can be summarised as

$P(B1) = P(G1) = 1/2$

$P(B2 \mid B1) = P(G2 \mid G1) = 0.6$

(It is easy to work out the values of $P(B2 \mid G1)$ and $P(G2 \mid B1)$.)

What now is the probability of a family having two boys? Half of all families will have a boy as their first child, and of them, 60% will have a boy on the second birth. Thus 30% (60% of 50%) of all families have two boys. This result is achieved by the rule

$$P(B1 \wedge B2) = P(B1) \times P(B2 \mid B1) \qquad [3.4]$$
$$= 0.5 \times 0.6$$
$$= 0.3$$

This rule is generally applicable and simplifies to rule [3.3] when *B*1 and *B*2 are independent, i.e. when $P(B2 \mid B1) = P(B2)$.

These rules are the 'building blocks' for working out the probability of compound events and, however complicated the event, it can (ultimately) be broken down to the simple events of which it is made up.

A slightly more difficult example is the following. What is the probability of a family having one child of each sex? This is the probability that they have a boy first *and* then a girl, *or* a girl first *and* then a boy. Both multiplication and addition rules need to be used since both operators 'and' and 'or' are used. Call a boy then a girl the event *E*1, and a girl then a boy *E*2. The required probability is given by

$P(E1 \vee E2)$

Since *E*1 and *E*2 are mutually exclusive

$$P(E1 \lor E2) = P(E1) + P(E2)$$

by the addition rule. What are the probabilities $E1$ and $E2$?

$$\begin{aligned} P(E1) &= P(B1 \land G2) \\ &= P(B1) \times P(G2 \mid B1) \end{aligned}$$

We continue to assume that these events are not independent, so the formula reduces no further. Clearly also

$$\begin{aligned} P(E2) &= P(G1 \land B2) \\ &= P(G1) \times P(B2 \mid G1) \end{aligned}$$

The simple probabilities are, as before:

$$P(B1) = P(G1) = 0.5$$

$$P(B2 \mid G1) = P(G2 \mid B1) = 0.4$$

Thus

$$\begin{aligned} P(E1) &= 0.5 \times 0.4 \\ &= 0.2 \end{aligned}$$

and

$$\begin{aligned} P(E2) &= 0.5 \times 0.4 \\ &= 0.2 \end{aligned}$$

so

$$\begin{aligned} P(E1 \lor E2) &= 0.2 + 0.2 \\ &= 0.4 \end{aligned}$$

which is the desired probability.

It is worthwhile and fairly straightforward to check this answer by remembering that the sum of the probabilities of all the events in the sample space must equal one. The probabilities of two boys (0.3) and a mixture of boys and girls (0.4) have so far been calculated. The only other possibility is of two girls. This probability can be immediately derived as 0.3, the same as the probability of two boys, since boys and girls are treated symmetrically in this problem. Thus the sum is $0.3 + 0.4 + 0.3 = 1$, as it must be.

Tree diagrams

Tree diagrams are useful as a means of clarifying a problem so that the use of the multiplication and addition rules can be applied. Their use will be illustrated by re-examining the problem of the sex of children. The tree diagram for this problem is shown in Fig. 3.2.

The tree diagram is an alternative way of enumerating all possible outcomes in the sample space and finding the attached probabilities. For example, to find the probability of two girls, follow the lowest path on the diagram and multiply the probabilities along it, to give $0.5 \times 0.6 = 0.3$. To find the probability of

Figure 3.2 Tree diagram for a two-child family

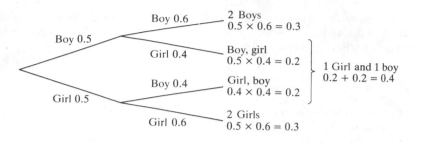

one child of each sex it is necessary to add the probabilities attached to the paths boy, girl and girl, boy, i.e. $(0.5 \times 0.4) + (0.5 \times 0.4) = 0.4$.

The tree diagram can obviously be extended to cover third, fourth and subsequent children, although the number of branches rapidly (geometrically) increases. The difficulty then becomes not the calculation of the probability attached to each outcome, but sorting out which branches should be taken into account in the calculation. For example, if there are five children of whom three are girls, then there are ten different 'routes' through the tree which lead to an outcome of three girls and two boys, each representing a different ordering of three girls and two boys. We frequently need to count how many of these 'routes' there are in a particular problem. Fortunately there are formulae which allow the rapid calculation of the number of such routes. These are the techniques of counting *permutations* and *combinations*.

Permutations and combinations

It was stated above that there are ten different ways (or orderings) of having three girls and two boys. How is this number arrived at? One way is to write down all the possible orderings:

GGGBB	GGBGB	GGBBG	GBGGB	GBGBG
GBBGG	BGGGB	BGGBG	BGBGG	BBGGG

In more complex problems this soon becomes tedious. The record number of children born to a British mother is 39, of whom 32 were girls. The appropriate tree diagram has over 5,000 billion routes, and a computer drawing one route per second would need 17,433 years to complete the task! Therefore, rather than draw the tree diagram, use is made of the *combinatorial* formula. Suppose that there are n children, r of them girls; then the number of orderings, denoted nCr, can be derived by using the combinatorial formula.

$$nCr = \frac{n!}{r!(n-r)!} = \frac{n \times (n-1) \times (n-2) \times \ldots \times 1}{r \times (r-1) \times \ldots \times 1 \times (n-r) \times (n-r-1) \times \ldots \times 1}$$

In the example above, $n = 5, r = 3$, hence

71

$$5C3 = \frac{5!}{3!(5-3)!} = \frac{5 \times 4 \times 3 \times 2 \times 1}{3 \times 2 \times 1 \times 2 \times 1} = 10$$

which is the result previously calculated. A second example will reinforce the message. Suppose there are four girls instead of three in the family, how many orderings are there? The formula gives $n = 5, r = 4$, so

$$5C4 = \frac{5!}{4!1!} = \frac{5 \times 4 \times 3 \times 2 \times 1}{4 \times 3 \times 2 \times 1 \times 1} = 5$$

This gives five possible orderings (i.e. the single boy could be born first, second, third, fourth or fifth). Why does this formula give the correct result?

Consider five empty boxes to fill, corresponding to the five births (in chronological order), and suppose there are three girls among the five children.

The three girls (call them Amanda, Bridget and Christine) have to be put into these five boxes. For Amanda there is a choice of five boxes. Having chosen one, there remain four empty boxes for Bridget, so there are $5 \times 4 = 20$ possibilities. There remain three empty boxes for Christine, making $20 \times 3 = 60$ possible orderings in all (the two boys go into the two remaining boxes). Sixty is the number of *permutations* of three named girls in five births. This is written $5P3$, or in general nPr (P standing for permutations, not probability in this case). Hence

$$5P3 = 5 \times 4 \times 3$$

or in general

$$nPr = n \times (n-1) \times \ldots \times (n-r+1)$$

An easier formula for nPr is obtained by multiplying top and bottom by $(n-r)!$

$$nPr = \frac{n \times (n-1) \times \ldots \times (n-r+1) \times (n-r)!}{(n-r)!}$$

$$= \frac{n!}{(n-r)!}$$

What is the difference between nPr and nCr? The 60 permutations contain many instances of double (or rather multiple) counting. For example consider the cases

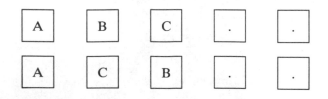

These are both the same, i.e. examples of three girls followed by two boys. A little thought should make it clear that *nPr* is too large, by a factor representing the number of ways of ordering the three girls. This factor is equal to $r! = 3! = 3 \times 2 \times 1 = 6$ (any of the three girls could be first, then there remain two who could come second and the one who remains is last). *nPr* must therefore be divided by $r!$, giving

$$\frac{nPr}{r!} = \frac{n!}{(n-r)!\ r!}$$

which is the formula given for *nCr* earlier.

Bayes' theorem

The differences between Bayesian and classical (frequentist) views of statistics have been mentioned above. It is now time to set out the basis of those differences. Bayes' theorem itself is an uncontroversial statement about probabilities which is accepted by Bayesian and classical statisticians alike. It is the use and interpretation of this result which is at the root of the argument.

The theorem itself is easily derived from first principles.

$$P(A \wedge B) = P(A \mid B) \times P(B) \qquad \text{(see eqn [3.4])}$$

Hence

$$P(A \mid B) = \frac{P(A \wedge B)}{P(B)}$$

Expanding both top and bottom of the right-hand side,

$$P(A \mid B) = \frac{P(B \mid A) \times P(A)}{P(B \mid A) \times P(A) + P(B \mid {\sim}A) \times P({\sim}A)} \qquad [3.5]$$

Equation [3.5] is known as *Bayes' theorem* and is a statement about the probability of event A, conditional upon event B having occurred. This is best seen via a simple example.

Two bags contain red and yellow balls. Bag A contains six red and four yellow balls, bag B has three red and seven yellow balls. A ball is selected at random from one of the bags and turns out to be red. What is the probability it came from bag A?

The following notation is used:

$P(A)$: the probability of selecting bag A at random. $P(A) = 1/2$, therefore.
$P(R \mid A)$: the probability of selecting a red ball from bag A. $P(R \mid A) = 6/10$.

The meanings and values of $P(B)$, $P(Y \mid A)$ etc. should be obvious. The question asks for the probability of bag A having been selected, given a red ball has been chosen. By Bayes' theorem this is

$$P(A \mid R) = \frac{P(R \mid A) \times P(A)}{P(R \mid A) \times P(A) + P(R \mid B) \times P(B)}$$

$$= \frac{6/10 \times 1/2}{6/10 \times 1/2 + 3/10 \times 1/2}$$

$$= \quad 2/3$$

(The reader should check that $P(B \mid R) = 1/3$, so that the sum of the probabilities is one.)

Bayes' theorem can be extended to cover more than two bags; if there are five bags, for example, labelled A to E then

$$P(A \mid R) = \frac{P(R \mid A) \times P(A)}{P(R \mid A) \times P(A) + P(R \mid B) \times P(B) + \ldots + P(R \mid E) \times P(E)}$$

In Bayesian language, $P(A)$ and $P(B)$ are known as the *prior* (to the drawing of a ball) probabilities, $P(R \mid A)$, etc. are known as the *likelihoods*, and $P(A \mid R)$ and $P(B \mid R)$ are the *posterior* probabilities. Bayes' theorem can alternatively be expressed as:

$$\text{posterior probability} = \frac{\text{likelihood} \times \text{prior probability}}{\Sigma \,(\text{likelihood} \times \text{prior probability})}$$

and is illustrated below, by reworking the above example

	Prior probabilities	Likelihood	Prior × likelihood	Posterior probabilities
A	0.5	0.6	0.3	0.3 / 0.45 = 2/3
B	0.5	0.3	0.15	0.15 / 0.45 = 1/3
			0.45	

The prior probabilities are $P(A)$ and $P(B)$, the likelihoods are $P(R \mid A)$ and $P(R \mid B)$, and the posterior probabilities are $P(A \mid R)$ and $P(B \mid R)$.

The general version of Bayes' theorem may be stated as follows. If there are n events (bags) labelled $E_1, \ldots E_n$, then the probability of the event i occurring, given the sample evidence R is:

$$P(E_i \mid R) = \frac{P(R \mid E_i) \times P(E_i)}{\Sigma P(R \mid E_i) \times P(E_i)}$$

As stated earlier, dispute arises over the interpretation of Bayes' theorem. In the above example there is no difficulty because the probability statements can be interpreted as relative frequencies. If the experiment of selecting a bag at random and choosing a ball from it were repeated many times, then of those occasions when a red ball is selected, in two-thirds of them bag A will have been chosen. However, consider an alternative interpretation of the symbols:

A: a coin is fair
B: a coin is unfair
R: the result of a toss is a head

Then given a toss (or series of tosses) of a coin, this evidence can be used to calculate the probability of the coin being fair. This makes no sense according to the frequentist school: either the coin is fair or it isn't; it is not a question of probability. The calculated value must therefore be interpreted as a degree of belief, and must be given a subjective interpretation. The differences between the two schools of thought will come up again later in the book.

The Binomial distribution

The Binomial distribution is just an extension of the problem dealt with above, so it is worthwhile considering it further. For simplicity, births are again considered to be independent events, so that the probability of a boy being born is equal to 0.5 whatever the sex of the previous child. We shall in turn calculate the probability of having no boys, one, two, etc. boys among five children. The probabilities for a single event (birth) are

$$P(B) = P(G) = 1/2$$

First consider the case of no boys, i.e. five girls. The desired probability is

$$P(G \wedge G \wedge G \wedge G \wedge G)$$

which, since they are independent events, is just

$$P(G) \times P(G) \times P(G) \times P(G) \times P(G) = P(G)^5$$
$$= (1/2)^5$$
$$= 1/32$$

Thus

$$P(\text{no boys}) = 1/32$$

For one boy

$$P(B \wedge G \wedge G \wedge G \wedge G)$$
$$= P(B) \times P(G) \times P(G) \times P(G) \times P(G) = P(B)^1 \times P(G)^4$$
$$= 1/2^1 \times (1/2)^4$$
$$= 1/32$$

But this only gives one ordering (of the five possible), that of the boy being the first. The nCr formula has to be used to find the number of possible orderings. In this case it is $5C1$. Thus

$$P(1 \text{ boy}) = 5C1 \ P(B)^1 \ P(G)^4$$
$$= \frac{5!}{1!4!} \times (1/2)^1 \times (1/2)^4$$
$$= 5/32$$

Similarly

$$P(2 \text{ boys}) = 5C2 \; P(B)^2 \; P(G)^3$$
$$= \frac{5!}{2!3!} \times (1/2)^2 \times (1/2)^3$$
$$= 10/32$$

And

$$P(3) = 5C3 \; P(B)^3 \; P(G)^2$$
$$= 10/32$$
$$P(4) = 5C4 \; P(B)^4 \; P(G)^1$$
$$= 5/32$$
$$P(5) = 5C5 \; P(B)^5 \; P(G)^0$$
$$= 1/32$$

(NB (a) 0! is defined to be 1; (b) check that the probabilities sum to one.)

A fairly clear pattern is emerging. The probability of *r* boys in *n* births is given by the formula

$$P(r) = nCr \; P(B)^r \; P(G)^{(n-r)}$$

This is known as the *Binomial* distribution and is commonly encountered in statistics. Whenever a simple event (e.g. birth, tossing a coin) has only two possible outcomes with known probabilities, and those probabilities do not alter from one trial to the next, then the Binomial distribution is appropriate. Indeed, in statistical terms, birth (or at least the sex of the baby) is equivalent to tossing a coin. The probability of three heads in five tosses is the same as three girls in five children.

The fact that it is called the Binomial *distribution* suggests that it is like the frequency distributions of Chapter 1. This is indeed the case. Since the area under the distribution (i.e. the sum of the probabilities) is one, the Binomial is a *probability* distribution. If probability is thought of as a relative frequency, then it is easy to see the relationship between a probability distribution and a relative frequency distribution. It is straightforward to draw the probability distribution, which is presented in Fig. 3.3.

The mean and variance of the data can also be calculated, taking the probabilities as frequencies (*r* is equivalent to *x*, $P(r)$ to $f(x)$), as in Table 3.1.
The mean of the distribution is given by:

$$\text{Mean} = \frac{\Sigma r \; P(r)}{\Sigma P(r)} = \frac{80/32}{1} = 2.5 \qquad \text{(equivalent to } \frac{\Sigma fx}{\Sigma f} \text{)}$$

and the variance by:

$$\text{Variance} = \frac{\Sigma r^2 \; P(r)}{\Sigma P(r)} - \text{mean}^2 \qquad \text{(equivalent to } \frac{\Sigma fx^2}{\Sigma f} - \bar{x}^2 \text{)}$$
$$= \frac{240/32}{1} - 2.5^2$$
$$= 1.25$$

Thus the mean number of boys in a family of five children is 2.5 (which seems intuitively obvious) and the variance 1.25 (which probably doesn't). It can be

Figure 3.3 The Binomial distribution, $n=5$, $p=\frac{1}{2}$

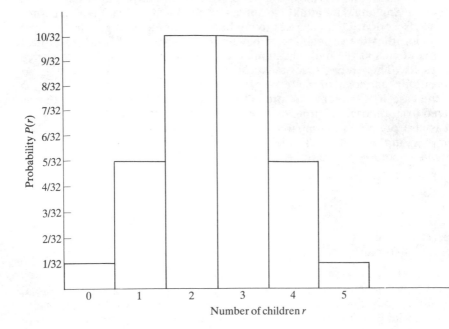

Table 3.1 The mean and variance of the Binomial distribution

r	$P(r)$	$r \times P(r)$	$r^2 \times P(r)$
0	1/32	0	0
1	5/32	5/32	5/32
2	10/32	20/32	40/32
3	10/32	30/32	90/32
4	5/32	20/32	80/32
5	1/32	5/32	25/32
	32/32	80/32	240/32

proven that the mean of a Binomial distribution is equal to nP and the variance equal to nPQ, where P is the probability of success in a single trial and Q the probability of failure. In this case $P = P(B) = 1/2$, $Q = P(G) = 1/2$ and $n = 5$. So

mean $= nP = 5 \times 1/2 = 2.5$

variance $= nPQ = 5 \times 1/2 \times 1/2 = 1.25$

77

It is interesting to note that this Binomial distribution has been obtained, its histogram drawn and the mean and variance calculated, just as in Chapter 1, without having any data at all! No survey of childbearing was conducted nor were any secondary data sources looked at. The point of departure was the assumption that the probability of having a boy was a half, and theoretical principles (such as the multiplication and addition rules) were used to derive the results. This shows that statistical distributions can either be derived theoretically, as above, or they can be obtained by examining empirical data, as was the case in Chapter 1. A probability distribution is always one that is derived from theoretical principles rather than from actual data.

It is also possible to compare theoretical and empirical distributions. For example, suppose that 500 families with five children were surveyed to see how many had one boy, two boys, etc. Suppose the data were as follows

No of boys	0	1	2	3	4	5	Total
No. of families	20	75	145	140	85	35	500
Expected no. of families (Binomial)	16	78	156	156	78	16	500

The last row gives the data one would expect to find according to the Binomial distribution (e.g. $500 \times 1/32 = 16$) and is fairly similar to the actual data. The Binomial probability distribution would appear to be good at explaining the distribution of boys in families with five children. If there were large differences between the theoretical and empirical distributions, then this would cast doubt upon the validity of the Binomial explanation. Perhaps the probability of a boy is not equal to a half, or successive births are not independent, as was assumed. Chapter 8 (on the Chi-squared distribution) will describe methods which can be used to decide whether the differences between the actual and expected values are significantly large.

The next chapter goes on to generalise the concept of probability distributions and looks at other distributions apart from the Binomial.

Problems

3.1 Given a standard pack of cards, calculate the following probabilities:
(a) – P(drawing an ace)
(b) – P(drawing a court card) (i.e. jack, queen, or king)
(c) – P(drawing a red card)
(d) – P(drawing three aces without replacement)
(e) – P(drawing three aces with replacement).

3.2 The following data give duration of unemployment by age, in July 1986 (it is an abridged version of the table in question 3 in Chapter 1).

| Age | Duration of unemployment (weeks) | | | | Total | Economically |
| | ≤ 8 | 8–26 | 26–52 | > 52 | (000s) | active |
	(percentage figures)					(000s)
16–19	27.2	29.8	24.0	19.0	273.4	1270
20–24	24.2	20.7	18.3	36.8	442.5	2000
25–34	14.8	18.8	17.2	49.2	531.4	3600
35–49	12.2	16.6	15.1	56.2	521.2	4900
50–59	8.9	14.4	15.6	61.2	388.1	2560
≥ 60	18.5	29.7	30.7	21.4	74.8	1110

The 'economically active' column gives the total of employed plus unemployed in each age category.

(a) In what sense may these figures be regarded as probabilities? What does the figure 27.2 (top left cell) mean following this interpretation?

(b) Assuming the validity of the probability interpretation, which of the following statements are true?

   (i) The probability of an economically active adult aged 25–34, drawn at random, being unemployed is 531.4/3,600.

   (ii) If someone who has been unemployed for over one year is drawn at random, the probability that they are aged 16–19 is 19%.

   (iii) For those aged 35–49 who became unemployed before July 1985, the probability of their still being unemployed is 56.2%.

   (iv) If someone aged 50–59 is drawn at random from the economically active population, the probability of their being unemployed for 8 weeks or less is 8.9%.

   (v) The probability of someone aged 35–49 drawn at random from the economically active population being unemployed for between 8 and 26 weeks is $0.166 \times 521.2/4{,}900$.

(c) A person is drawn at random from the population and found to have been unemployed for over one year. What is the probability that they are aged between 16 and 19?

3.3 Manchester United beat Liverpool 4–2 at soccer, but you do not know the order in which the goals were scored. Draw a tree diagram to display all the possibilities and use it to find (a) the probability that the goals were scored in the order L, MU, MU, MU, L, MU and (b) the probability that the score was 2–2 at some stage.

3.4 Three per cent of firms in a particular industry go bankrupt in a given year. What is the probability of a randomly chosen firm surviving for five years? What assumption about the probability of going bankrupt in each year are you making. Does this seem to be a reasonable assumption to make? If not, is the answer likely to over– or underestimate the true probability?

3.5 Which of the following events are independent?
(a) Two flips of a fair coin.
(b) Two flips of a biased coin.

(c) Rainfall on two successive days.
(d) Rainfall on 1 April and 1 October.
(e) The profits of computer firms IBM and DEC next year showing an increase over the previous year.

3.6   The French national lottery works as follows. Six numbers from the range 0 to 49 are selected at random. If you have correctly guessed all six you win the first prize. What are your chances of winning (you are only allowed to guess six numbers)? A single entry like this costs one franc. For 210 francs you can choose ten numbers and you win if the six selected numbers are among them. Is this better value than the single entry?

3.7   An important numerical calculation on a spacecraft is carried out independently by three computers. If all arrive at the same answer it is deemed correct. If one disagrees it is over-ruled. If there is no agreement, then a fourth computer does the calculation, and if its answer agrees with any of the others, it is deemed correct. The probability of an individual computer's getting the right answer is 99%.

(a) What is the probability of the first three computers' getting the right result?
(b) What is the probability of getting the right result?
(c) What is the probability of getting the wrong result?

3.8   A student takes a multiple-choice examination paper. Each question has four choices from which the answer must be selected. The student has a 60% probability of knowing the answer to any particular question. If he doesn't know he chooses at random. The paper contains six questions.

(a) What is the probability of the student getting more than half marks?
        53% ?   60% ?   74% ?   81% ?
(b) Another student has a 50% chance of knowing the right answer to a question. If the two students work together, guessing any answers they don't know, what is the probability they get over half marks? (Assume the probabilities are independent.)
        55% ?   75% ?   85% ?   95% ?
(c) A class of five students, all with a 60% probability of knowing the right answer, has taken the test. The teacher has not worked out the answers in advance so decides to accept an answer as correct if obtained by a majority of the class. What is the probability of the correct answer being obtained by this method?
        24% ?   44% ?   64% ?   84% ?
(d) If a student obtains exactly half marks, is it possible to calculate the probability of his knowing the correct answer to a question?
        Yes, 1/3 ?   Yes, 1/2 ?   Yes, 2/3 ?   No ?

4 Probability distributions

Introduction

The next step towards an understanding of statistical inference is the concept of a probability distribution, which is the subject of this chapter. The probability distribution was introduced at the end of the previous chapter and illustrated using the Binomial distribution. The Binominal is only one of a number of probability distributions, several of which are examined in this book. In this chapter the Binomial distribution will be examined in more detail and another important distribution will be introduced, the Normal distribution. The relationship between these two distributions will also be set out. A third probability distribution, the Poisson, is also introduced.

In order to understand fully the idea of a probability distribution a new concept is first introduced, that of a random variable. As will be seen later in the chapter, an important random variable is the sample mean, and to understand how to draw inferences from the sample mean it is important to recognise it as a random variable.

Random variables

Examples of random variables have already been encountered in the previous chapter, for example the result of the toss of a coin, or the number of boys in a family of five children. A random variable is one whose outcome or value is the result of chance and is therefore unpredictable, although the range of possible outcomes and the probability of each outcome is known. It is impossible to know in advance the outcome of a toss of a coin for example, but it must be either heads or tails, each with probability one-half. The number of boys in the example in the previous chapter must be an integer in the range 0 to 5, with the probabilities given by Table 3.1.

The concept of a random variable is therefore best understood in terms of the sample space. The sample space lists all possible outcomes of an experiment, and attaching a probability to each outcome completely defines the random variable. The random variable 'the result of a toss of a coin' is therefore defined by:

Outcome	Heads	Tails
Probability	1/2	1/2

The random variable 'the number of boys in a family of five children' is defined by:

Outcome	0	1	2	3	4	5
Probability	1/32	5/32	10/32	10/32	5/32	1/32

Random variables abound in everyday life, as well as in statistical theory. The time of arrival of a train is a random variable. It may be timetabled to arrive at 11.15, but it probably (almost certainly!) won't arrive at *exactly* that time. If a sample of ten basketball players were taken, and their average height calculated, this would be a random variable. In this latter case, it is the process of taking a sample that introduces the variability which makes the resulting average a random variable. If the experiment were repeated, a different sample and a different value of the random variable would be obtained.

The above examples can be contrasted with some things which are not random variables. If one were to take *all* basketball players and calculate their average height, the result would not be a random variable. This time there is no sampling procedure to introduce variability into the result. If the experiment were repeated, the same result would be obtained, since the same people would be measured the second time (this assumes that the population does not change, of course). Just because the value of something is unknown does not mean it qualifies as a random variable. This is an important distinction to bear in mind, since it is legitimate to make probability statements about random variables ('the probability that the average height of a sample of basketball players is over 6 feet 4 inches is 60%) but not about parameters ('the probability that the Pope is over 6 feet 4 inches is 60%). Here again there is a difference of opinion between frequentist and subjective schools of thought. The latter group would argue that it *is* possible to make probability statements about the Pope's height. It is a way of expressing lack of knowledge about the true value.

Particular probability distributions

As stated above, although the exact value of a random variable cannot be predicted in advance, it is possible to have some idea of the range of possible values, and the probabilities with which each is likely to occur. The train is most likely to arrive at close to 11.15, the average height of basketball players is likely to be around 6 feet 6 inches and, as found in the previous chapter, the most likely number of boys in a family of five children is two or three. This leads on naturally to the idea of the *distribution* of a random variable, for example the Binomial distribution associated with the number of boys in a family. This is termed the *probability distribution* of the random variable, i.e. the range of possible values that the random variable can take and the probability associated with each of those values. A probability distribution can be presented in a number of ways, descriptive, graphical or mathematical. The three forms of presentation for the Binomial distribution are:

Descriptive

Number of boys	0	1	2	3	4	5
Probability	1/32	5/32	10/32	10/32	5/32	1/32

Graphical

Figure 4.1

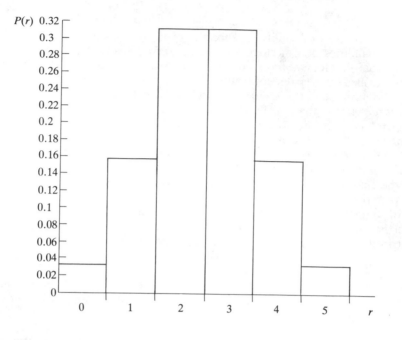

Mathematical

$$P(r) = nCr\ P(G)^r\ P(B)^{(n-r)}$$
$$= 5Cr\ (1/2)^r\ (1/2)^{(n-r)}$$

Each of these formulations expresses precisely the same information in different ways. The choice between them is a matter of convenience, though the mathematical presentation has the advantage that the other forms can be derived from it, while the reverse is not true (or at least not so straightforward).

Thus a random variable has associated with it a probability distribution which is the *theoretical* distribution, which can be compared with the empirical (or sample) distribution, i.e. the actual outcome of an experiment or series of experiments. There is a large number of different probability distributions, of which the Binomial is one; others will be encountered in the ensuing chapters, these being the Normal, Poisson, *t*, chi-squared and *F* distributions. It is important to know which is the appropriate probability distribution to associate with a given random variable in order to be able to draw correct statistical inferences; this will become apparent as each of the probability distributions is encountered. In the rest of this chapter three probability distributions, the Binomial, Normal and Poisson, will be examined; others are reserved for later chapters.

The Binomial distribution

This distribution should be becoming familiar by now. Recall that the formula for the Binomial is

$$P(r) = nCrP^rQ^{n-r}$$

where P is the probability of success, Q is the probability of failure and the probabilities do not change between trials. This formula shows that the Binomial is in fact a *family* of distributions, each member of the family being distinguished by the values of P and n. Since Q is equal to $1-P$, it does not serve to distinguish members of the family independently of P. P and n are known as the *parameters* of the distribution. The Binomial is thus a distribution with two parameters, and once these are known the distribution is completely determined (i.e. $P(r)$ can be calculated for all values of r). To illustrate the difference between members of the family of the Binomial distribution, Fig. 4.2 presents four Binomial distributions, for different values of P and n. It can be seen that for the value of $P = 1/2$ the distribution is symmetric, while for all other values it skewed either to the left or right.

Since the Binomial distribution depends only upon the two values P and n, a shorthand notation can be used. A random variable r, which has a Binomial distribution with the parameters P and n, can be written

$$r \sim B(n, P).$$

('$\sim$' means 'is distributed', not 'is the complement of' used earlier). Thus for the previous example of children, where r represents the number of boys

$$r \sim B(5, 1/2)$$

This is simply a brief and convenient way of writing down the information available: it involves no new problems of a conceptual nature.

The Binomial distribution can be used to solve a variety of problems. For example, if a die is thrown four times, what is the probability of getting two or more sixes? This is a problem involving repeated experiments (rolling the die) with but two types of outcome for each roll: success (a six) or failure (anything but a six). The probability of success (one-sixth) does not vary from one experiment to another, and so use of the Binomial distribution is appropriate. The values of the parameters are $P=1/6$ and $n=4$. Denote by r the random variable 'the number of sixes in four rolls of the die'; then

$$r \sim B(4, 1/6)$$

Hence

$$P(r) = nCrP^rQ^{n-r}$$

where $P=1/6$, $n=4$ and $Q=1-P=5/6$.

The probability of two sixes is then

$$P(2) = 4C2 \ (1/6)^2 \ (5/6)^2 = 0.116$$

The probability of three sixes is

$$P(3) = 4C3 \ (1/6)^3 \ (5/6)^1 = 0.015$$

Figure 4.2 Four different Binomial distributions

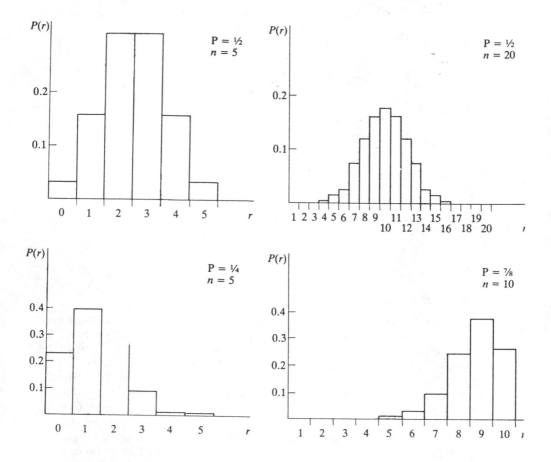

and four sixes

$$P(4) = 4C4 \ (1/6)^4 = 0.00077$$

Since these events are mutually exclusive, the probabilities can simply be added together to get the desired result, which is 0.132, or 13.2%. This is the probability of two or more sixes in four rolls of a die. What has been calculated is the area in the right-hand tail of the appropriate Binomial distribution, as illustrated in Fig. 4.3. Many similar problems can be solved by calculating the area under the appropriate part of the Binomial distribution.

Having examined one particular probability distribution we now move on to probably the most important of all probability distributions, the Normal.

Figure 4.3 The Binomial distribution P=1/6, *n*=4

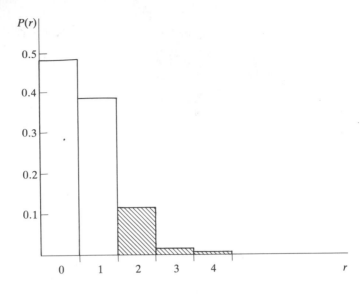

The Normal distribution

The Normal distribution is the most common and important distribution in statistics. It was discovered by the German mathematician Gauss in the nineteenth century (hence it is also known as the Gaussian distribution), in the course of his work on regression (see Chapter 9). When does a random variable follow the Normal distribution rather than, say, the Binomial? A Normal distribution tends to emerge when the random variable is influenced by many small and independent factors. For example, the heights of adult males follow a Normal distribution, since they are influenced by many factors such as heredity, diet, environmental quality, etc. The heights of all adults (both male and female) are not Normally distributed, however, since the factors influencing males' heights tend to be different from those influencing females'. It is obvious from empirical observation that this distribution is bimodal.

Another example is of a machine producing bolts with a nominal length of 5 cm which will actually produce bolts of slightly varying length (these differences would probably be extremely small) owing to factors such as wear in the machinery, slight variations in the pressure of the lubricant, etc. These would result in bolts whose length is Normally distributed. This sort of process is extremely common, with the result that the Normal distribution often occurs in everyday problems.

Having introduced the Normal distribution, what does it look like? It is presented below in mathematical and graphical forms. If *X* is a random variable which is Normally distributed, its probability distribution is given in mathmatical form by the formula

$$P(X) = \frac{1}{\sigma\sqrt{2\pi}} \, e^{-\frac{1}{2}[(X-\mu)/\sigma]^2}$$ [4.1]

The mathematical formulation is not so formidable as it appears. μ and σ are parameters of the distribution, like P and n for the Binomial; π is 3.1416 and e is the natural number 2.7183. If the formula is evaluated using different values of x (try $X = -1.5$, -1, -0.5, 0, 0.5, 1, 1.5), the values of $P(X)$ obtained will map out a Normal distribution (setting $\mu = 0$ and $\sigma = 1$ makes the calculation fairly easy with a calculator).

The Normal distribution mapped out by this process will look like the one drawn in Fig. 4.4 (all values of X have been evaluated rather than just a few, so the distribution is a continuous one, unlike the Binomial which is discrete).

Figure 4.4 The Normal distribution

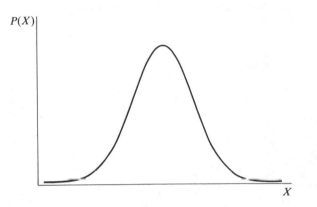

It should be noted that the Normal distribution

(i) is unimodal
(ii) is symmetric
(iii) is bell shaped
(iv) extends continuously over all the values of X from minus infinity to plus infinity, though the value of $P(X)$ becomes extremely small as these values are approached (the pages of this book being of only finite width, this last characteristic is not faithfully represented!).

Like the Binomial, the Normal is a family of distributions differing from one another only in the values of the parameters μ and σ. Several Normal distributions are drawn in Fig. 4.5 for different values of the parameters.

Whatever value of μ is chosen turns out to be the centre of the distribution. Since the distribution is symmetric, μ is its mean. The effect of varying σ is to narrow (small σ) or widen (large σ) the distribution. σ turns out to be the standard deviation of the distribution. The Normal is another two-parameter family of distributions like the Binomial, and once the mean, μ, and the standard deviation, σ, (or equivalently the variance, σ^2) are known the whole

Figure 4.5(a) The Normal distribution with mean μ=20 and variance σ²=25

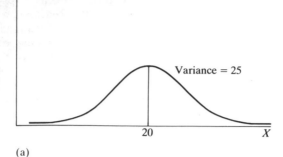

(a)

Figure 4.5(b) The Normal distribution with mean μ=15 and variance σ²=4

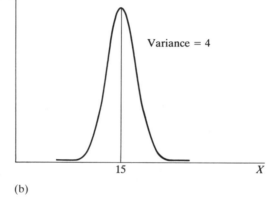

(b)

Figure 4.5(c) The Normal distribution with mean μ=0 and variance σ²=16

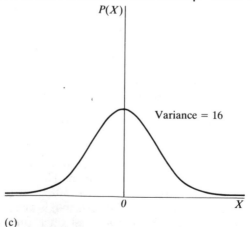

(c)

of the distribution can be drawn. The shorthand notation for a Normal distribution is

$$X \sim N(\mu, \sigma^2)$$

meaning 'the variable X is Normally distributed with mean μ the variance σ^2'. This is similar in form to the expression for the Binomial distribution, though the meaning of the parameters is different.

The Normal distribution can be used in practice to solve a wide variety of problems; a simple one is as follows. The height of adult males is Normally distributed with mean height $\mu = 174$ cm and standard deviation $\sigma = 9.6$ cm. Let X represent the height of adult males; then

$$X \sim N(174, \ 92.16)$$

Figure 4.6 Distribution of the heights of adult males

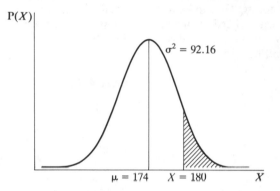

What proportion of adult males are over 180 cm in height? This requires calculating the area under the Normal distribution to the right of $X = 180$, i.e. the shaded area in Fig. 4.6 One way to find this would be to make use of eqn [4.1], but this requires the use of sophisticated mathematics.

Since this is a frequently encountered problem, the answers have been tabulated in the tables of the *standard Normal distribution*. Since there is an infinite number of Normal distributions (for every combination of μ and σ^2), it would be an impossible task to tabulate them all. The standard Normal distribution, which has a mean of zero and a variance of one, is therefore used to represent all Normal distributions. Before the table can be consulted, therefore, the data has to be transformed so that it accords with the standard Normal distribution. This means that the z-score of the data must be calculated, as in Chapter 1. The method is now demonstrated.

Using the standard Normal distribution table

First the z-score of $X = 180$ is calculated

$$z = \frac{X - \mu}{\sigma} = \frac{180 - 174}{9.6} = 0.63$$

89

This means that 180 is 0.63 standard deviations above the mean, 174, of the distribution. The problem now is to find the area under the Normal distribution to the right of 0.63 standard deviations above the mean. This answer can be read off directly from the table of the standard Normal distribution, Table A2. The left-hand column gives the z-score to one place of decimals. The appropriate row of the table is the one for $z = 0.6$. The appropriate column depends upon the second place of decimals in the z-score. This is 3 in the above calculation, so the column headed '3' is the one wanted. The cell in the row labelled 0.6 and the column headed '3' contains the value 0.2643 which is the area desired. In other words, 26.43% of the distribution lies to the right of 0.63 standard deviations above the mean. Therefore 26.43% of adult males are over 180 cm in height.

Use of the standard Normal table is possible because although there is an infinite number of Normal distributions, they are all fundamentally the same, so that the area to the right of 0.63 standard deviations above the mean is the same for all of them. The process of standardisation turns all Normal distributions into a Normal distribution with a mean of zero and a variance of one. This is what is known as the standard Normal distribution. This process is illustrated in Fig. 4.7 a and b.

Figure 4.7 (a)   **Figure 4.7 (b)**

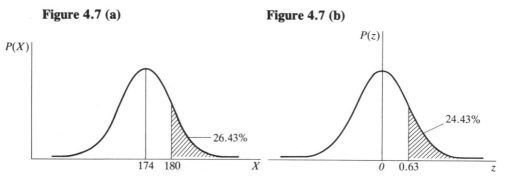

The area in the right-hand tail is the same for both distributions. It is the distribution on the right which is tabulated in Table A2. To demonstrate how standardisation turns all Normal distributions into the standard Normal, the earlier problem will be repeated but taking all measurements in inches. The answer should obviously be the same. Taking 1 in = 2.54 cm the figures are

$$X = 70.87 \qquad \sigma = 3.78 \qquad \mu = 68.50$$

What proportion of men are over 70.87 in in height? The appropriate Normal distribution is now

$$X \sim N(68.50, \ 3.78^2)$$

The z-score is

$$z = \frac{70.87 - 68.50}{3.78} = 0.63$$

which is the same z-score as before.

Since a great deal of use is made of the standard Normal tables, it is worth working through a couple more examples to reinforce the method. We have so far calculated that $P(z \geq 0.63) = 0.2643$. Since the total area under the graph equals one (i.e. the sum of probabilities must be one), the area to the left of $z = 0.63$ must equal 0.7357, i.e. 73.57% of men are under 180 cm. It is fairly easy to manipulate areas under the graph to arrive at the required area, for example, what proportion of men are between 174 and 180 cm in height? It is helpful to refer to Fig. 4.8 at this point. The size of area A is required. Area B has already been calculated as 0.2643. Since the distribution is symmetric, the area $A + B$ must equal 0.5, since 174 is at the centre (mean) of the distribution. Area A is therefore $0.5 - 0.2643 = 0.2357$, and 23.57% is the desired result.

Figure 4.8

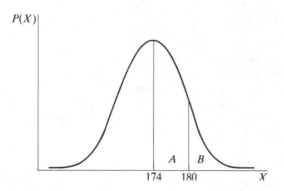

As a final exercise consider the question of what proportion of men are between 172 and 178 cm tall. As shown in Figure. 4.9 area $C + D$ is wanted.

Figure 4.9

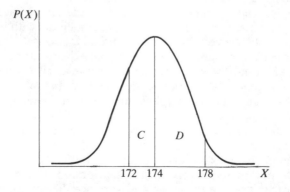

The only way to find this is to calculate the two areas separately and then add them together. For area D the z-score associated with 178 is:

$$z_D = \frac{178 - 174}{9.6} = 0.42$$

Table A2 indicates that the area in the right-hand tail, beyond $z = 0.42$, is 0.3372, so area $D = 0.5 - 0.3372 = 0.1628$. For C, the z-score is

$$z_C = \frac{172 - 174}{9.6} = -0.21$$

The minus sign indicates that it is the left-hand tail of the distribution, below the mean, which is being considered. Since the distribution is symmetric, it is the same as if it were the right-hand tail, so the minus sign may be ignored when consulting the table. Looking up $z = 0.21$ in Table A2 gives an area of 0.4168 in the tail, so area C is therefore $0.5 - 0.4168 = 0.0832$. Adding areas C and D gives $0.1628 + 0.0832 = 0.2460$. So approximately one-quarter of men are between 172 and 178 cm in height. It is worth practising a few of these calculations to become proficient in them.

An alternative interpretation of the results obtained above is that if a man is drawn at random from the adult population, the probability that he is over 180 cm tall is 26.43%. This is in line with the frequentist school of thought. Since 26.43% of the population is over 180 cm in height, that is the probability of a man over 180 cm being drawn at random.

The sample mean as a Normally distributed variable

One of the main concepts in statistical inference is the probability distribution of the mean of a random sample. Suppose that, from the population of adult males, a random sample of size $n = 36$ was taken, that their heights were measured, and that the mean height of the sample was calculated. This sample mean is a random variable because of the chance element of random sampling (different samples would yield different values of the sample mean). Since the sample mean is a random variable it must have associated with it a probability distribution. It can be proven (though it is beyond the scope of this book to do so) that under certain conditions this probability distribution is Normal. As stated earlier, a Normal distribution tends to emerge when a random variable is influenced by a large number of independent factors. In the case of the sample mean, each observation in the sample counts as an influencing factor, and as long as the observations are independently drawn, this ensures that the sample mean is Normally distributed. Normality is only guaranteed if the number of influences, the sample size, is sufficiently large.

Since the sample mean is Normally distributed, it is natural to ask what are the values of the parameters of this Normal distribution. The two parameters of the Normal distribution are the mean and variance. These are obtained from the following theorem, which is stated without proof.

Theorem: The sample mean, $\bar{x}$, drawn from a population which follows a Normal distribution with mean μ and variance of σ^2, has a sampling distribution which is Normal, with mean μ and variance σ^2/n, where n is the sample size, i.e.

$X \sim N\ (\mu, \sigma^2)$ Population distribution
$\bar{x} \sim N\ (\mu, \sigma^2/n)$ Distribution of sample means

The meaning of this theorem is as follows. First of all it is *assumed* that the population from which the samples are to be drawn is itself Normally distributed (this assumption will be relaxed in a moment), with mean μ and variance σ^2 (see Fig. 4.10).

Figure 4.10 The population distribution

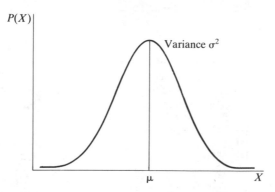

From this population many samples are drawn, each of sample size n, and the mean of each sample is calculated. The samples are independent, meaning that the observations selected for one sample do not influence the selection of observations in the other samples. This gives many sample means, $\bar{x}_1 . \bar{x}_2 \ldots$ etc. If these sample means are treated as a new set of observations, then the probability distribution of these observations can be drawn. The theorem states that this distribution is Normal, with the sample means centred around μ, the population mean, and with variance σ^2/n. The argument is set out diagrammatically as in Fig. 4.11.

Intuitively this theorem can be understood as follows. If the height of adult males is a Normally distributed random variable with mean $\mu = 174$ cm and variance $\sigma^2 = 92.16$, then it would be expected that a random sample of (say) 20 males would yield a sample mean height of around 174 cm, perhaps a little more, perhaps a little less. In other words, the sample mean is centred around 174 cm, or the mean of the distribution of sample means is 174 cm.

The larger is the size of the individual samples (i.e. the large n), the closer the sample mean would tend to be to 174 cm. For example, if the sample size is only two, a sample of two very tall people is quite possible, with a high sample mean as a result, well over 174 cm, e.g. 182 cm. But if the sample size were 20, it is very unlikely the 20 very tall males would be selected, and the sample mean is likely to be much closer to 174. This is why the sample size n appears in the formula for the variance of the distribution of the sample mean, σ^2/n.

93

Figure 4.11 The distribution of sample means

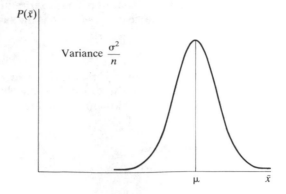

The above theorem can be used to solve a range of statistical problems. For example, what is the probability that a random sample of nine adult males will have a mean height greater than 180 cm? The height of all adult males is known to be Normally distributed with mean $\mu = 174$ cm and variance $\sigma^2 = 92.16$. The theorem can be used to derive the probability distribution of the sample mean $\bar{x}$:

$$X \sim N(\mu, \sigma^2) \quad \text{i.e.}$$
$$X \sim N(174,\ 92.16)$$

Hence

$$\bar{x} \sim N\ (\mu, \sigma^2/n) \quad \text{i.e.}$$
$$\bar{x} \sim N\ (174,\ 92.16/9)$$

This is represented diagrammatically in Fig. 4.12.

Figure 4.12 Distribution of the sample mean ($n=9$) from a population with $\mu=174$ and $\sigma^2=92.16$

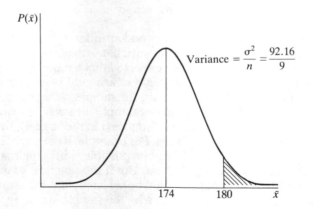

To answer the question posed, the area to the right of 180, shaded in Fig.4.12, has to be found. This should by now be a familiar procedure. First the z-score is calculated:

$$z = \frac{\bar{x} - \mu}{\sqrt{\sigma^2/n}} = \frac{180 - 174}{\sqrt{92.16/9}} = \frac{6}{3.20} = 1.88$$

Note that the divisor in the formula for the z-score now is $\sqrt{\sigma^2/n}$, not $\sqrt{\sigma^2}$. This is because it is the distribution of sample means which is being used, which has a variance of σ^2/n, not σ^2 which is the population variance. $\sqrt{\sigma^2/n}$ is known as the *standard error*, to distinguish it from σ, the standard deviation of the population.

Looking up the value of $z = 1.88$ in Table A2 gives an area of 0.0301 in the right-hand tail of the Normal distribution beyond $z = 1.88$. Thus 3.01% of sample means will be greater than or equal to 180 cm when the sample size is nine. The desired probability is therefore 3.01%.

This probability is quite small, and it is interesting to consider the reasons for this. There are two possibilities:

(i) through bad luck, the sample collected is not very representative of the population as a whole, or

(ii) the sample is representative of the population, but the population mean is not 174 cm after all.

Only one of these two possibilities can be correct. How to decide between them will be taken up later on, in Chapter 6 on hypothesis testing.

It is interesting to examine the difference between the answer for a sample size of nine (3.01%) and the one obtained earlier for a single individual (26.43%). The latter may be considered as a sample of size one from the population. The examples illustrate the fact that the larger the sample size, the closer the sample mean is likely to be to the population mean. Thus larger samples tend to give better estimates of the population mean.

Sampling from a non-Normal population

The previous theorem and examples relied upon the fact that the population followed a Normal distribution. But what happens if it is not Normal? After all, it is not known for certain that the heights of all adult males are Normally distributed, and there are many populations which are not Normal (e.g. the height of all persons, male or female). What can be done in these circumstances? The answer is to use another theorem about the distribution of sample means (again presented without proof). This is known as the *Central Limit Theorem* (in fact, it is one version of the theorem, which appears in many slightly different guises).

Theorem 2: The sample mean $\bar{x}$, drawn from a population with mean μ and variance σ^2, has a sampling distribution which approaches a Normal distribution with mean μ and variance σ^2/n, as the sample size approaches infinity.

This is a very useful theorem, since it allows the assumption that the

95

population is Normally distributed to be dropped. Note that the distribution of sample means is only Normal as long as the sample size is infinite; for any finite sample size the distribution is only approximately Normal. However, the approximation is close enough for practical purposes if the sample size is larger than 25 or so observations. If the population distribution is itself nearly Normal, then a smaller sample size would suffice. If the population distribution is particularly skewed, then more than 25 observations would be desirable. Twenty-five observations constitutes a rule of thumb that is adequate in most circumstances. This is another illustration of statistics as an inexact science. It does not provide absolutely clear-cut answers to questions, but, used judiciously, it helps us to arrive at sensible conclusions.

As an example of the use of this second theorem, suppose the average income per capita of a country is μ = £5,000 p.a. with standard deviation σ = £1,000. The actual shape of the income distribution is unknown (in practice, income distributions tend to be skewed to the right, so are not Normal). A sample of 50 people is drawn from this population. What is the probability that the mean income of the sample will be at least £5,200? Since the sample size n is greater than 25, the theorem can safely be applied. Hence

$$\bar{x} \sim N(\mu, \sigma^2/n)$$
$$\bar{x} \sim N(5,000, 1,000^2/50)$$

This is represented diagrammatically in Fig. 4.13.

Figure 4.13 Distribution of the sample mean (n=50) from a population with μ=5,000 and σ^2=1,000^2

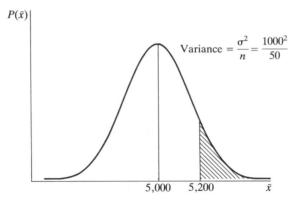

The size of the shaded area needs to be found.

$$z = \frac{\bar{x} - \mu}{\sqrt{\sigma^2/n}} = \frac{5,200 - 5,000}{\sqrt{1,000^2/50}} = 1.41$$

Referring to the standard Normal tables, the area in the tail is found to be 7.93%. So, if the parameters for the population are correct (μ = 5,000,

$\sigma = 1{,}000$), there is a chance of 7.93% of finding a sample mean of £5,200 or greater with a sample of size 50.

The relationship between the Binomial and Normal distributions

Most statistical distributions are related to one another in some way. This means that many problems can be solved by a variety of different methods (using different distributions), though usually one is more convenient than the others. This point may be illustrated by looking at the relationship between the Binomial and Normal distributions.

Recall that, if a random variable r follows a Binomial distribution, then

$$r \sim B\ (n,\ P),$$

and the mean of the distribution is nP and the variance nPQ. It turns out that, as n gets larger, the Binomial distribution is approximately the same as a Normal distribution with mean nP and variance nPQ. This approximation is valid as long as $nP \geq 5$ and $nQ \geq 5$, so the approximation may not be very good (even for large values of n) if P is very close to zero or one. The following problem can therefore be solved using both the Binomial and Normal distributions.

Forty students take an exam in statistics which is simply graded pass/fail. If the probability, P, of any individual student passing is 60%, what is the probability of at least 30 students passing the exam?

The sample data are:

$P = 0.6$
$Q = 1 - P = 0.4$
$n = 40$

Binomial method

To solve the problem using the Binomial distribution it is necessary to find the probability of exactly 30 students passing, plus the probability of 31 passing, plus the probability of 32 passing, etc. up to the probability of 40 passing (the fact that the events are mutually exclusive allows this). The probability of 30 passing is

$$P(30) = nCrP^rQ^{n-r}$$
$$= 40C30 \times 0.6^{30} \times 0.4^{10}$$
$$= 0.020$$

(NB This calculation assumes that the probabilities are independent, i.e. no copying!). This by itself is quite a tedious calculation (a computer was used to do it), but $P(31)$, $P(32)$, etc. still have to be calculated. Calculating these and summing them gives the result of 3.52% as the probability of at least 30 passing. (It would be a useful exercise for you to do, if only to appreciate how long it takes. It should be done no more than once in a lifetime.)

97

Figure 4.14 The Normal approximation to the Binomial distribution for $n=40$ and $P=0.6$

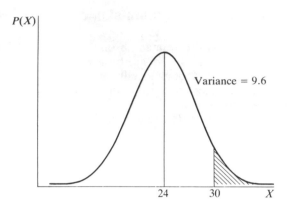

Normal method

As already stated, the Binomial distribution can be approximated by a Normal distribution with mean nP and variance nPQ. nP in this case is 24 and nQ is 16, both greater than five, so the approximation can be safely used. Thus

$$r \sim N \ (nP, \ nPQ) \quad \text{i.e.}$$
$$r \sim N \ (24, \ 9.6)$$

Diagrammatically the situation is as shown in Fig. 4.14. The usual methods are used to find the shaded area. However, before doing so, there is one adjustment to be made (this *only* applies when approximating the Binomial distribution by the Normal). The Normal distribution is a continuous one whereas the Binomial is discrete. Thus '30' in the Binomial distribution is represented by the area under the Normal distribution between 29.5 and 30.5, and '31' is represented by 30.5 to 31.5, etc. Thus it is the area under the Normal distribution to the right of 29.5, not 30, which must be calculated. This is known as the *continuity correction*. Remember that this is *only* used when approximating the Binomial by the Normal distribution. Hence

$$z = \frac{29.5 \ - \ 24}{\sqrt{9.6}} = 1.78$$

This gives a shaded area of 3.75%, not far off the correct answer as calculated by the Binomial distribution. The time saved and ease of calculation would seem to be worth the slight loss in accuracy.

Other examples can be constructed to test this method, using different values of P and n. Small values of n, or values of nP or nQ less than 5, will give poor results, i.e. the Normal approximation to the Binomial will not be very good.

The Poisson distribution

The section above showed how the Binomial distribution could be approximated by a Normal distribution under certain circumstances. The approximation does not work particularly well for very small values of P, when nP is less than five. In these circumstances the Binomial may be approximated by the Poisson distribution, which is given by the formula

$$P(X) = \frac{\mu^X \, e^{-\mu}}{X!} \qquad\qquad [4.2]$$

where μ is the mean of the distribution (like μ for the Normal distribution and nP for the Binomial). Like the Binomial, but unlike the Normal, the Poisson is a discrete probability distribution, so that eqn [4.2] is only defined for integer values of X. Furthermore, it is applicable to a series of trials which are independent, as in the Binomial case.

The use of the Poisson distribution is appropriate when the probability of 'success' is very small and the number of trials is large. Its use is illustrated by the following example. A manufacturer gives a two-year guarantee on the TV tubes he makes. From past experience he knows that 0.5% of his tubes will be faulty and fail within the guarantee period. What is the probability that of a consignment of 500 tubes (a) none will be faulty, (b) more than three are faulty?

The mean of the Poisson distribution in this case is $\mu = 2.5$ (0.5% of 500). Therefore

$$P(0) = \frac{2.5^0 \, e^{-2.5}}{0!} = 0.082$$

giving a probability of 8.2% of no failures. The answer to this problem via the Binomial method is

$$P(0) = 0.995^{500} = 0.0816$$

Thus the Poisson method gives a reasonably accurate answer from the much simpler calculation. The Poisson approximation to the Binomial is satisfactory if nP is less than about seven.

The probability of more than three tubes expiring is calculated as

$$P(X > 3) = 1 - P(0) - P(1) - P(2) - P(3)$$

$$P(1) = \frac{2.5^1 \, e^{-2.5}}{1!} = 0.205$$

$$P(2) = \frac{2.5^2 \, e^{-2.5}}{2!} = 0.256$$

$$P(3) = \frac{2.5^3 \, e^{-2.5}}{3!} = 0.214$$

So $P(X > 3) = 1 - 0.082 - 0.205 - 0.256 - 0.214$
$$= 0.242$$

Thus there is a probability of about 24% of more than three failures. The Binomial calculation is much more tedious, but gives an answer of 24.4% also.

The Poisson distribution is also useful for queuing-type problems. If a shop receives, on average, 20 customers per hour, what is the probability of no customers within a five-minute period while the owner takes a coffee break?

The average number of customers per five-minute period is $20 \times 5/60 = 1.67$. The probability of a free five-minute spell is therefore

$$P(0) = \frac{1.67^0 \ e^{-1.67}}{0!} = 0.189$$

a probability of about 19%. Note that this problem cannot be solved by the Binomial method since n and P are not known separately, only their product.

Expected value and variance operators

A useful shorthand when referring to the mean and variance of a random variable is to use the E (expected value) and V (variance) operators. As well as being a useful form of notation, there are simple rules for manipulating these operators which allow certain problems to be solved quickly and elegantly.

Let X represent a random variable, such as the result of throwing a die. This experiment has six possible outcomes, the integers one to six, each with the same probability of occurring, namely one-sixth. The expected value of this experiment, $E(X)$, is the mean of the probability distribution, as calculated in Table 4.1.

Table 4.1 Calculation of the expected value and variance for the throw of a die

X	$P(X)$	$X\,P(X)$	$X^2\,P(X)$
1	1/6	1/6	1/6
2	1/6	2/6	4/6
3	1/6	3/6	9/6
4	1/6	4/6	16/6
5	1/6	5/6	25/6
6	1/6	6/6	36/6
	1	21/6	91/6

The formula for the expected value is

$$E(X) = \Sigma \ X \ P(X)$$

Thus $E(X) = 21/6 = 3.5$, as might be expected. (Since $P(X)$ is the same as the relative frequency $f/\Sigma f$,

$$E(X) = \frac{\Sigma X\ f(X)}{\Sigma\ f(X)}$$

which is the more familiar formula for the mean (see eqn [1.2]).)

An alternative way of thinking about this example is as follows. You roll the die and receive in £s the number showing. How much would you expect to receive? The answer is £3.50, the expected value of the distribution. Note that on a single roll of the die you would not get this amount (it has to be an integer amount), but if the experiment were repeated many times you would receive an average of £3.50 on each roll.

Rules for manipulating expected values

If k is a constant, then

(i) $E(k) = k$ The expected value of a constant is itself. If you receive £2 ($k=2$) whatever the score on the die, you expect to receive £2.

(ii) $E(X+k) = E(X) + k$ If you receive the score on the die plus £2 ($k=2$) then you would expect to receive £5.50.

The proof of this is straightforward:

$$
\begin{aligned}
E(X+k) &= \Sigma\ (X + k)\ P(X) \\
&= \Sigma\ X\ P(X) + \Sigma k\ P(X) \\
&= E(X) + k \qquad \text{(since } \Sigma\ P(X) = 1)
\end{aligned}
$$

(iii) $E(kX) = kE(X)$ You receive ten times the score on the die ($k=10$). You expect to receive £35.

Proof:

$$
\begin{aligned}
E(kX) &= \Sigma\ kX\ P(X) \\
&= k\ \Sigma\ X\ P(X) \\
&= kE(X)
\end{aligned}
$$

If b is another constant, then

(iv) $E(kX+b) = kE(X) + b$ Using rules (i), (ii) and (iii). You receive ten times ($k=10$) the score plus £5 ($b=5$). You expect £40.

Rules involving two random variables

Let Y be a second random variable, e.g. the score on a second die. Then

(v) $E(X+Y) = E(X) + E(Y)$ You receive the aggregate score on the two dice. You expect to receive £7.

(vi) $E(kX+bY) = kE(X) + bE(Y)$ Using (iii) and (v).

The variance operator

The notation $V(X)$ is used to represent the variance of the variable X. Let X be a random variable with mean μ, i.e.

$E(X) = \mu$. Then
$V(X) = E(X - E(X))^2$

is the definition of the variance operator. It looks more familiar if it is expanded:

$$V(X) = E(X - \mu)^2$$
$$= 1/n\ \Sigma(X - \mu)^2$$

This is the same as eqn [1.3] for the variance save that n is used in the formula rather than $n-1$ since the formula above is not being applied to sample data. Similarly μ is used for the mean of the random variable to distinguish it from the sample mean.

Let X again represent the score on a die. What is $V(X)$? This is most easily calculated using the following formula

$$V(X) = \Sigma X^2 P(X) - (E(X))^2$$

Using the results in Table 4.1 gives

$$V(X) = 91/6 - (21/6)^2$$
$$= 2.92$$

This is the variance of the score on the die, and the standard deviation is therefore $\sqrt{2.92} = 1.71$. Receiving in £ the score on the die, you would expect £3.50 but with a standard deviation of £1.71.

Rules for manipulating the variance operator

Let X and Y be random variables as before, and k and b be constants. Then

(vii) $V(k) = 0$ A constant has no variance.

(viii) $V(X+k) = V(X)$ The addition of a constant to every observation makes no difference to the variance.

(ix) $V(kX) = k^2 V(X)$ Multiplying all observations by k multiplies the variance by k^2, *not* k.

Proof

$$
\begin{aligned}
V(kX) &= E(kX - E(kX))^2 \\
&= E(kX - kE(X))^2 \\
&= E(kX - k\mu)^2 && \text{Since } E(X) = \mu \\
&= E(k^2 X^2 - 2k^2\mu X + k^2\mu^2) && \text{Squaring the bracket} \\
&= E(k^2 X^2) - 2k^2\mu E(X) + k^2\mu^2 && \text{Note that } E(\mu^2) = \mu^2 \\
&= k^2 E(X^2) - 2k^2\mu^2 + k^2\mu^2 \\
&= k^2\ (E(X^2) - \mu^2) \\
&= k^2\ (E(X - \mu)^2) \\
&= k^2\ V(X)
\end{aligned}
$$

As long as X and Y are independent, then

102

(x) $V(X+Y) = V(X) + V(Y)$
(xi) $V(X-Y) = V(X) + V(Y)$ Note: plus not minus!

The usefulness of these operators will be shown later when the mean and variance of certain random variables is required, such as of the difference between two sample means.

Problems

4.1 If the random variable r follows a Binomial distribution with the probability of success in a single trial $P = 0.75$, calculate the probabilities of the following in a series of six trials:

(a) $P(r = 3)$
(b) $P(r = 4)$
(c) $P(r \geq 4)$
(d) $P(r \leq 3)$

4.2 If the probability of a boy in a single birth is 1/2 and is independent of the sex of previous babies, then the number of boys in a family of 10 children follows a Binomial distribution with mean 5 and variance 2.5. In each of the following instances, describe how the distribution of the number of boys differs from the Binomial described above.

(a) The probability of a boy is 6/10.
(b) The probability of a boy is 1/2 but births are not independent. The birth of a boy makes it more than an even chance that the next child is a boy.
(c) As (b) above, except that the birth of a boy makes it less than an even chance that the next child will be a boy.
(d) The probability of a boy is 6/10 on the first birth. The birth of a boy makes it a more than even chance that the next baby will be a boy.

4.3 A firm receives components from a supplier in large batches, for use in its production process. Production is uneconomic if a batch containing 10% or more defective components is used. The firm checks the quality of each incoming batch by taking a sample of 15 and rejecting the whole batch if more than one defective component is found.

(a) If a batch containing 10% defectives is delivered what is the probability of it being accepted?
(b) How could the firm reduce this probability of erroneously accepting bad batches?
(c) If the supplier produces components with an average proportion of 3% defective, what is the probability of the firm sending back a satisfactory batch?
(d) What role does the assumption of a 'large' batch play in the calculation?

4.4   For the standard Normal variable z, find

(a) $P(z \geq 1.64)$
(b) $P(z \geq 0.5)$
(c) $P(z \geq -1.5)$
(d) $P(-2 \leq z \leq 1.5)$
(e) $P(z \leq -0.75)$

Find the values of z which cut off

(f) The top 10% of the distribution;
(g) The bottom 15%;
(h) The middle 50%.

4.5   If $X \sim N(10, 9)$ find

(a) $P(X \geq 12)$
(b) $P(X \leq 7)$
(c) $P(8 \leq X \leq 15)$
(d) $P(11 \leq X \leq 17)$
(e) $P(X = 10)$

4.6   If $X \sim N(100, 100)$ and samples of size 9 are taken, find

(a) $P(\bar{x} \geq 105)$
(b) $P(\bar{x} \leq 95)$
(c) $P(93 \leq \bar{x} \leq 102)$

where $\bar{x}$ is the sample mean.

4.7   From a population with mean 60 and standard deviation 48 are drawn samples of size 36. Find

(a) $P(\bar{x} \geq 70)$
(b) $P(56 \leq \bar{x} \leq 100)$
(c) $P(\bar{x} \leq 50)$

4.8   If IQ is Normally distributed with mean 100 and variance 400, find the following probabilities:

(a) Drawing an individual at random from the population with an IQ higher than 120
(b) Drawing ten people at random from the population whose average IQ turns out to be higher than 120.

4.9   If a country's average income is £10,000 per annum with standard deviation £2,000, find the following probabilities

(a) Drawing an individual at random from the population with an income over £12,000;
(b) Drawing ten individuals at random whose average income is under £8,000;
(c) Drawing 40 individuals at random whose average income is between £9,500 and £10,500.

104

4.10 A manufacturer claims that his tyres last 20,000 miles on average with a standard deviation of 2,000 miles. A consumer organisation tests a random sample of 48 tyres and reports an average mileage of 19,200. What do you think of the manufacturer's claim?

4.11 A department store sells on average three sets of an expensive brand of television per week. At the beginning of each week it brings its stock up to five sets. In how many weeks of the year (50 weeks) can it expect to have to turn away disappointed customers?

4.12 Given

$$E(X) = 10 \quad V(X) = 4 \quad a = 6$$
$$E(Y) = -3 \quad V(Y) = 7 \quad b = 10$$

evaluate

(a) $E(aX)$
(b) $E(Y/b)$
(c) $E((X + Y)/b)$
(d) $E(a^2X)$
(e) $V(aX)$
(f) $V(Y/b)$
(g) $V(X + 2Y/b)$

Make clear any assumptions you make in deriving these answers.

4.13 A firm is considering investing in one of two risky projects, whose returns are given in the accompanying table:

Project A Outcome	Profit (£m)	Probability
1	5	0.2
2	2	0.7
3	−1	0.1

Project B Outcome	Profit	Probability
1	8	0.2
2	2	0.7
3	−4	0.1

Thus for project A there is a 20% chance of a £5 m. profit, 70% chance of £2 m., etc. Calculate the expected profit from each project. Does this indicate that the firm should go for project B? What additional information is provided by the variance of the profit?

4.14   A firm invests in two risky projects simultaneously, in two different countries. The return on the projects depends on the growth rate in each country, as follows:

Country A project		
Growth rate	Profit (£m.)	Probability
High	5	0.5
Low	−2	0.5

Country B project		
Growth rate	Profit (£m.)	Probability
High	8	0.5
Low	−3	0.5

(a) Calculate the expected profit and its variance for each project.
(b) If high growth in A is always associated with high growth in B, determine the expected profit to the firm (i.e. from both projects), and its variance.
(c) If high growth in A is never associated with high growth in B, determine the expected profit to the firm and its variance.
(d) If the growth rate in A is completely independent of the growth in B, determine the expected profit and its variance.
(e) What properties of expected value and variance operators are illustrated by (i)–(iv) above?

4.15   A firm's income this year and next is unknown, but has the following mean and variance

	Mean income	Variance
Year 1	£500,000	£40,000 m.
Year 2	£660,000	£66,550 m.

The firm wishes to discount next year's income by 10% to make it comparable to this year's.

(a) Find the mean and variance of year 2 income once discounted.
(b) Find the mean and standard deviation of total discounted income, assuming the income flows are independent.

5 Estimation and confidence intervals

Introduction

We now come to the heart of the subject of statistical inference. Until now the following type of question has been examined: given the population parameters μ and σ, what is the probability of the sample mean $\bar{x}$, from a sample of size n, being greater than some specified value? The parameters μ and σ are assumed to be known, and the objective is to try to form some conclusions about possible values of $\bar{x}$. However, in practice it is usually the sample values $\bar{x}$ and s that are known, while the population parameters μ and σ are not. Thus a more interesting question to ask is: given the values of $\bar{x}$ and s, what can be said about μ and σ? Sometimes the population standard deviation (σ) is known, and inferences have to be made about μ alone. For example, a sample of 50 British families found an average weekly expenditure on food ($\bar{x}$) of £37.50 with a standard deviation (s) of £6.00; what can be said about the average expenditure (μ) of *all* British families?

Schematically the situation is as shown in Fig. 5.1.

Figure 5.1.

Sample information	inferences about	Population parameters
$\bar{x}, s$	$\longrightarrow$	μ, σ

This chapter will be concerned only with inferences about μ. Inferences about σ will be covered in Chapter 8. This chapter covers the *estimation* of μ, and Chapter 6 describes *testing hypotheses* about μ. The two procedures are very closely related.

Point and interval estimation

There are basically two ways in which an estimate of a parameter can be presented. The first of these is as a point estimate, i.e. a single value which is the best estimate of the parameter of interest. The point estimate is the one which is most prevalent in everyday usage; for example, the average Briton drinks 4.5 cups of tea per day. Although this is presented as a fact, it is actually an estimate, obtained from a survey of people's drinking habits. Since it is obtained from a sample there must be some doubt about its accuracy: the sample will probably not exactly represent the whole population. For this reason interval estimates are also used, which give some idea of the likely accuracy of the estimate. If the sample size is small, for example, then it is quite possible that the estimate will not be very close to the true value and this would be reflected in a wide interval estimate, for example that the average Briton drinks between 3 and 6 cups of tea per day. A larger sample, or a better method of estimation, would allow a narrower interval to be derived and thus a more precise estimate of the parameter to be obtained, such as an average consumption of between 4 and 5 cups. Interval estimates are better for the consumer of the statistics, since they not only show the estimate of the parameter but also give an idea of the confidence which the researcher has in that estimate. The following sections describe how to construct both types of estimate.

Rules and criteria for finding estimates

In order to estimate a parameter such as the population mean, a rule (or set of rules) is required which describes how to derive the estimate of the parameter from the sample data. Such a rule is known as an *estimator*. An example of an estimator for the population mean is 'use the sample mean'. It is important to distinguish between an estimator, a rule, and an estimate, which is the value derived as a result of applying the rule to the data.

There are many possible estimators for any parameter, so it is important to be able to distinguish between good and bad estimators. The following are all possible estimators of the population mean

(i) the sample mean
(ii) the smallest observation in the sample
(iii) a randomly chosen observation from the sample

A set of criteria is needed for discriminating between good and bad estimators. Two important criteria by which to judge estimators are *bias* and *precision*.

Bias

It is impossible to know if a single estimate of a parameter, derived by applying a particular estimator to the sample data, gives a correct estimate of the parameter or not. The estimate might be too low or too high and, since the parameter is unknown, it is impossible to check this. What *is* possible, however, is to say whether an estimator gives the correct answer *on average*. An estimator which gives the correct answer on average is said to be unbiased. Another way of expressing this is to say that an unbiased estimator does not *systematically* mislead the researcher away from the correct value of the parameter. It is important to remember, though, that even using an unbiased estimator does not guarantee that a single use of the estimator will yield a correct estimate of the parameter.

Formally, an estimator is unbiased if its expected value is equal to the parameter being estimated. Consider trying to estimate the population mean using the three estimators suggested above. Taking the sample mean first, we have already learned that its expected value is μ, i.e.

$$E(\bar{x}) = \mu$$

which immediately shows that the sample mean is an unbiased estimator.

The second estimator (the smallest observation in the sample) can easily be shown to be biased, using the result derived above. Since the smallest sample observation must be less than the sample mean, its expected value must be less than μ. Denote the smallest observation by x_1, then

$$E(x_1) < \mu$$

so this estimator is biased downwards. It underestimates the population mean. The size of the bias is simply the difference between the expected value of the estimator and the value of the parameter, so the bias in this case is

$$\text{Bias} = E(x_1) - \mu$$

For the sample mean the bias is obviously zero.

Turning to the third rule, this can be shown to be another unbiased estimator. Choosing a single observation at random from the sample is equivalent to taking a random sample of size one from the population in the first place. Thus the single observation may be considered as the sample mean from a random sample of size one. Since it is a sample mean it is unbiased, as demonstrated above.

Precision

Two of the estimators above were found to be unbiased, and in fact there are many unbiased estimators (the sample median is another). Some way of choosing between the set of unbiased estimators is therefore required, which is where the second criterion of precision comes in. Unlike bias, precision is a relative concept, comparing one estimator with another. Given two estimators, A and B, A is more precise than B if the estimates it yields (from all possible samples) are less spread out than those of estimator B. A precise estimator will tend to give similar estimates for all possible samples.

Consider the two unbiased estimators found above: how do they compare on the criterion of precision? It turns out that the sample mean is the more precise of the two, and this is not difficult to understand why. Taking just a single sample observation means that it is quite likely to be unrepresentative of the population as a whole, and thus leads to a poor estimate of the population mean. The sample mean, on the other hand, is based on all the sample observations and it is unlikely that all of them are unrepresentative of the population. The sample mean is therefore a good estimator of the population mean, being more precise than the single observation estimator.

Just as bias was related to the expected value of the estimator, so precision can be defined in terms of the variance. One estimator is more precise than another if it has a smaller variance. Recall that the probability distribution of the sample mean is

Figure 5.2 The probability distributions of two estimators of the population mean: A (the sample mean), B (sample observation)

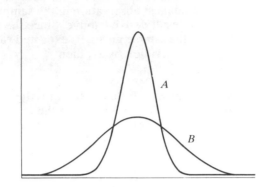

$$\bar{x} \sim N\ (\mu,\ \sigma^2/n)$$

in large samples, so the variance of the sample mean is

$$V(\bar{x}) = \sigma^2/n$$

As the sample size n gets larger, therefore, the variance of the sample mean becomes smaller, so the estimator becomes more precise. For this reason large samples give better estimates than small samples, and so the sample mean is a better estimator than taking just one observation from the sample. The two estimators can be compared in a diagram (see Fig. 5.2) which draws the probability distributions of the two estimators. It is easily seen that the sample mean yields estimates which are on average closer to the population mean.

For the case of the population variance it is fairly easy to show (using the E and V operators) that an unbiased estimate is provided by the sample variance, as long as the latter is calculated using eqn [1.4], i.e.

$$s^2 = \frac{\Sigma f_i(x_i - \bar{x})^2}{n - 1}$$

It should be noted that just because an estimator is biased does not necessarily mean that it is imprecise. Sometimes there is a trade-off between an unbiased but imprecise estimator and a biased but precise one. Figure 5.3 illustrates. Although estimator B is biased, it will nearly always yield an estimate which is fairly close to the true value; even though the estimate is expected to be wrong, it is not likely to be far wrong. Estimator A, though unbiased, can give estimates which are far away from the true value, so that B might be the preferred estimator. In the rest of this book only unbiased estimators are considered, the most important being the sample mean.

Figure 5.3 Two estimators of μ: A (unbiased) and B (biased, but more precise)

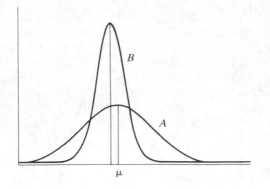

Estimation with large samples

For the type of problem encountered in this chapter the method of estimation differs according to the size of the sample. 'Large' samples, by which is meant sample sizes of 25 or more, are dealt with first, and small samples are considered in the following section. The reason why different methods are required will be dealt with in the later section.

Estimating a mean

Consider the example given at the beginning of the chapter, where a sample of 50 families found an average weekly food expenditure of £37.50, with standard deviation £6.00. What can be inferred about the population mean μ?

For the point estimate of μ the sample mean is a good candidate since it is unbiased, and it is more precise than other sample statistics such as the median. The point estimate of μ is therefore simply £37.50.

The interval estimate will be centred around the sample mean, so the width of the interval needs to be calculated. To do this requires the probability distribution of $\bar{x}$, which was found in Chapter 4 to be

$$\bar{x} \sim N\ (\mu,\ \sigma^2/n)$$

From this, it can be calculated that there is a 95% probability of the sample mean lying within 1.96 standard errors of μ, i.e.

$$P\ (\mu - 1.96\sqrt{\sigma^2/n} \leq \bar{x} \leq \mu + 1.96\sqrt{\sigma^2/n}) = 0.95$$

(1.96 is the *z*-score which cuts off the extreme 5% of the distribution, 2.5% each tail). This statement can be turned around to say that μ lies within 1.96 standard errors of $\bar{x}$ with 95% confidence, i.e. one can be 95% confident that

$$\bar{x} - 1.96\sqrt{\sigma^2/n} \leq \mu \leq \bar{x} + 1.96\sqrt{\sigma^2/n}$$

Diagrammatically these two arguments may be presented as shown in Figs 5.4 (a) and (b).

Figure 5.4(a) The 95% probability interval for $\bar{x}$ around the population mean μ

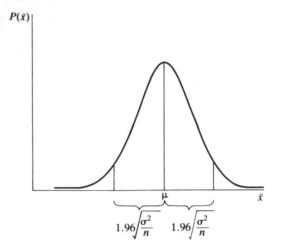

Figure 5.4(b) The 95% confidence interval for μ around the sample mean $\bar{x}$

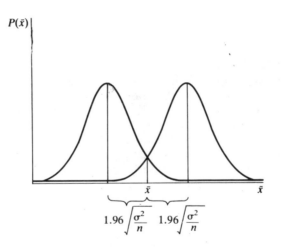

The interval

$$[\ \bar{x} - 1.96\sqrt{\sigma^2/n} \ , \ \bar{x} + 1.96\sqrt{\sigma^2/n} \ ] \qquad\qquad [5.1]$$

is called the *95% confidence interval* and this is the interval estimate. In this example the value of σ^2 is unknown, but in large ($n \geq 25$) samples it can be replaced by s^2 from the sample. s^2 is here used as an estimate of σ^2; as stated above it is unbiased, and it is sufficiently precise in large samples. The 95% confidence interval is therefore

$$[\bar{x} - 1.96\sqrt{s^2/n}, \; \bar{x} + 1.96\sqrt{s^2/n} \;] \qquad\qquad [5.2]$$
$$= [37.50 - 1.96\sqrt{6^2/50}, \; 37.50 + 1.96\sqrt{6^2/50} \;]$$
$$= [35.84, \; 39.16]$$

Thus we are 95% confident that the true average weekly expenditure on food lies between £35.84 and £39.16. It should be noted that £37.50 lies exactly at the centre of the interval.

By examining eqn [5.2] one can see that the confidence interval is wider

(i) the smaller the sample size
(ii) the greater the standard deviation of the sample.

The greater uncertainty which is associated with smaller sample sizes is manifested in a wider confidence interval estimate of the population mean. Greater variation in the sample data also leads to greater uncertainty about the population mean and a wider confidence interval. Note that the width of the confidence interval does not depend upon the population size: a sample of 50 observations reveals as much about a population of 10,000 as it does about a population of 10,000,000. This point will be discussed in more detail in Chapter 7 on sampling methods.

A question which arises at this point is why the term 'confidence' rather than 'probability' is used. Why not say that μ lies within the interval with 95% probability? The answer to this goes back to the definition of probability. According the frequentist view, probability statements can be made about random variables but not about population parameters. Since μ is a parameter, one cannot make probability statements about it. The true value of μ either lies in the interval or it does not; it cannot be 95% in it. To emphasise this point the term 'confidence' rather than 'probability' is used. This may seem like a semantic difference, but it is important to understand the reason for it. Those who adhere to the subjective belief definition of probability and use Bayesian methods of analysis would regard it as legitimate to talk of a probability interval, reflecting one's belief about the location of μ. Classical statistics continues to emphasise the difference between a random variable, with its probability distribution, and a population parameter.

A second question is why use a probability (and hence a confidence level) of 95%? In fact, one can choose any confidence level, and thus confidence interval. The 90% confidence level can be obtained by finding the *z*-score which cuts off 10% of the Normal distribution (5% in each tail). From Table A2 this is $z = 1.64$, so the 90% confidence interval is

$$[\bar{x} - 1.64\sqrt{\sigma^2/n}, \; \bar{x} + 1.64\sqrt{\sigma^2/n}]$$
$$= [37.50 - 1.64\sqrt{6^2/50}, \; 37.50 + 1.64\sqrt{6^2/50}]$$
$$= [36.11, \; 38.89]$$

Notice that this is narrower than the 95% confidence level. The greater the degree of confidence required, the wider the interval has to be. Any confidence level may be chosen, and by judicious choice of this level the confidence interval can be made as wide or as narrow as wished. This would seem to undermine the purpose of calculating the confidence interval, which is to obtain some idea of the uncertainty attached to the estimate. This is not the case, however, because the reader of the results can interpret them appropriately as long as the confidence level is made clear. To simplify matters, the 95% and 99% confidence levels are the most commonly used and serve as conventions. Beware of the researcher who calculates the 76% confidence interval: this may have been chosen in order to obtain the desired answer rather than in the spirit of scientific inquiry! The general formula for the (100–x)% confidence interval is

$$[\bar{x} - z_x\sqrt{\sigma^2/n}, \ \bar{x} + z_x\sqrt{\sigma^2/n}] \qquad \text{[.5.3]}$$

where z_x is the z-score which cuts off the extreme x% of the Normal distribution.

Estimating a sample proportion

One of the most common uses of this technique is opinion polls, which attempt to estimate the proportion of the population intending to vote for a political party on the basis of a sample of about 1,000 voters. Opinion polls are not proper random samples, however, so are not an appropriate subject for this section (they are discussed further in Chapter 7). Instead we shall use an example relating to home ownership where it is assumed that a proper sampling technique has been used.

A random sample of 100 families finds 60 own their own homes. What proportion of the population own their own homes?

This is a question about estimating π, the population proportion, given data from a sample. The sample data are

$$p = 60 \, / \, 100 = 0.60$$
$$n = 100$$

The symbol p (lower case) is used for the sample proportion to distinguish it from the probability of an event, P.

The key to solving this problem is recognising p as a random variable just like the sample mean. This is because its value depends upon the sample drawn and will vary from sample to sample. Once the probability distribution of this random variable is known, the problem is quite easy to solve using the same methods as were used for the mean.

The sampling distribution of p is derived in the appendix to this chapter, and is given by

$$p \sim N \ (\pi, \ \pi Q/n) \qquad \text{[5.4]}$$

where π is the population proportion and $Q = 1 - \pi$.

Having derived the probability distribution of p the same methods of estimation can be used as for the sample mean. Since the expected value of p is π, the sample proportion is an unbiased estimate of the population parameter. The point estimate of π is therefore simply p. Thus it is estimated that 60% of the population are home-owners.

Given the sampling distribution for p in eqn [5.4], the formula for the 95% confidence interval for π can immediately be written down as:

114

$$[p - 1.96\sqrt{\pi Q/n} \, , \, p + 1.96\sqrt{\pi Q/n} \,] \tag{5.5}$$

Since the value of π is unknown, the confidence interval cannot yet be calculated, so the sample value of 0.6 has to be used instead. Like the case of the sample mean above, this is acceptable in large samples. Thus the 95% confidence interval is

$$[p - 1.96\sqrt{p \, Q/n} \, , \, p + 1.96\sqrt{p \, Q/n} \,] \tag{5.6}$$

$$= [0.6 - 1.96\sqrt{\frac{0.6 \times 0.4}{100}} \, , \, 0.6 + 1.96\sqrt{\frac{0.6 \times 0.4}{100}} \,]$$

$$= [0.504 \, , \, 0.696]$$

We say that we are 95% confident that the true proportion of home-owners lies between 50.4% and 69.6%.

It can be seen that these two cases apply a common method. In fact all confidence intervals are calculated according to similar principles and are based upon the probability distribution of the random variable. Finding this probability distribution is the crucial step, for once found the problem can be quickly solved. For example, for the cases of the sample mean and sample proportion we have

random variable	$\bar{x}$	p
mean of the random variable	μ	π
standard error of the random variable	$\sigma/\sqrt{n}$	$\sqrt{\pi Q/n}$

The probability distributions of the random variables are

$$\bar{x} \sim N(\mu, \, \sigma^2/n) \qquad p \sim N(\pi, \, \pi Q/n)$$

The confidence intervals are given by

For μ:
$$[\bar{x} - z \, \sqrt{\sigma^2/n} \, , \, \bar{x} + z \, \sqrt{\sigma^2/n}]$$

For π:
$$[p - z \, \sqrt{\pi Q/n} \, , \, p + z \, \sqrt{\pi Q/n} \,] \tag{5.7}$$

where z is the z-score appropriate for the desired level of confidence. With this knowledge two further cases can be swiftly dealt with.

Estimating the difference between two means

Sixty pupils from school 1 scored an average mark of 62% in an exam, with a standard deviation of 18%. Thirty-five pupils from school 2 scored an average of 70% with standard deviation 12%. Estimate the true difference between the two schools in the average mark obtained.

This is a more complicated problem than those previously treated since it involves two samples rather than one. Estimates need to be found for $\mu_1 - \mu_2$ (the true difference in the mean marks of the schools), in the form of both point and interval estimates. The pupils taking the exams may be thought of as samples of all pupils in the schools who could potentially take the exams.

Notice that this is a problem about sample means, not proportions, even though the question deals in percentages. The point is that each observation in the sample (i.e. each student's mark) can take a value between 0 and 100, and one can calculate the standard deviation of the marks. For this to be a problem of sample proportions the mark for each pupil would have to be of the pass/fail type, so that one could only calculate the proportion who passed.

It might be thought that the way to approach this problem is to derive one confidence interval for each sample (along the lines set out above), and then to somehow combine them; for example, the degree of overlap of the two confidence intervals could be assessed. This would be the wrong approach. It is sometimes a good strategy, when faced with an unfamiliar problem to solve, to translate it into a more familiar problem and then solve it using known methods. This is the procedure which will be followed here. The essential point is to keep in mind the concept of a random variable and its probability distribution.

Problems involving a single random variable have already been dealt with above. The current problem deals with two samples and therefore there are two random variables to consider: the two samples means $\bar{x}_1$ and $\bar{x}_2$. Since the aim is to estimate $\mu_1 - \mu_2$, an obvious candidate for an estimator is the difference between the two sample means, $\bar{x}_1 - \bar{x}_2$. This is the difference between two random variables so is itself a random variable. It can be proven that this random variable follows a Normal distribution. Its mean and variance can be found using the E and V operators. Letting

$$E(\bar{x}_1) = \mu_1, \quad V(\bar{x}_1) = \sigma_1^2/n_1 \text{ and}$$
$$E(\bar{x}_2) = \mu_2, \quad V(\bar{x}_2) = \sigma_2^2/n_2$$

Then

$$\begin{aligned} E(\bar{x}_1 - \bar{x}_2) &= E(\bar{x}_1) - E(\bar{x}_2) \\ &= \mu_1 - \mu_2 \\ V(\bar{x}_1 - \bar{x}_2) &= V(\bar{x}_1) + V(\bar{x}_2) \quad \text{assuming } \bar{x}_1 \text{ and } \bar{x}_2 \text{ are independent} \\ & \qquad\qquad\qquad\qquad\qquad \text{random variables} \\ &= \frac{\sigma_1^2}{n_1} + \frac{\sigma_2^2}{n_2} \end{aligned}$$

It is probably reasonable to assume independence in this case since the marks in one school are unlikely to affect those in the other. The probability distribution of $\bar{x}_1 - \bar{x}_2$ can therefore be summarised as

$$\bar{x}_1 - \bar{x}_2 \sim N\left(\mu_1 - \mu_2, \frac{\sigma_1^2}{n_1} + \frac{\sigma_2^2}{n_2}\right) \qquad\qquad [5.8]$$

This is illustrated in Fig. 5.5.

Equation [5.8] shows that $\bar{x}_1 - \bar{x}_2$ is an unbiased estimator of $\mu_1 - \mu_2$, since its expected value (the mean of the distribution) is $\mu_1 - \mu_2$. The difference between the sample means will therefore be used as the point estimate of $\mu_1 - \mu_2$. Thus the point estimate of the true difference between the schools is

$$\bar{x}_1 - \bar{x}_2 = 62 - 70 = -8\%$$

116

Figure 5.5 The distribution of $\bar{x}_1 - \bar{x}_2$

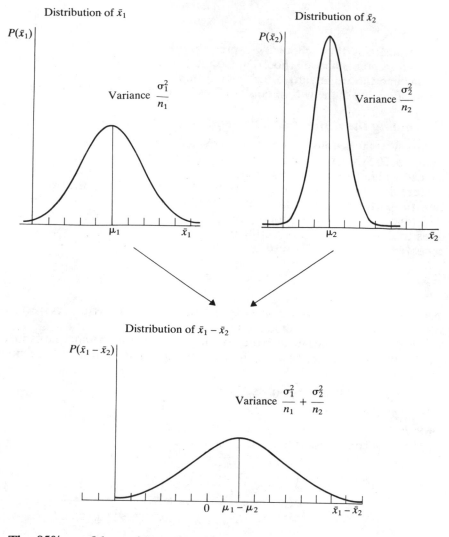

The 95% confidence interval estimate is derived in the same manner as before, making use of the standard error of the random variable. The formula is

$$\left[(\bar{x}_1 - \bar{x}_2) - 1.96 \sqrt{\frac{{\sigma_1}^2}{n_1} + \frac{{\sigma_2}^2}{n_2}} \ , \ (\bar{x}_1 - \bar{x}_2) + 1.96 \sqrt{\frac{{\sigma_1}^2}{n_1} + \frac{{\sigma_2}^2}{n_2}} \right]$$

$$[5.9]$$

The 95% confidence interval for $\mu_1 - \mu_2$ is therefore

117

$$\left[(62 - 70) - 1.96 \sqrt{\frac{18^2}{60} + \frac{12^2}{35}} \; , \; (62 - 70) + 1.96 \sqrt{\frac{18^2}{60} + \frac{12^2}{35}} \right]$$

$[- 14.05, \; - 1.95]$

The estimate is that school 2's average mark is between 1.95 and 14.05 percentage points above school 1's. Notice that the confidence interval does not include the value zero, which would imply equality of the two schools' marks. Equality of the two schools can thus be ruled out with 95% confidence.

Estimating the difference between two proportions

A survey of 80 Britons showed that 23 owned personal computers. A similar survey of 50 Swedes showed 10 with computers. Are personal computers more widespread in Britain than Sweden?

Here the aim is to estimate $\pi_1 - \pi_2$, the difference between the two population proportions, so the probability distribution of $p_1 - p_2$ is needed, the difference of the sample proportions. The derivation of this follows similar lines to those set out above for the difference of two sample means, so is not repeated. The probability distribution is

$$p_1 - p_2 \sim N \left(\pi_1 - \pi_2, \frac{\pi_1 Q_1}{n_1} + \frac{\pi_2 Q_2}{n_2} \right) \qquad [5.10]$$

Again, the two samples must be independently drawn for this to be correct (it is difficult to see how they could not be in this case).

Since the difference between the sample proportions is an unbiased estimate of the true difference, this will be used for the point estimate. The point estimate is therefore

$p_1 - p_2 = 23/80 - 10/50$
$\qquad = 0.0875$

or 8.75%.

The 95% confidence interval is given by

$$\left[(p_1 - p_2) - 1.96 \sqrt{\frac{\pi_1 Q_1}{n_1} + \frac{\pi_2 Q_2}{n_2}} \; , \right.$$
$$\left. (p_1 - p_2) + 1.96 \sqrt{\frac{\pi_1 Q_1}{n_1} + \frac{\pi_2 Q_2}{n_2}} \right] \qquad [5.11]$$

π_1 and π_2 are unknown so have to be replaced by p_1 and p_2 for purposes of calculation, so the interval becomes

$$\left[(0.29 - 0.20) - 1.96 \sqrt{\frac{0.29 \times 0.71}{80} + \frac{0.20 \times 0.80}{50}} \; , \right.$$
$$\left. (0.29 - 0.20) + 1.96 \sqrt{\frac{0.29 \times 0.71}{80} + \frac{0.20 \times 0.80}{50}} \right]$$

$= [\; -0.061, \; 0.236 \;]$

The 95% confidence interval is fairly wide in this case, ranging from a negative to a positive value. We cannot even be 95% confident that there is any true difference at all between the two countries.

Estimation with small samples

So far only large samples (defined as sample sizes in excess of 25) have been dealt with, which means that (by the Central Limit theorem) the sampling distribution of $\bar{x}$ follows a Normal distribution, whatever the distribution of the parent population. Remember, from the two theorems of Chapter 4, that

(a) if the population follows a Normal distribution, $\bar{x}$ is also Normally distributed, and
(b) if the population is not Normally distributed, $\bar{x}$ is approximately Normally distributed in large samples ($n \geq 25$).

In the confidence interval formulae, s^2 was used in place of σ^2 since the latter was unknown.

When dealing with small samples, two problems can arise:

(a) if the population distribution is non-Normal, the distribution of $\bar{x}$ will also be non–Normal, and the methods of the previous section will not be correct. The correct confidence interval might be larger or smaller than the one calculated.
(b) if the population is Normally distributed, but σ is unknown, then the use of s to estimate it means that $\bar{x}$ is no longer approximately Normally distributed. The above methods will result in too narrow confidence intervals.

In case (a) recourse has to be made to non-parametric methods, i.e. methods which make no assumptions about the shape of the parent population. These methods are not covered in this book.

In case (b) there is a solution, which is to use the t distribution rather than the Normal in constructing the confidence interval.

Which distribution to use when constructing a confidence interval around $\bar{x}$ therefore depends upon the shape of the parent population (Normal or non-Normal) and upon the size of the sample. Table 5.1 sets out the possible circumstances which can arise, and the correct distribution to use.

The t distribution was derived by W.S. Gossett in 1908 while conducting tests on the average strength of Guinness beer (who says statistics has no impact on the real world?). He published his work under the pseudonym 'student', since the company did not allow its employees to publish under their own names, so the distribution is sometimes also known as the student's distribution.

The t distribution is in many ways similar to the Normal, insofar as it is

(a) unimodal
(b) symmetric
(c) bell shaped

119

Table 5.1 Distribution of $\bar{x}$

Sample Size	Population distribution	
	Normal	Not Normal
Large	Normal	approx. Normal
Small	Normal (if σ known) t (s known)	not known

The differences are that it is more spread out than the equivalent Normal distribution and has three parameters rather than two: the mean, the variance and the degrees of freedom, denoted by the Greek letter ν (pronounced 'nu'). Thus for small samples, where σ is unknown and the population is Normally distributed, instead of

$$\bar{x} - N\ (\mu,\ \sigma^2/n)$$

we have[1]

$$\bar{x} \sim t_\nu\,(\mu,\ s^2/n) \qquad\qquad [5.12]$$

and the number of degrees of freedom, ν, is one less than the sample size:

$$\nu = n - 1$$

As the number of degrees of freedom increases the t distribution becomes more and more like a Normal distribution. This is why, in large samples (where ν is also large), the Normal distribution can be used instead of the t. The t distribution is drawn in Fig. 5.6 for various values of the parameters. Thus, in calculating confidence intervals, tables for the t distribution need to be consulted, rather those for the Normal distribution. Apart from this, the methods are exactly as before. The methods are illustrated by the following examples.

Estimating a mean

The following would seem to be an appropriate example. A sample of 15 bottles of beer showed an average specific gravity of 1,035.6, with standard deviation 2.7. Estimate the true specific gravity of the brew.

Figure 5.6 The *t* distribution drawn for differing degrees of freedom

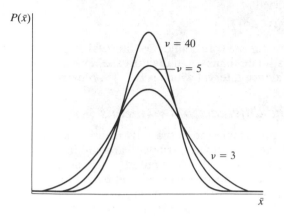

The sample information may be summarised as

$\bar{x}$ = 1,035.6
s = 2.7
n = 15

Since σ is unknown, the sample size is small and it can be assumed that the specific gravity of all bottles of beer is Normally distributed (numerous small random factors affect the specific gravity), then $\bar{x}$ follows a *t* distribution:

$\bar{x} \sim t_v (\mu, s^2/n)$
$v = n - 1$

Hence

$\bar{x} \sim t_{14} (1,035.6, 2.7^2/15)$

The sample mean is still an unbiased estimator of μ, since its expected value is μ, so it serves as point estimate of μ. The point estimate of μ is therefore 1,035.6.

The 95% confidence interval estimate is given by

$$[\bar{x} - t_v^{5\%} \sqrt{s^2/n} , \ \bar{x} + t_v^{5\%} \sqrt{s^2/n}] \qquad [5.13]$$

Where $t_v^{5\%}$ is the value of *t* which cuts off the extreme 5% (2.5% in each tail) of the *t* distribution with v degrees of freedom. From Table A3 this can be read off as 2.145 (see Appendix B of this chapter for how to read the table of the *t* distribution).

Thus the confidence interval is

$$[1,035.6 - 2.145 \ \sqrt{2.7^2/15} , \ 1,035.6 + 2.145 \ \sqrt{2.7^2/15}]$$

which when evaluated gives

[1,034.10, 1,037.10]

121

If the Normal distribution had (incorrectly) been used for this problem, then the t-score of 2.145 would have been replaced by a z-score of 1.96, giving a confidence interval of

[1,034.23, 1,036.97]

This underestimates the true confidence interval and gives the impression of a more precise estimate than is actually the case. Use of the Normal distribution leads to a confidence interval which is 8.7% too narrow.

Estimating the difference of two means

As in the case of a single mean the t-distribution needs to be used in small samples when the population variances are unknown. Again, both parent populations must be Normally distributed and in addition it must be assumed that the population variances are equal, i.e. $\sigma_1^2 = \sigma_2^2$ (this is required in the mathematical derivation of the t distribution). This latter assumption was not required in the large sample case using the Normal distribution. Consider the following example.

A sample of 20 Labour-controlled local authorities showed that they spent an average of £175 per taxpayer on administration with a standard deviation of £25. A similar survey of 15 Conservative-controlled authorities found an average figure of £158 with standard deviation of £30. Estimate the true difference in expenditure between Labour and Conservative authorities.

The sample information available is

$$\bar{x}_1 = 175 \qquad \bar{x}_2 = 158$$
$$s_1 = 25 \qquad s_2 = 30$$
$$n_1 = 20 \qquad n_2 = 15$$

We wish to estimate $\mu_1 - \mu_2$. The sample sizes are small and the population variances unknown, so the t distribution has to be used. It is assumed that the population variances are Normal and that the samples have been independently drawn. We also assume that the population variances are equal, which seems justified since s_1 and s_2 do not differ by much (Chapter 8 shows how to test this assumption). Since $\mu_1 - \mu_2$ is to be estimated, the sampling distribution of $\bar{x}_1 - \bar{x}_2$ is required. This is as follows:

$$\bar{x}_1 - \bar{x}_2 \sim t_v \left(\mu_1 - \mu_2, \ \frac{S^2}{n_1} + \frac{S^2}{n_2} \right) \qquad [5.14]$$

where

$$S^2 = \frac{(n_1 - 1)\, s_1^2 + (n_2 - 1)\, s_2^2}{n_1 + n_2 - 2} \qquad [5.15]$$

and the number of degrees of freedom, v, is

$$v = n_1 + n_2 - 2$$

S^2 is known as the *pooled* variance, and is an estimate of the (common value of) the population variances. It would be inappropriate to have the differing values

s_1^2 and s_2^2 in the formula for the t distribution, for this would be denying the assumption that $\sigma_1^2 = \sigma_2^2$, which is essential for the use of the t distribution. The estimate of the common population variance is just the weighted average of the sample variances, using degrees of freedom as weights. Each sample has $n_i - 1$ degrees of freedom, i=1,2 and the total number of degrees of freedom for the problem is the sum of the degrees of freedom in each sample.

Returning to the problem, $\bar{x}_1 - \bar{x}_2$ is an unbiased estimate of $\mu - \mu_2$, so the point estimate of the true difference in expenditure is $175 - 158 = £17$. The 95% confidence interval is given by

$$\left[(\bar{x}_1 - \bar{x}_2) - t_v^{5\%} \sqrt{\frac{S^2}{n_1} + \frac{S^2}{n_2}} \right. ,$$

$$\left. (\bar{x}_1 - \bar{x}_2) + t_v^{5\%} \sqrt{\frac{S^2}{n_1} + \frac{S^2}{n_2}} \right] \quad [5.16]$$

Evaluating S^2 first

$$S^2 = \frac{(20 - 1)\, 25^2 + (15 - 1)\, 30^2}{20 + 15 - 2}$$

$$= 741.66$$

Inserting this into eqn [5.16] gives

$$\left[(175 - 158) - 2.042 \sqrt{\frac{741.66}{20} + \frac{741.66}{15}} \right. ,$$

$$\left. (175 - 158) + 2.042 \sqrt{\frac{741.66}{20} + \frac{741.66}{15}} \right]$$

$$= [-1.99, 35.99]$$

Thus the true difference is quite uncertain and the evidence is even consistent with Conservative authorities spending more than Labour authorities. The large degree of uncertainty arises because of the small sample sizes and the quite wide variation within each sample.

One should be careful about the conclusions drawn from this test. The greater expenditure on administration could be either because of inefficiency of because of a higher level of services provided. To find out which is the case would require further investigation. The statistical test carried out here examines the levels of expenditure, but not whether they are productive or not.

Estimating a sample proportion

Estimating sample proportions when the sample size is small cannot be done with the t distribution. Recall that the distribution of p was derived from the distribution of r, which followed a Binomial distribution. In large samples the distribution of r is approximately Normal, thus giving a Normally distributed sample proportion. In small samples it is inappropriate to approximate the Binomial distribution with the *t* distribution, and indeed it is unnecessary, since the Binomial itself can be used. Small sample methods for the sample proportion should therefore be based on the Binomial distribution, as set out in Chapter 4. These methods are not therefore, discussed further here.

Calculating the required sample size

Before collecting sample data it is obviously necessary to know how large the sample size has to be. This can be decided using the methods of this chapter. The required sample size will depend upon two factors:

(a) the desired level of precision of the estimate;
(b) the funds available to carry out the survey.

The greater the precision required, the larger the sample size needs to be, *ceteris paribus*. But a larger sample will obviously cost more to collect and this might conflict with a limited amount of funds available. There is therefore a trade-off between the two desirable objectives of high precision and low cost. The following example shows how these two objectives conflict.

A firm producing sweets wishes to find out the average amount of pocket money children receive per week. It wants to be 99% confident that the estimate is within 10 pence of the correct value. How large a sample is needed?

The problem is one of estimating a confidence interval, turned on its head. Instead of having the sample information $\bar{x}$, s and n, and calculating the confidence interval for μ, the desired width of the confidence interval is given and it is necessary to find the sample size n which will ensure this. The formula for the 99% confidence interval, assuming a Normal rather than t distribution (i.e. it is assumed that the required sample size will be large) is

$$[\bar{x} - 2.58 \sqrt{\frac{s^2}{n}} , \bar{x} + 2.58 \sqrt{\frac{s^2}{n}}] \qquad [5.17]$$

Diagrammatically this can be represented as shown in Fig. 5.7. The firm wants the distance between $\bar{x}$ and μ to be no more than 10 pence in either direction, which means that the confidence interval must be 20 pence wide. The value of n which makes the confidence interval 20 pence wide has to be found. This can be done by solving the equation

$$10 = 2.58 \sqrt{\frac{s^2}{n}} , \text{ hence by rearranging}$$

$$n = \frac{2.58^2 s^2}{10^2} \qquad [5.18]$$

All that is now required to solve the problem is the value of s^2, the sample variance; but since the sample hasn't yet been taken this is not available. There are a number of ways of trying to get round this problem:

Figure 5.7 The desired width of the confidence interval

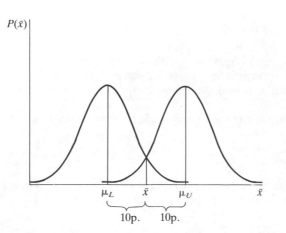

(a) using the results of existing surveys if available;
(b) conducting a small, preliminary survey;
(c) guessing.

These may not seem very satisfactory (particularly the last), but something has to be done and some intelligent guesswork should give a reasonable estimate of s^2. Suppose, for example, that a survey of children's *spending* taken five years previously showed a standard deviation of 15 pence. It might be reasonable to expect that the standard deviation of spending would be similar to the standard deviation of income, so 15 pence (updated for inflation) can be used as an estimate of the standard deviation. Suppose that five years' inflation turns the 15 pence into 25 pence (see Chapter 2, Index numbers). Using $s = 25$ we obtain

$$n = \frac{2.58^2 \times 25^2}{10^2}$$

$$= 41.60$$

giving a required sample size of 42 (the sample size has to be an integer). This is a large ($n \geq 25$) sample size so the use of the Normal distribution was justified.

Is the firm willing to pay for such a large sample? Suppose it was willing to pay out £500 in total for the survey, which cost £300 to set up and then £3 per person sampled. The total cost would be £300 + 42 × 3 = £426, which is within the firm's budget. If the firm wished to spend less than this, it would have to accept a smaller sample size and thus a lower precision or a lower level of confidence. For example, if only a 95% confidence level were required, the appropriate z-score would be 1.96, yielding

125

$$n = \frac{1.96^2 \times 25^2}{10^2}$$

$$= 24.01$$

A sample size of 24 would only cost £300 + 3 × 24 = £372. (At this sample size the assumption that $\bar{x}$ follows a Normal distribution becomes less tenable, so the results should be treated with caution. Use of the t distribution is tricky, because the appropriate t value depends upon the number of degrees of freedom which in turn depends on sample size, which is what is being looked for!)

The general formula for finding the required sample size is

$$n = \frac{z_x^2 s^2}{a^2}$$
[5.19]

where z_x is the z-score appropriate for the $(100 - x)\%$ confidence level and a is the desired accuracy (10 pence in this case).

Problems

5.1 Explain the difference between an estimate and an estimator. Is it true that a good estimator always leads to a good estimate?

5.2 Explain why an unbiased estimator is not always to be preferred to a biased one.

5.3 Given the sample data

$$\bar{x} = 40 \qquad s = 10 \qquad n = 36$$

calculate the 99% confidence interval estimate of the true mean. If the sample size were 20, how would the method of calculation and width of the interval be altered?

5.4 An insurance company knows that on average 5% of its customers have a car accident in any given year; in each case it has to pay out £1,000. The actuarially fair premium would therefore be £50, but the firm charges £60 to cover risk and profit. The firm will obviously go bankrupt if more than 6% of its customers have accidents.

(a) If the firm has 1,000 customers, calculate the probability of the firm's going bankrupt.
(b) Calculate the same probability if the firm has 10,000 customers.
(c) Why should you feel happier dealing with a large insurance company?
(d) Is a larger company more profitable in the long run?

5.5 A random sample of 100 record shops found that the average weekly sale of a particular record was 260 copies, with standard deviation 96. Find the 95%

126

confidence interval estimate for the true average sale for all shops. To compile the record chart it is necessary to know the correct average weekly sale to within 5% of its true value. How large a sample size is required?

5.6 Given the sample data

$$\bar{x}_1 = 25 \qquad \bar{x}_2 = 22$$
$$s_1 = 12 \qquad s_2 = 18$$
$$n_1 = 80 \qquad n_2 = 100$$

estimate the true difference between the means with 95% confidence.

5.7 A sample of 200 women from the labour force found an average wage of £6,000 p.a. with standard deviation £2,500. A sample of 100 men found an average wage of £8,000 with standard deviation £1,500. Estimate the true difference in wages between men and women. A different survey, of men and women doing similar jobs, obtained the following results:

$$\bar{x}_W = £7,200 \qquad \bar{x}_M = £7,600$$
$$s_W = £1,225 \qquad s_M = £750$$
$$n_W = 75 \qquad n_M = 50$$

Estimate the difference between male and female wages using this new data. What can be concluded from the results of the two surveys?

5.8 A sample of 954 adults in early 1987 found that 23% of them hold shares. Given a UK adult population of 41 million and assuming a proper random sample was taken, find the 95% confidence interval estimate for the number of shareholders in the UK. A 'similar' survey the previous year had found a total of 7 million shareholders. Assuming 'similar' means the same sample size, find the 95% confidence interval estimate of the increase in shareholders between the two years.

Appendix A: Derivation of the sampling distribution of *p*

The sampling distribution can be easily derived from the distribution of *r*, the number of successes in *n* trials of an experiment. The problem in the text concerns the number of home-owners ('successes') in a sample of 100. Thus $r = 60$ and $n = 100$. The sample proportion *p* is given by $p = r/n = 0.6$.

The distribution of *r* is (from Chapter 4)

$$r \sim B\,(n,\ P) \text{ or}$$
$$r \sim N\,(nP,\ nPQ)$$

in large samples where *P* is approximately 0.5. Both these conditions are satisfied in this case.

Knowing the distribution of *r*, is it possible to find that of *p*? Since *p* is simply *r* multiplied by a constant, $1/n$, it is also Normally distributed. The mean and variance of the distribution can be derived using the *E* and *V* operators. First, however, note that *P* (the probability of being a home-owner) may be replaced

127

by π (the proportion of home-owners in the population). This is justified since, according to the frequentist approach to probability, they are equivalent. Therefore

$$r \sim N(n\pi, n\pi Q)$$

The expected value of r is therefore

$$E(r) = n\pi$$

Hence

$$E(p) = E(r/n)$$

and since n is a constant

$$E(p) = E(r/n) = 1/n \; E(r) = 1/n \; n\pi$$
$$= \pi$$

The expected value of the sample proportion is equal to the population proportion. p is therefore unbiased as an estimator of π.
For the variance:

$$V(r) = n\pi Q$$

Hence

$$V(p) = V(r/n) = 1/n^2 \; V(r) = 1/n^2 \; n\pi Q$$
$$= \pi Q/n$$

Hence the distribution of p is given by

$$p \sim N(\pi, \pi Q/n)$$

Appendix B: Using tables of the t distribution

Using tables of the t distribution is similiar to using the Normal distribution, expect that account must be taken of degrees of freedom, v. This is best illustrated by example. Suppose the value of the t distribution corresponding to the 95% confidence level is required, for 15 degrees of freedom. The t value is found in Table A3, in the column headed 0.025 (2.5% in each tail), in the row labelled 15. The value is $t = 2.13$. Similarly the t value for the 99% confidence level is found from the 0.005 column in the same row. This value is $t = 2.95$.

Values of the t distribution for different confidence levels and degrees of freedom may be found in an analogous manner. As the number of degrees of freedom increases, the t distribution approaches the Normal, which may be seen by examining the final row of Table A3, which is identical to the Normal distribution.

6 Hypothesis testing

Introduction

This chapter deals with problems very similar to those of the previous chapter on estimation, but examines them in a slightly different way. The estimation of population parameters and the testing of hypotheses about those parameters are similar techniques (indeed they are formally equivalent in a number of respects), but there are important differences in the interpretation of the results arising from each method. The process of estimation is appropriate when measurement is involved, such as measuring the true average expenditure on food; hypothesis testing is better when decision making is involved, such as whether to accept that a supplier's products are up to a specified standard. Hypothesis testing is also used to make decisions about the truth or otherwise of different theories, such as whether rising prices are caused by rising wages; and it is here that the issues become contentious. It is sometimes difficult to interpret correctly the results of hypothesis tests in these circumstances. This is discussed further below.

The concepts of hypothesis testing

As on many previous occasions we proceed by means of an example. The example is slightly artificial, but serves to illustrate the principles involved. A company buys bolts from two different suppliers, call them firms A and B. From past experience it is known that firm A supplies bolts of average length 5.00 cm with standard deviation 0.05 cm. Firm B is known to supply bolts of average length 5.02 cm with standard deviation 0.075 cm. One day a consignment of 50 bolts is delivered, but with no indication of which supplier they came from. How is it to be decided whether the consignment is from A or B? The obvious answer of telephoning each company to ask if they've sent a consignment is ruled out; the answer has to be decided on statistical grounds alone.

In this problem the available evidence consists of the sample of $n = 50$ bolts and from this the delivery has to be assigned to supplier A or B. The sample evidence we shall use is x, the sample mean, in this case the average length of the 50 bolts, along with the sample size. Suppose the sample mean is 5.009 cm. The information available is

Population	or
$\mu_A = 5.00$ cm	$\mu_B = 5.02$ cm
$\sigma_A = 0.05$ cm	$\sigma_B = 0.075$cm

Sample
$$\bar{x} = 5.009 \text{ cm}$$
$$n = 50$$

Using this information the technique of estimation set out in the previous chapter could be used to construct a confidence interval for μ. However, this would not be very useful for deciding between supplier A and supplier B. Suppose both μ_A *and* μ_B were in the confidence interval (the significance level could always be raised to ensure this were true). Further, should σ_A, σ_B or the sample standard deviation (not given here) be used in constructing the interval? The unequal population standard deviations pose something of a problem. The technique of estimation is not of great help in a context in which a decision has to be made.

It has to be decided whether the sample comes from population (supplier) A or from population (supplier) B. Some form of decision rule has to be devised which enables this to be done, and this decision rule is conventionally called a hypothesis test. Here (as in all statistical testing) there are two competing hypotheses, the first being that the sample comes from A (this hypothesis is called H_0), the second that it comes from B (hypothesis H_1). This is written

$$H_0 : \mu = \mu_A \quad \text{or} \quad H_0 : \mu = 5.00$$
$$H_1 : \mu = \mu_B \qquad\qquad H_1 : \mu = 5.02$$

μ here means the mean of the population from which the sample comes, and so must be either μ_A or μ_B. The question is which of these hypotheses is correct and which is false.

It can never be certain whether the right answer has been obtained (as long as phone calls are ruled out!); only an informed guess can be made. It is known that, on average, firm A produces shorter bolts than firm B. A sample of 'short' bolts would tend to favour the conclusion that the delivery came from firm A, but the difficulty arises in answering the tautological question, 'How short is "short"?' Even so, it is possible for firm B to produce (by chance) a sample of 'short' bolts (the figures for the standard deviations indicate that neither firm produces bolts of exactly uniform length). Thus it is quite possible to come to the wrong decision and assign the sample to supplier B when *in fact* it came from A. This error is termed (convention again) a Type I error. Assigning the sample to A when it comes in fact from B is known as a Type II error. Schematically this can be represented as shown in Fig. 6.1.

Obviously a good decision rule gives a good chance of making correct decisions and rules out errors as far as possible. Unfortunately it is impossible to eliminate completely the possibility of errors. As the decision rule is changed to reduce the probability of a Type I error, the probability of making a Type II error inevitably increases. The skill comes in balancing these two types of error. Again a diagram is useful in illustrating this. Figure 6.2 shows the sampling distribution of $\bar{x}$ under H_0 (i.e. *assuming H_0 is true*) and under H_1 (assuming H_1 is true).

Each of these is a Normal distribution (by the Central Limit theorem of Chapter 4) and is constructed in exactly the same way as the sampling distributions in the previous chapter. In other words, *if* the sample came from supplier A, then the sample mean is distributed:

Figure 6.1 Type I and Type II errors

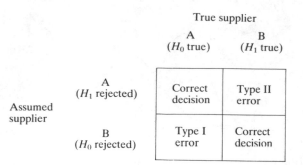

Figure 6.2 The sampling distributions of $\bar{x}$ under H_0 and under H_1

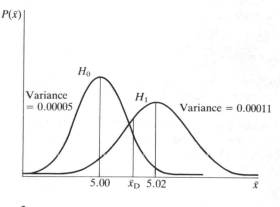

$$\bar{x} \sim N\ (\mu_A,\ \sigma_A^2/n)$$
i.e.
$$\bar{x} \sim N\ (5.00,\ 0.00005)$$

On the other hand, if the sample came from supplier B, the sample mean would be distributed:

$$\bar{x} \sim N\ (\mu_B,\ \sigma_B^2/n)$$
i.e.
$$\bar{x} \sim N\ (5.02,\ 0.00011)$$

The decision rule amounts to choosing a point on the horizontal axis in Fig. 6.2. If the particular sample mean lies to the right of this point, the sample is assigned to supplier B, if to the left to supplier A. Such a point is represented by $\bar{x}_D$ (D for decision rule) in Fig. 6.2. Suppose that $\bar{x}_D$ is arbitrarily chosen to be 5.01 cm. A sample mean length greater than this means the sample is assigned to supplier B; if less then 5.01, to supplier A.

Based on this decision rule, the probabilities of Type I and Type II errors can now be calculated. Recall that a Type I error means rejecting H_0 when it is true.

Figure 6.3 The probability of a Type I error

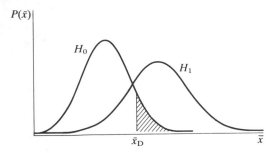

This means that a sample mean greater than or equal to 5.01 cm was obtained, even though H_0 was true.

The probability of a Type I error is therefore the area under the Normal distribution associated with H_0, to the right of $\bar{x}_D$. This is illustrated in Fig. 6.3. This area is straightforward to calculate:

$$z = \frac{5.00 - 5.01}{\sqrt{0.00005}} = -1.41$$

which, from Table A2, gives an area of 7.93%. Thus the probability of wrongly assigning the sample to supplier B, a Type I error, is 7.93%, given this particular decision rule.

A Type II error assigns the sample to supplier A, though in fact it comes from B. This type of error is found from the distribution of $\bar{x}$ under H_1 and is illustrated in Fig. 6.4. The area representing a Type II error is again shaded and can be calculated as

$$z = \frac{5.02 - 5.01}{\sqrt{0.00011}} = 0.95$$

which gives the probability of a Type II error as 17.11%.

Figure 6.4 The probability of a Type II error

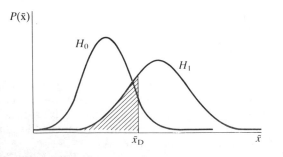

What is the best decision rule (i.e. what value of x_D) to adopt? Trying to avoid a Type I error by having a high value of $\bar{x}_D$ inevitably means incurring a high probability of making a Type II error. It is here that subjective judgement (by the statistician or by the decision maker) plays a role. If it is felt that the two types of error are equally undesirable, then the probabilities of the two types of error could be equalised. Setting $\bar{x}_D = 5.008$ cm would give a probability of approximately 13% for both types of error. Alternatively, it might be felt that making a Type I error is more costly to the firm than a Type II error. Suppose supplier B is very slow to refund money, so that paying him by mistake (Type I error) would mean a long wait for a refund (and he can't be telephoned to complain, remember . . .). In this case the balance of probabilities could be shifted against a Type I error and thus the decision rule would be altered. If a Type I error was felt to be twice as costly as a Type II error, then it might be appropriate to make the probability of a Type I error half that of a Type II error (it would involve a few trial-and-error calculations to find the value of $\bar{x}_D$ that achieved this).

There are several points to note about this procedure. First of all it does involve some subjective judgement in the choice of $\bar{x}_D$. It might be argued that, since it is subjective, why not just make a subjective decision without calculating the probabilities of different types of error? The counter-argument is that these calculations do at least lead to an *informed* decision, even if subjective. The knowledge that one decision rule might be leading towards a likely and costly error is surely valuable knowledge.

The second point to note is that there is not a consistent relationship between the probabilities of Type I and Type II errors. It is *not* the case, for example, that the sum of these probabilities is one. In the example above, they sum to 25.29%. Nor is it the case that they always sum to the same amount. When the two error probabilities are equalised, their sum came to 26%. It is impossible to say, in general, how the probability of a Type II error decreases as that of a Type I error increases. It all depends upon the particular problem. Some examples are illustrated in Fig. 6.5

It can be seen that, for a fixed probability of a Type I error, the probability of a Type II error is greater:

(a) the closer together are the two hypothesised population means, μ_A and μ_B (compare (b) and (c))
(b) the greater the variance σ_B^2/n (compare (a) and (b)).

In other words, it is easier to make the correct decision:

(a) the greater the difference in the average length of bolts made by A and B (if $\mu_A = 5$ cm, $\mu_B = 50$ cm the problem would be very easy!);
(b) the more accurately and consistently the bolts were made, e.g. if *all* A's bolts were exactly 5.00 cm and B's exactly 5.02 cm (i.e. $\sigma_A = \sigma_B = 0$).
(c) the larger the sample size. Large n makes σ^2/n small, so the sampling distributions are narrow, as in Fig. 6.5 (a). It is always beneficial to have a larger sample size for this reason. The drawback is that larger samples cost more money and/or time to collect, which may not be available. Sometimes sampling actually destroys the product (e.g. crash-testing of

Figure 6.5 Different Type II error probabilities for a constant Type I error probability

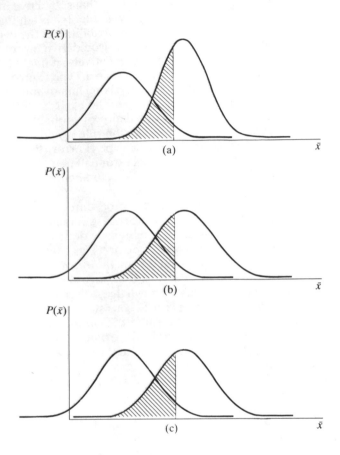

motor vehicles) so is expensive in this way also. (Rolls-Royce is exempt from some of the US crash tests for this very reason.)

Another way of looking at types of error is to consider the *power* of a hypothesis test. This is defined as

Power = 1 − probability (Type II error)

Since a Type II error is defined as accepting H_0 when false (equivalent to rejecting H_1 when true), power is the probability of rejecting H_0 when false. (If H_0 is false, it must be *either* accepted *or* rejected. Hence these probabilities sum to one.) This is one of the correct decisions as identified earlier, associated with the lower right-hand box in Fig. 6.1. A powerful test is therefore desirable, and hypethesis tests should, if possible, be set up to maximise power. This involves, as shown above, looking for large effect sizes (μ_A and μ_B being far apart), using large samples, and trying to obtain accurate samples (small variances). Unfortunately, in economics and business the data are very often given in advance and there is little or no control over the sampling procedure. This leads to a neglect of considerations of power, unlike (for example) psychology, where experiments can be designed and carried out. The gathering of sample data will be discussed further in Chapter 7.

Hypothesis testing in practice: large samples

The above discussion presented a rather idealised treatment of the subject of hypothesis testing (hence the slightly artificial example), but it served to illustrate the principles. In practice, matters are somewhat different, which means that although the method of calculation of the results is the same, the interpretation of these results has to be more cautious.

As in the case of estimation, the methods of analysis differ slightly, depending upon whether the sample is large ($n \geq 25$) or not. The principles are exactly the same as in estimation: where the sample size is small and the population variance (σ^2) is unknown and therefore has to be estimated by the sample variance (s^2), the t-distribution rather than the Normal has to be used. Large sample problems are dealt with first.

The type of problem that usually arises is not so clear cut as the previous example. A more likely type of problem is the following: a firm receives a consignment of 5,000 bolts from its sole supplier, who claims that his bolts are of average length 5.00 cm. Measuring a random sample of 50 bolts yields an average length of 5.009 cm with a standard deviation of 0.05 cm. Should the consignment be sent back?

The difference now is that there is only one supplier and the question is to decide whether the batch is faulty or not. Telephones can now be permitted, since they would be useless anyway! The starting point, as before, is to define the two hypotheses. This is now more difficult, since there is no firm B to provide the second hypothesis. Instead we write

$H_0 : \mu = 5.00$
$H_1 . \mu \neq 5.00$

H_0 is referred to as the null hypothesis, H_1 as the alternative hypothesis. It can be seen that the latter is now very vague; μ is not equal to 5.00, but it is not known what it *is* equal to. Unfortunately it is impossible to be more precise. The null hypothesis states that the bolts come from the supplier *and* meet the specification; the alternative hypothesis is that the sample comes from a different supplier (population) and does not meet the specification. Even though the bolts obviously do come from the usual supplier, they do not meet the specification, and so might be thought of as coming from a different, hypothetical, supplier who supplies bolts of a different length.

The methodological procedure we shall adopt is as follows. It is first *assumed* that the null hypothesis is true, and the statistical tests are performed on that basis. If the null hypothesis fails these tests (i.e. the hypothesis test), the null hypothesis is *rejected* in favour of the alternative hypothesis. At no stage in the

135

procedure is the alternative hypothesis actually put to the test, and indeed it would would be difficult to do so, since it is so vaguely specified. If the null hypothesis passes the tests, then it is 'not rejected' by the data. It is (strictly) incorrect to say the hypothesis is 'accepted', although this usage is quite common and does little harm as long as one is aware of its correct interpretation.

This approach is in the spirit of the work of Karl Popper, who argued that theories (hypotheses) could never be conclusively proved to be true, but only proved to be false (rejected). Thus, for example, the Newtonian theory of mechanics was believed to be true until it was proved false by Einstein's theory of relativity.

To decide upon the decision rule it is helpful to look at the two types of error that could be made

Type I : reject the null hypothesis when in fact it is true (i.e. send back a consignment which is in fact satisfactory)

Type II : reject the alternative hypothesis when in fact it is true (i.e. accept a faulty consignment).

If the cost of accepting a faulty consignment were high (e.g. the bolts were a vital part of cars' braking systems), then a low probability of a type II error (and consequently a high probability of a Type I error) would be desirable. If the bolts were not used in critical applications, and costs of returning a consignment were high, then it would be wise to try to avoid a Type I error.

Unfortunately, since the exact value of μ under the alternative hypothesis is unknown, the probability of a Type II error cannot be calculated (nor, therefore, the power of the test). This is illustrated in Fig. 6.6. The position of the sampling distribution of $\bar{x}$ under H_0 is well defined, but that under H_1 is not, and is therefore drawn with a dashed line (two possible H_1 distributions are drawn). The only course of action open is to choose (arbitrarily) some Type I error probability, use that to derive the decision rule, and ignore the probability of a Type II error.

Figure 6.6 The sampling distribution of $\bar{x}$ under H_0 and under H_1

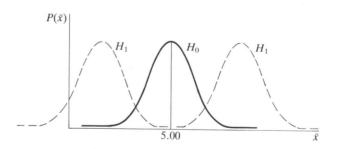

The convention (again!) is to take 5% as the Type I error probability, or 1% if one wants especially to guard against rejecting true null hypotheses. This probability is known as the *significance level* of the test.

Significance level: The probability of rejecting the null hypothesis when it is in fact true.

The *confidence level* is then defined as:

Confidence level $= 1 -$ significance level

so a 5% significance level (i.e. Type I error probability) corresponds to a 95% confidence level. This is the same as the confidence level concept used in the previous chapter on estimation. Either form of expression is acceptable. There is not much reason to support the 5% significance level apart from the fact that it is a convention and thus widely used, in the same way as the 95% confidence interval. If each researcher could independently choose her significance level it would be easy to arrive at any desired decision, simply through judicious choice of significance level. Beware the researcher who rejects a hypothesis at the 11.5% significance level!

With this in mind, the distribution under H_0 can be divided up into the rejection region (5% of the total area) and the acceptance (strictly, non-rejection) region (95%) as in Fig. 6.7.

Figure 6.7 The rejection regions for H_0 at the 5% significance level

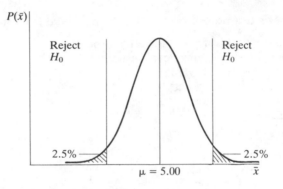

There are in fact two rejection regions, one in either tail of the distribution, because the alternative hypothesis could be either to the right or to the left of H_0. Each rejection region constitutes 2.5% of the distribution, making 5% in total. This is known as a *two tail* hypothesis test, because both sides (above and below μ) are involved. If the sample mean falls into either rejection region, then the null hypothesis is rejected in favour of the alternative hypothesis.

Rather than deal with the distribution of $\bar{x}$ it is easier to use the standard Normal distribution, introduced in Chapter 4. The z-score associated with the simple mean is calculated and is compared with the value of z which cuts off the outer 5% of the standard Normal distribution. This latter value of z is known as the *critical value* of the test, denoted by z^*, and from Table A2 this can be read off as $z^* = 1.96$. If the calculated z-score falls into the rejection region, then the null hypothesis is rejected. This is illustrated in Fig. 6.8. The z-score in this case is

Figure 6.8 The critical values of z and the rejection regions under the standard Normal distribution

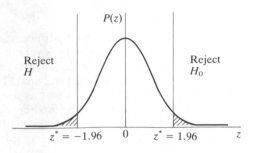

$$z = \frac{\overline{x} - \mu}{\sqrt{\sigma^2/n}} = \frac{5.009 - 5.00}{\sqrt{0.05^2/50}} = 1.27$$

which is less than the critical value, 1.96, indicating that the z-score lies in the acceptance region. H_0 is therefore not rejected. The bolts do meet the specification.

The hypothesis test procedure can thus be broken down into five steps:

Step 1: Set up the null and alternative hypotheses
Step 2: Choose the significance level, usually 5%
Step 3: Look up the critical value, z^*
Step 4: Calculate the test statistic

$$z = \frac{\overline{x} - \mu}{\sqrt{\sigma^2/n}} \qquad\qquad [6.1]$$

Step 5: Decision rule
If $z > z^*$ or $z < -z^*$ then
reject H_0 in favour of H_1.

Another example, shorn of detailed explanation, should reinforce the method, and also illustrates the usage of a one tail test.

The average price of houses in the centre of London is £60,000. It is to be expected that houses in Outer London are cheaper. A random sample of 40 finds an average price of £56,000 with standard deviation £12,000. Is this data consistent with the hypothesis?

Step 1: Null and alternative hypotheses

These are

H_0: $\mu = 60,000$
H_1: $\mu < 60,000$

Although houses are believed to be cheaper in Outer London, the null hypothesis is that they are the same price. This is because the null is the basis for

138

calculations and so has to be precise. Saying that houses are 'cheaper' is not sufficiently precise for the null hypothesis. The rule is that the null hypothesis must *always* have the '=' sign in it.

The researcher's belief that prices are cheaper outside the centre is consigned to the alternative hypothesis. Notice that in this case it is '$\mu < 60,000$' rather than 'not equal to'. It is very unlikely that prices are higher outside the centre, so this possibility is excluded *a priori*. This is therefore a *one tail* test: only one tail of the distribution is relevant. One tail tests use *either* of the relationships < (less than, as above) or > (greater than) in the alternative hypothesis. The choice of whether or not to use a one tail test should *not*, however, be based on the sample evidence. Just because the sample mean happens to be less than the hypothesised value does not mean that a one tail test with '<' in the alternative hypothesis should be used. This would be using the sample data to determine the hypothesis, which is then tested against the sample data! The circularity of the argument should be clear. The choice of alternative hypothesis should be based upon evidence apart from the sample data. In this case, economic theory would suggest that the supply of housing is less constrained outside the city centre, resulting in lower house prices. If in doubt it is safer to use a two tail test.

The only difference between one and two tail tests as far as the calculation is concerned is that for the one tail case the rejection region is concentrated in one tail of the distribution; in this example it is the left hand tail, as illustrated in Fig. 6.9.

Figure 6.9 The rejection region for a one tail test at the 5% significance level

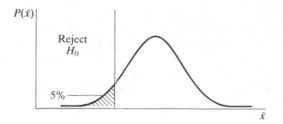

Step 2: significance level: 5% is chosen.

Step 3: critical value: The value of z which cuts off 5% in *one* tail of the distribution has to be found. From the standard Normal table this is shown to be $z^* = -1.64$.

Step 4: calculation of the test statistic:

$$z = \frac{\bar{x} - \mu}{\sqrt{\sigma^2/n}} = \frac{56,000 - 60,000}{\sqrt{12,000^2/40}} = -2.11 \qquad [6.2]$$

Step 5: comparison z and z^*:

$z- < z^*$ so H_0 is rejected in favour of H_1.

The test does support the expectation of cheaper houses in Outer London, at the 5% significance level. Another way of putting this is to say that the hypothesis that houses are no cheaper in Outer London than in Inner London can be rejected with 95% confidence. This can be interpreted as: if house prices were no lower in Outer London than Inner London, then the chance of obtaining a random sample of 40 houses in Outer London, with $\bar{x} \leq 56{,}000$ and $s = 12{,}000$ is less than 5%. Therefore, *either* a rather unlikely event has occurred, *or* houses are cheaper outside the centre. The second of these possibilities is chosen. Note that it is not *certain* that houses are cheaper in Outer London; this cannot be established unless *every* house in Outer London is valued, a prohibitively expensive task.

Testing a sample proportion

Having learned, in the previous chapter, the sampling distributions of the sample mean, the sample proportion, and the difference of two sample means and of two proportions, the different types of hypothesis test can be quickly and easily examined. The test statistic is always given by

$$\frac{\text{Value of the random variable } - \text{ Hypothesised value}}{\text{Standard error of the random variable}}$$

Thus in the previous section the test statistic for the sample mean was

$$z = \frac{\bar{x} - \mu}{\sqrt{\sigma^2/n}}$$

Therefore, as with estimation, once the sampling distribution of the random variable is known, the hypothesis test should be straightforward.

Consider the following problem about a sample proportion: a car manufacturer claims that no more than 10% of its cars should need repairs in the first three years of their life. A random sample of 50 three-year-old cars found that eight had required attention. Does this contradict the maker's claim?

From Chapter five (eqn [5.4]), the sampling distribution of the sample proportion in large samples is given by

$$p \sim N\ (\pi,\ \pi Q/n), \text{Where } Q\ =\ 1\ -\ \pi \qquad\qquad [6.3]$$

The sample data are

$$p\ =\ 8/50\ =\ 0.16$$
$$n\ =\ 50$$

The hypothesis test is set out along the same lines as for a sample mean.

Step 1: the null and alternative hypothesis

$H_0: \pi\ =\ 0.10$

$H_1: \pi\ >\ 0.10$ (the only concern is the manufacturer not matching his claim)

Step 2: significance level: 5%

Step 3: critical value of the Normal distribution for a one tail test at the 5% significance level, $z^* = 1.64$

Step 4: test statistic

$$z = \frac{p - \pi}{\sqrt{\dfrac{\pi(1 - \pi)}{n}}} \tag{6.4}$$

$$= \frac{0.16 - 0.10}{\sqrt{\dfrac{0.1 \times 0.9}{50}}}$$

$$= 1.41$$

Step 5: decision rule. Since the test statistic is less than the critical value, it falls into the acceptance region. The null hypothesis is not rejected by the data. The manufacturer's claim is not unreasonable.

It is interesting to think about how this problem would have been handled by the technique of estimation. How would this have altered the view of the problem and the evidence?

Testing the difference of two sample means

Suppose a company wishes to compare the performance of its two factories producing a standard product, say golf balls. The factories are equipped with the same machinery but their outputs might differ due to managerial ability, labour relations, etc. Senior management wishes to know if there is a difference between the two factories. Output is monitored for 30 days, with the following results

	Factory 1	Factory 2
Average daily output	2,560	2,490
Standard deviation of daily output	89	104

Does this produce sufficient evidence of a real difference between the factories? The information at our disposal may be summarised as

$$
\begin{array}{ll}
\bar{x}_1 = 2{,}560 & \bar{x}_2 = 2{,}490 \\
s_1 = 89 & s_2 = 104 \\
n_1 = 30 & n_2 = 30
\end{array}
$$

The hypothesis test to be conducted concerns the difference between the factories' outputs, so the appropriate random variable to examine is $\bar{x}_1 - \bar{x}_2$. From Chapter 5 (eqn [5.8]), this has the following distribution, in large samples:

$$\bar{x}_1 - \bar{x}_2 \sim N\left(\mu_1 - \mu_2, \frac{\sigma_1^2}{n_1} + \frac{\sigma_2^2}{n_2}\right) \qquad [6.5]$$

The population variances, σ_1^2 and σ_2^2, may be replaced by their sample estimates, s_1^2 and s_2^2, if the former are unknown, as here. The hypothesis test is therefore as follows.

Step 1: H_0: $\mu_1 - \mu_2 = 0$
$\quad\quad\quad H_1$: $\mu_1 - \mu_2 \neq 0$

Step 2: significance level 1%. This is chosen since the management does not want to interfere unless it is really confident of some difference between the factories.

Step 3: the critical value is $z^* = 2.57$

Step 4: the test statistic is

$$z = \frac{(\bar{x}_1 - \bar{x}_2) - (\mu_1 - \mu_2)}{\sqrt{\dfrac{s_1^2}{n_1} + \dfrac{s_2^2}{n_2}}} \qquad [6.6]$$

$$= \frac{(2{,}560 - 2{,}490) - 0}{\sqrt{\dfrac{89^2}{30} + \dfrac{104^2}{30}}}$$

$$= 2.80$$

Step 5: decision rule. The test statistic falls into the rejection region. There does appear to be a significant difference between the two factories which merits investigation.

A number of remarks about this example should be made. First it should be noted that it is not necessary for the two sample sizes to be equal (although they are in the example). For example, 45 days' output from factory 1 and 35 days from factory 2 could have been sampled. Secondly, the values of s_1^2 and s_2^2 do not have to be equal. They are respectively estimates of σ_1^2 and σ_2^2, and although the null hypothesis asserts that $\mu_1 = \mu_2$ it does not assert that the variances are equal. Management wants to know if the *average* levels of output are the same; it is not concerned about daily fluctuations in output. Chapter 8 will provide a test of the hypothesis of equal variances.

The final point to consider is whether all the necessary conditions for the correct applications of this test have been met. One doubt might be whether the sample observations are truly independent within each sample and whether the two samples themselves are truly independent of each other. Since the samples are of 30 consecutive days' output from each factory, one day's output might not be independent of the previous day's output. Suppose that factory 2 suffered a breakdown of some kind which took three days to fix. Output would be reduced on three successive days and factory 2 would almost inevitably appear less efficient than factory 1. The fact that the standard deviation for factory 2 is higher than for factory 1 lends support to the suspicion that this might have occurred. A look at the individual sample observations might therefore be worthwhile. It would have been altogether better if the samples had been collected on randomly chosen days over a longer time period to reduce the danger of this type of problem.

If the two factories both obtain their supplies from a common, but limited, source, then the output of one factory might not be independent of the output of the other. A high output of one factory would tend to be associated with a low output from the other, which has little to do with their relative efficiencies. This might leave the average difference in output unchanged but might increase the variance substantially (either a very high positive value of $\bar{x}_1 - \bar{x}_2$ or a very high negative value is obtained). This would lead to a low value of the test statistic and the conclusion of no difference in output. Any real difference in the efficiency is being masked by the common supplier problem.

Testing the difference of two sample proportions

In a comparison of two holiday companies' customers, of the 75 who went with Happy Days Tours, 45 said they were satisfied, and 48 of the 90 who went with Fly by Night Holidays were satisfied. Is there a significant difference between the companies?

This problem can be handled by a hypothesis test on the difference of two sample proportions. The procedure is as follows. The sample evidence is

$p_1 = 45/75 \qquad n_1 = 75$ (the subscript 1 refers to Happy Days
$p_2 = 48/90 \qquad n_2 = 90$ Tours)

The hypothesis test is as follows:

Step 1: H_0: $\pi_1 - \pi_2 = 0$
       H_1: $\pi_1 - \pi_2 \neq 0$

Step 2: significance level: 5%

Step 3: critical value: $z^* = 1.96$

Step 4: test statistic. The distribution of $p_1 - p_2$ (see eqn [5.10]) is

$$p_1 - p_2 \sim N\left(\pi_1 - \pi_2, \ \frac{\pi_1(1 - \pi_1)}{n_1} + \frac{\pi_2(1 - \pi_2)}{n_2}\right) \qquad [6.7]$$

so the test statistic is

$$z = \frac{(p_1 - p_2) - (\pi_1 - \pi_2)}{\sqrt{\dfrac{\pi_1(1 - \pi_1)}{n_1} + \dfrac{\pi_2(1 - \pi_2)}{n_2}}} \qquad [6.8]$$

π_1 and π_2 in the denominator of eqn [6.8] have to be replaced by estimates from the samples. However, they cannot simply be replaced by p_1 and p_2 because they are unequal; to do so would contradict the null hypothesis that they *are* equal. Since the null hypothesis is assumed to be true (for the moment), it doesn't make sense to use a test statistic which explicitly supposes the null hypothesis to be false. Therefore π_1 and π_2 are replaced by an estimate of their common value which is denoted $\hat{\pi}$ and whose formula is

$$\hat{\pi} = \frac{n_1 \, p_1 + n_2 \, p_2}{n_1 + n_2} \qquad\qquad [6.9]$$

This yields

$$\frac{75 \times 0.60 + 90 \times 0.533}{75 + 90}$$

$$= 0.564$$

This in fact is just the proportion of all customers who were satisfied, 93 out of 165.

The test statistic therefore becomes

$$z = \frac{(p_1 - p_2) - (\pi_1 - \pi_2)}{\sqrt{\dfrac{\hat{\pi}\,(1 - \hat{\pi})}{n_1} + \dfrac{\hat{\pi}\,(1 - \hat{\pi})}{n_2}}} \qquad\qquad [6.10]$$

$$= \frac{0.60 - 0.533}{\sqrt{\dfrac{0.564 \times 0.436}{75} + \dfrac{0.564 \times 0.436}{90}}}$$

$$= 0.86$$

Step 5: the test statistic is less than the critical value so the null hypothesis cannot be rejected with 95% confidence. There is not sufficient evidence to prove any difference between the two companies' performance.

Hypothesis tests with small samples

As with estimation, slightly different methods have to be employed when the sample size is small ($n < 25$) and the population variance is unknown. When both of these conditions are satisfied the t distribution must be used rather than the Normal, so a t-test is conducted rather than a z-test. This means consulting tables of the t distribution to obtain the critical value of a test, but otherwise the methods are similar. These methods will be applied to hypotheses about sample means only, since they are inappropriate for tests of a sample proportion.

Testing the sample mean

A large chain of supermarkets sells 5,000 packets of cereal in each of its stores each month. It decides to test-market a different brand of cereal in 15 of its stores. After a month the 15 stores have sold an average of 5,200 packets each, with a standard deviation of 500 packets. Should all supermarkets switch to selling the new brand?

The sample information is

$$\bar{x} = 5,200$$
$$s = 500$$
$$n = 15$$

From Chapter 5 (see eqn [5.12]) the distribution of the sample mean from a small sample when the population variance is unknown is

$$\bar{x} \sim t_v (\mu, s^2/n) \tag{6.11}$$

With $v = n - 1$ degrees of freedom. The test statistic is therefore

$$t_{n-1} = \frac{\bar{x} - \mu}{\sqrt{s^2/n}} \tag{6.12}$$

The hypothesis test is

Step 1: $H_0 : \mu = 5,000$
$H_1 : \mu > 5,000$ (only an improvement in sales is relevant)

Step 2: significance level: 1% (chosen because the cost of changing brands is high)

Step 3: the critical value of the t distribution for a one tail test at the 1% significance level with $v = n - 1 = 14$ degrees of freedom is $t^* = 2.62$. Note that this value is obtained from the '0.01' column of Table A3, because the rejection region is concentrated in one tail of the distribution.

Step 4: the test statistic is

$$t_{14} = \frac{\bar{x} - \mu}{\sqrt{s^2/n}}$$

$$= \frac{5,200 - 5,000}{\sqrt{500^2/15}}$$

$$= 1.55$$

Step 5: the null hypothesis is not rejected since the test statistic is less than the critical value. It would probably be unwise to switch over to the new brand of cereals.

Testing the difference of two sample means

A survey of 20 British companies found an average annual expenditure on research and development of £3.7 m. with a standard deviation of £0.6 m. A survey of 15 similar German companies found an average expenditure on research and development of £4.2 m. with standard deviation £0.9 m. Does this evidence lend support to the view often expressed that Britain does not invest enough in research and development?

This is a question about the difference of two sample means, $\bar{x}_1 - \bar{x}_2$, whose sampling distribution in small samples, with population variances unknown, is (see eqn [5.14])

$$\bar{x}_1 - \bar{x}_2 \sim t_v \left(\mu_1 - \mu_2, \frac{S^2}{n_1} + \frac{S^2}{n_2} \right) \qquad [6.13]$$

where

$$S^2 = \frac{(n_1 - 1) \, s_1^2 + (n_2 - 1) \, s_2^2}{n_1 + n_2 - 2} \qquad [6.14]$$

and the number of degrees of freedom, v, is given by

$$v = n_1 + n_2 - 2$$

The hypothesis test is as follows

Step 1: H_0: $\mu_1 - \mu_2 = 0$
 H_1: $\mu_1 - \mu_2 < 0$

Step 2: significance level: 5%.

Step 3: the critical value of the t distribution at the 5% significance level for a one tail test with $v = n_1 + n_2 - 2 = 33$ degrees of freedom is approximately $t^* = -1.69$.

Step 4: the test statistic is

$$t = \frac{\bar{x}_1 - \bar{x}_2 - (\mu_1 - \mu_2)}{\sqrt{\dfrac{S^2}{n_1} + \dfrac{S^2}{n_2}}} \qquad [6.15]$$

$$S^2 = \frac{(n_1 - 1) \, s_1^2 + (n_2 - 1) \, s_2^2}{n_1 + n_2 - 2} \qquad [6.16]$$

$$= \frac{19 \times 0.6^2 + 14 \times 0.9^2}{33}$$

$$= 0.55$$

Hence

$$t = \frac{(3.7 - 4.2) - 0}{\sqrt{\dfrac{0.55}{20} + \dfrac{0.55}{15}}} = -1.97$$

Step 5: the test statistic is less than critical value so the null hypothesis is rejected. The data does support the view that Britain spends less on R & D than Germany.

Independent and dependent samples

The following example illustrates the differences between independent samples (as encountered so far), and dependent samples where slightly different methods of analysis are required. The example also illustrates how a particular problem can often be analysed by a variety of statistical methods.

A company introduces a training programme to raise the productivity of its clerical workers, which is measured by the number of invoices processed per day. The company wants to know if the training programme is effective. How should it monitor the programme? There are a variety of ways of going about the task, as follows:

(a) take two (random) samples of workers, one trained and one not trained, and compare their productivity;
(b) take a sample of workers and compare their productivity before and after training;
(c) take two samples of workers, one to be trained and the other not. Compare the improvement of the trained workers with any change in the other group's performance over the same period.

We shall go through each method in turn, pointing out any possible difficulties.

Two random samples: Suppose a group of ten workers is trained and compared with a group of ten non-trained workers, with the following data being relevant:

$$\bar{x}_T = 25.5 \qquad \bar{x}_N = 21.00$$
$$s_T = 2.55 \qquad s_N = 2.91$$
$$n_T = 10 \qquad n_N = 10$$

Thus trained workers process 25.5 invoices per day compared with only 21 by non-trained workers. The question is whether this is significant, given that sample sizes are quite small.

The appropriate test here is a *t*-test of the difference of two sample means, as follows:

$$H_0: \mu_T - \mu_N = 0$$
$$H_1: \mu_T - \mu_N > 0$$

147

$$t_{18} = \frac{25.5 - 21.00}{\sqrt{\dfrac{7.49}{10} + \dfrac{7.49}{10}}} = 3.68$$

(7.49 is S^2, the pooled variance). The t statistic leads to rejection of the null hypothesis; the training programme does seem to be effective.

One problem with this test is that the two samples might not be truly random and thus might not properly reflect the effect of the training programme. Poor workers might have been reluctant (and have refused) to take part in training, departmental managers might have selected better workers for training as some kind of reward, or better workers may have simply volunteered. In a well designed experiment this should not be allowed to happen, of course, but this does not rule out the possibility. There is also the 5% (significance level) chance of unrepresentative samples being selected and a Type I error occurring.

Paired samples: This is the situation where a sample of workers is tested before and after training. The sample data are as follows:

Worker	1	2	3	4	5	6	7	8	9	10
Before	21	24	23	25	28	17	24	22	24	27
After	23	27	24	28	29	21	24	25	26	28

One could proceed by assuming these are two independent samples and conduct a t-test. The summary data and results are

$$\bar{x}_B = 23.50 \qquad \bar{x}_A = 25.5$$
$$s_B = 3.10 \qquad s_A = 2.55$$
$$n_B = 10 \qquad n_A = 10$$

The resulting test statistic is $t_{18} = 1.58$ which is not significant at the 5% level.

There are two problems with this test and its result. First, the two samples are not truly independent, since the before and after measurements refer to the same group of workers. Secondly, nine out of ten workers in the sample have shown an improvement, which is odd in view of the result found above of no significant improvement. If the training programme really has no effect, then the probability of a single worker showing an improvement is 1/2. The probability of nine or more workers showing an improvement is, by the Binomial Method, $(1/2)^{10}10C9 + (1/2)^{10}$, which is about one in a hundred. A very unlikely event seems to have occurred. Note here how the Binomial distribution may be used to gain some insight into the problem.

The t-test used above is inappropriate because it does not make full use of the information in the sample. It does not reflect the fact, for example, that the before and after scores 21 and 23 relate to the same worker. The Binomial calculation above does reflect this fact. A re-ordering of the data would not affect the t-test result, but would affect the Binomial, since a different number of workers would now show an improvement. Of course the Binomial does not use all the sample information either: it dispenses with the actual productivity data for each worker and replaces it with 'improvement' or 'no improvement'. It disregards the amount of improvement for each worker.

The best use of the sample data comes by measuring the improvement for each worker, as follows (if a worker had deteriorated, this would be reflected by a negative number):

Worker	1	2	3	4	5	6	7	8	9	10
Improvement	2	3	1	3	1	4	0	3	2	1

This new data can be treated by single sample methods, and account is taken both of the actual data values and of the fact that the original samples were dependent (re-ordering of the data would produce different improvement figures). The summary statistics of the new data are as follows:

$$\bar{x} = 2.00$$
$$s = 1.247$$
$$n = 10$$

The null hypothesis of no improvement can now be tested as follows:

$$H_0: \mu = 0$$
$$H_1: \mu > 0$$

$$t_9 = \frac{2.00 - 0}{\sqrt{\dfrac{1.247^2}{10}}} = 5.07$$

This is significant at the 5% level so the null hypothesis of no improvement is rejected. The correct analysis of the sample data has thus reversed the previous conclusion.

Matters do not end here, however. Although we have discovered an improvement, this might be due to other factors apart from the training programme. For example, if the before and after measurements were taken on different days of the week (that Monday morning feeling . . .), or if one of the days were sunnier, making people feel happier and therefore more productive, this would bias the results. These may seem trivial examples but these effects do exist, for example the 'Friday afternoon car', which has more faults than the average.

The way to solve this problem is to use a control group, so called because extraneous factors are controlled for so as to isolate the effects of the factor under investigation. In this case, the productivity of the control group would be measured (twice) at the same times as that of the training group, though no training would be given to them. Suppose that the average improvement of the control group were 0.5 invoices per day with standard deviation 1.0 (again for a group of ten). This can be compared with the improvement of the training group via the two-sample *t*-test, giving

$$t_{18} = \frac{2.00 - 0.5}{\sqrt{\dfrac{1.13^2}{10} + \dfrac{1.13^2}{10}}} = 2.97$$

(1.13^2 is the pooled variance). This confirms the finding that the training programme is of value.

149

Discussion of hypothesis testing

The preceding exposition has served to illustrate how to carry out a hypothesis test and the rationale behind it. However, the methodology has been subject to criticism and it is important to understand this since it gives a greater insight into the meaning of the results of a hypothesis test.

In the previous examples the problem has been posed as a decision-making one, e.g. whether or not to send back a consignment of goods. However, statistical inference is very often used not so much to aid decision making as to provide evidence for or against a particular theory, to alter one's degree of belief in the truth of the theory. For example, a theory might assert that rising prices are caused by rising wages (the cost-push theory of inflation). The null and alternative hypotheses would be

H_0: there is no connection between rising wages and rising prices
H_1: there is some connection between rising wages and rising prices.

(Note that the null has 'no' connection. 'Some' connection is too vague to be the null hypothesis.) Data could be gathered to test this hypothesis (the appropriate methods will be discussed in the chapter on correlation and regression). But what 'decision' rests upon the result of this test? It might be thought that government might make a decision to impose a prices and incomes policy, but if every academic study of inflation led to the imposition or abandonment of a prices and incomes policy there would have been an awful lot of policies! (In fact there were a lot of such policies, but not as many as the number of studies of inflation.) No single study is decisive ('more research is needed' is a very common phrase), but each does influence the climate of opinion which may eventually lead to a policy decision. But if a hypothesis test is designed to influence opinion, how is the significance level to be chosen?

It is difficult to trade off the costs of Type I and Type II errors and the probability of making those errors. A Type I error in this case means concluding that rising wages do cause rising prices when in fact they do not. So what would be the cost of this error, i.e. imposing a prices and incomes policy when in fact it is not needed? It is extremely difficult, if not impossible, to put a figure on it. It would depend on what type of prices and incomes policy were imposed: would wages be frozen or allowed to rise with productivity, how fast would prices be allowed to rise, would company dividends be frozen? The costs of the Type II error would also be problematic (not imposing a needed prices and incomes policy), for they would depend on, among other things, what alternative policies might be adopted.

Therefore the 5% (or 1%) significance level really does depend upon convention; it cannot be justified by reference to the relative costs of Type I and Type II errors (it is too much to believe that everyone does consider these costs and independently arrives at the conclusion that 5% is the appropriate significance level!). However, the 5% convention does impose some sort of discipline upon research; it sets some kind of standard against which all theories (hypotheses) are measured. But then suppose a result is significant at the 4.95% level (i.e. it just meets the 5% convention) and the null hypothesis is rejected. A *very* slight change in the sample could have meant the result being significant at only the 5.05% level, and the null hypothesis being accepted. Would we really be happy to completely alter our belief on such fragile results? Most researchers (but not all!) would be cautious if their results were only just significant (or fell just short of significance). This suggests that results are best presented by giving the significance level of the test so that the reader can make his own judgement; or at least the calculated z-score should be given so that the significance level can be derived. Just giving the all-or-nothing result that the null hypothesis was or was not rejected is not very satisfactory.

Bayesian statisticians would argue that their methods do not suffer from this problem, since the result of the analysis (termed a *posterior probability*) gives the degree of belief which the researcher has in the truth of the null hypothesis. However, this posterior probability does in part depend upon the prior probability (i.e. before the statistical analysis) that the researcher attaches to the null hypothesis. As noted in Chapter 3, the derivation of the prior probabilities can be difficult.

In practice, most people do not regard the results of a hypothesis test as all-or-nothing proof, but interpret the result on the basis of the quality of the data, the care the researcher has taken in analysing the data, personal experience, and a multitude of other factors. Both schools, classical and Bayesian, introduce subjectivity into the analysis and interpretation of data; classical statisticians in the choice of the significance level (and choice of one or two tail test), Bayesians in their choice of prior probabilities. It is not clear which method is superior, but classical methods have the advantage of being simpler.

Another criticism of hypothesis testing is that it is based on weak methodological foundations. Earlier in the chapter the connection was mentioned between the principles of hypothesis testing and the work of Popper, who argued that theories can never be proved true, but can be proved false. Further, Popper argued that theories should be rigorously tested against the evidence, and that strenuous efforts should be made to try to falsify the theory. This methodology is not strictly followed in hypothesis testing, where the researcher's hypothesis is actually the alternative. The conclusion is arrived at by default, because of the failure of the null hypothesis to survive the evidence.

Consider the researcher who believes that health standards have changed in the last decade. This may be tested by gathering data on health and testing the null hypothesis of no change in health standards against the alternative hypothesis of some change. The researcher's theory thus becomes the alternative hypothesis and is never actually tested against the data. No attempt is made to falsify the (alternative) hypothesis: it gets accepted by default if the null hypothesis fails. *Only* the null hypothesis ever gets tested.

A further problem is the asymmetry between the null and alternative hypotheses. The null hypothesis is that there is *exactly* no change in health standards whereas the alternative hypothesis contains all other possibilities, from a large deterioration to a large improvement. The dice seem loaded against the null hypothesis. Indeed, if a large enough sample is taken, the null hypothesis is almost certain to be rejected, because there is bound to have been *some* change, however small. The large sample size leads to a small standard error (σ^2/n) and thus a large z-score. This suggests that the significance level of a test should decrease as the sample size increases.

These particular problems are avoided by the technique of estimation, which measures the size of the change and focuses attention upon that, rather than upon some accept/reject decision. As the sample size gets larger, the confidence interval narrows and an improved measure of the true change in health standards is obtained. Zero (i.e. no change) might be in the confidence interval or it might not; it is not the central issue. Thus the techniques of estimation and hypothesis testing put different emphasis upon interpretation of the results, even though they are formally identical. In the earlier example of London house prices, the hypothesis of no difference between prices in Inner and Outer London was rejected at the 5% significance level. This means that the 95% confidence interval estimate of the difference would not contain zero (i.e. no difference). A confidence interval contains all values which would not be rejected by a (two tail) hypothesis test at the same significance level.

On some occasions a confidence interval is inferior to a hypothesis test, however. Consider the following case. In the UK only 17 out of 465 judges are women (3.7%). The Equal Opportunities Commission commented that since the appointment system is so secretive it is impossible to tell if there is discrimination or not. What can the statisticians say about this? No discrimination (in its broadest sense) would mean that half of all judges would be women. Thus the hypotheses are

$$H_0: \pi = 0.5$$
$$H_1: \pi < 0.5$$

The sample data is $p = 0.037$, $n = 465$. The z-score is

$$z = \frac{p - \pi}{\sqrt{\dfrac{\pi(1 - \pi)}{n}}}$$

$$z = \frac{0.037 - 0.5}{\sqrt{\dfrac{0.5 \times 0.5}{465}}}$$
$$= -19.97$$

This is clearly significant, so the null hypothesis is rejected. There is some form of discrimination somewhere against women (unless women choose not to be judges). But a confidence interval estimate of the 'true' proportion of female judges would be meaningless. To what population is this 'true' proportion related? The lesson from all this is that there exist differences between confidence intervals and hypothesis tests, despite their formal similarity. Which technique is more appropriate is a matter of judgement for the researcher. With hypothesis testing, the rejection of the null hypothesis at some significance level might actually mean a small (and unimportant) deviation from the hypothesised value. It should be remembered that the rejection of the null hypothesis based on a large sample of data is also consistent with the true value and hypothesised value being quite close together.

Summary of test statistics

This section collects together all the test statistics formulae for easy reference.

Large samples

Sample mean:

$$z = \frac{\bar{x} - \mu}{\sqrt{\sigma^2/n}} \quad \text{or} \quad z = \frac{\bar{x} - \mu}{\sqrt{s^2/n}}$$

Sample proportion:

$$z = \frac{p - \pi}{\sqrt{\dfrac{\pi(1 - \pi)}{n}}}$$

Difference of two sample means:

$$z = \frac{(\bar{x}_1 - \bar{x}_2) - (\mu_1 - \mu_2)}{\sqrt{\dfrac{\sigma_1^2}{n_1} + \dfrac{\sigma_2^2}{n_2}}}$$

or

$$z = \frac{(\bar{x}_1 - \bar{x}_2) - (\mu_1 - \mu_2)}{\sqrt{\dfrac{s_1^2}{n_1} + \dfrac{s_2^2}{n_2}}}$$

Difference of two sample proportions:

$$z = \frac{(p_1 - p_2) - (\pi_1 - \pi_2)}{\sqrt{\dfrac{\pi(1 - \pi)}{n_1} + \dfrac{\pi(1 - \pi)}{n_2}}}$$

Small samples with population variance unknown

Sample mean:

$$t_v = \frac{\bar{x} - \mu}{\sqrt{s^2/n}}$$

where $v = n - 1$

153

Difference of two sample means:

$$t_v = \frac{\bar{x}_1 - \bar{x}_2 - (\mu_1 - \mu_2)}{\sqrt{\dfrac{S^2}{n_1} + \dfrac{S^2}{n_2}}}$$

where

$$S^2 = \frac{(n_1 - 1)\,s_1^2 + (n_2 - 1)\,s_2^2}{n_1 + n_2 - 2}$$

$$v = n_1 + n_2 - 2$$

Problems

6.1 Given the following sample data

$$\bar{x} = 15 \qquad s^2 = 270 \qquad n = 30$$

test the null hypothesis that the true mean is equal to 12, against a two-sided alternative hypothesis. Draw the distribution of $\bar{x}$ under the null hypothesis and indicate the rejection regions for this test.

6.2 Answer true or false, with reasons if necessary.

(a) There is no way of reducing the probability of a Type I error without simultaneously increasing the probability of a Type II error.
(b) The probability of a Type I error is associated with an area under the distribution of $\bar{x}$ assuming the null hypothesis to be true.
(c) It is always desirable to minimise the probability of a Type I error.
(d) A larger sample, *ceteris paribus*, will increase the power of a test.
(e) The significance level is the probability of a Type II error.
(f) The confidence level is the probability of a Type II error.

6.3 Given the two hypotheses

$$H_0: \mu = 400$$
$$H_1: \mu = 415$$

and $\sigma^2 = 1{,}000$ (for both hypotheses), draw the distribution of $\bar{x}$ under both hypotheses. If the decision rule is chosen to be: reject H_0 if $\bar{x} \geq 410$ from a sample of size 40, find the probability of a Type II error and the power of the test. What happens to these answers as the sample size is increased? Draw a diagram to illustrate.

6.4 Given the following data from two independent samples

$$\bar{x}_1 = 115 \qquad \bar{x}_2 = 105$$
$$s_1 = 21 \qquad s_2 = 21$$
$$n_1 = 49 \qquad n_2 = 63$$

test the hypothesis of no difference between the population means against the alternative that the mean of population 1 is greater than the mean of population 2.

6.5 A pharmaceutical company testing a new type of pain reliever administered the drug to 30 volunteers experiencing pain. Sixteen of them said that it eased their pain. Does this evidence support the claim that the drug is effective in combating pain? A second group of 40 volunteers were given a placebo instead of the drug. Thirteen of them reported a reduction in pain. Does this new evidence cast doubt upon your previous conclusion?

6.6 A consumer organisation is testing two different brands of battery. A sample of 15 of brand A shows an average useful life of 410 hours with a standard deviation of 20 hours. For brand B, a sample of 20 gave an average useful life of 391 hours with standard deviation 26 hours. Test whether there is any significant difference in battery life. What assumptions are being made about the population in carrying out this test?

6.7 A supermarket receives perishable goods from a supplier which are kept in stock before going on sale. From past experience it is known that 5% of all batches deteriorate and have to be thrown away. A new storeman is employed, who later reports that nine out of 100 batches had to be thrown away. What conclusions can be drawn? If, over the relevant time period, demand had risen so that goods spent less time in stock before going on sale, how would this alter your judgement?

6.8 A firm receives components from a supplier, which it uses in its own production. The components are delivered in batches of 2,000. The supplier claims that there are only 1% defective components on average from its production. However, production occasionally gets out of control and a batch is produced with 10% defective components. The firm wishes to intercept these low quality batches, so a sample of size 50 is taken from each batch and tested. If two or more defectives are found in the sample, then the batch is rejected.

(a) Describe the two types of error the firm might make in assessing batches of components.
(b) Calculate the probability of each type of error given the data above.
(c) If, instead, samples of size 30 were taken and the batch rejected if one or more rejects were found, how would the error probabilities be altered?
(d) The firm can alter the two error probabilities by choice of sample size and rejection criteria. How should it set the relative sizes of the error probabilities
  (i) if the components might affect consumer safety;
  (ii) if there are many competitive suppliers of components;
  (iii) if the costs of replacement under guarantee are high?

7 Sampling methods

Introduction

Much of the text has been concerned with the analysis of sample evidence and discussing the inferences that can be drawn from it. It has been stressed that this evidence must come from randomly drawn samples and, although the notion of randomness was discussed in Chapter 4, the precise nature of a random sample has not been set out. This chapter remedies the omission and discusses the various types of random sample and how they are collected.

When conducting statistical research, there are two ways of proceeding:

(a) use secondary data sources, such as the *UN Yearbook*, or
(b) collect the data personally

(there is a third and better way, which is to employ a research assistant). In the first case it is important to know how the data were collected in order to use the appropriate methods of statistical analysis. This will usually mean consulting a handbook describing the survey. For example, the UK Family Expenditure Survey is fully described in W.F.F. Kemsley, R.U. Redpath and M. Holmes (1980). To use the methods of analysis outlined in this book it is important that the samples collected were proper random samples. If not, the data may still be of some use (it might be possible to work out the direction of any bias, for example) but should be treated with caution. Advice about the use of the secondary data sources was given in Chapter 1.

This chapter is therefore mainly concerned with the problems of collecting survey data prior to its analysis. The decision to collect the data personally depends upon the type of problem faced, the current availability of data relating to the problem and the time and cost needed to conduct a survey. It should not be forgotten that the first question that needs answering is whether the answer obtained is worth the cost of finding it. It is probably not worthwhile the government spending £50,000 to find out how many biscuits people eat, on average (this is not to say this hasn't been done . . .). The sampling procedure is therefore always subject to some limit on cost, and the researcher is trying to obtain the best value for money.

The importance of sampling methods

The probability distributions which have been used as the basis of the techniques of estimation and hypothesis testing rely upon the sample having been drawn at random from the population. If this is not the case, then the formulae for confidence intervals, hypothesis tests, etc. are incorrect and not strictly applicable (they may be reasonable approximations but it is difficult to know how reasonable). In addition, the results about the bias and precision of estimators will be incorrect. For example, suppose an estimate of the average expenditure on repairs and maintenance by car owners is obtained from a sample survey. A poor estimate would arise if only Rolls-Royce owners were included in the sample, since they are not representative of the population as a whole. The precision of the estimator (the sample mean, $\bar{x}$) is likely to be poor because the mean of the sample could either be very low (Rolls-Royce cars are very reliable so rarely need repairs) or very high (if they do break down the high quality of the car necessitates a costly repair). This means the confidence interval estimate will be very wide and thus imprecise. It is not immediately obvious if the estimator would be biased upwards or downwards.

Thus some form of random sampling method is needed to be able to use the theory of the probability distributions of random variables. It should not be believed that these problems of non-random sampling can be ignored if a very large sample is taken, as the following cautionary tale shows. In 1936 the *Literary Digest* tried to predict the result of the forthcoming US election by sending out 10 million (*sic*) mail questionnaires. Two million were returned, but even with this enormous sample size Roosevelt's vote was incorrectly estimated by a margin of 19% points. The problem is that those who respond to questionnaires are not a random sample of those who receive them.

The meaning of random sampling

The definition of random sampling is that every element of the population should have a known, non-zero probability of being included in the sample. The problem with the sample of cars above was that Ford cars (for example) had a zero probability of being included. Many sampling procedures give an *equal* probability of being selected to each member of the population but this is not an essential requirement. It is possible to adjust the sample data to take account of unequal probabilities of selection. If, for example, Roll-Royces had a much greater chance of being included than Fords, then the estimate of the population mean would be calculated as a weighted average of the sample observations, with greater weight being given to 'Ford' observations than to 'Rolls-Royce' observations. A very simple illustration of this is given below

	Rolls-Royce	Ford
Number in population	1	2
Annual repair bill	£400	£100 (each)
Average repair bill £200	$(= \dfrac{400 + 2 \times 100}{3})$	

Suppose the sample is constrained to have one observation from each make.

	Rolls-Royce	Ford
Number in sample	1	1
Probability of selection	100%	50%
Repair bill	£400	£100
Sample weight (to compensate for unequal probabilities)	1	2

Weighted sample mean £200 $(= \dfrac{1 \times 400 + 2 \times 100}{3})$

Thus, making the sample weight equal to the inverse of the probability of selection redresses the balance. As long as the probability of being in the sample is known, the weight can be derived; but if the probability is zero, this procedure breaks down. Having equal probabilities of selection usually makes the analysis simpler, but is not an essential requirement.

Other theoretical assumptions necessary for deriving the probability distribution of the sample mean or proportion are that the population is of infinite size and that each observation is independently drawn. In practice the former condition is never satisfied since no population is of infinite size, but most populations are large enough that it does not matter. For each observation to be independently drawn (i.e. the fact of one observation being drawn does not alter the probability of others in the sample being drawn) strictly requires that sampling be done with replacement, i.e. each observation drawn is returned to the population before the next observation is drawn. Again in practice this is often not the case, sampling being done without replacement, but again this is of negligible practical importance.

On occasion the population is quite small and the sample constitutes a substantial fraction of it. In these circumstances the *finite population correction* (fpc) can be applied to the formula for the variance of $\bar{x}$, the fpc being given by

$$\text{fpc} = (1 - n/N)$$

where N is the population size and n is the sample size. The table below illustrates its usage:

Variance of $\bar{x}$ from infinite pop.	Variance of $\bar{x}$ from finite pop.	Example values of fpc			
		$n =20$ $N=50$	25 100	50 1,000	100 10,000
σ^2/n	$\sigma^2/n\,(1 - n/N)$	0.60	0.75	0.95	0.99

The finite population correction serves to narrow the confidence interval because a sample size of (say) 25 reveals more about a population of 100 than about a population of 100,000, so there is less uncertainty about population parameters. When the sample size constitutes only a small fraction of the population (e.g. 5% or less), the finite population correction can be ignored in practice. If the whole population is sampled ($n = N$), then the variance becomes zero and there is no uncertainty about the population mean.

158

A further important aspect of random sampling occurs when there are two samples to be analysed, when it is important that the two samples are independently drawn. This means that the drawing of the first sample does not influence the drawing of the second sample. This is a necessary condition for the derivation of the probability distribution of the difference between the sample means (or proportions).

Types of random sample

The meaning and importance of randomness in the context of sampling has been explained. However, there are various different types of sampling, all of them random, but which have different statistical properties. Some methods lead to greater precision of the estimates, while others can lead to considerable cost savings in the collection of the sample data, but at the cost of lower precision. The aim of sampling is usually to obtain the most precise estimates of the parameter in question, but the best method of sampling will depend on the circumstances of each case. If it is costly to sample individuals, a sampling method which lowers cost may allow a much larger sample size to be drawn and thus good (precise) estimates to be obtained, even though the method is inherently not very precise. These issues will be examined in more detail below, as a number of different sampling methods are examined.

Simple random sampling

This type of sampling has the property that every possible sample that could be obtained from the population has an equal chance of being selected. It is also the case that each element of the population has an equal probability of being included in the sample, but this is *not* the defining characteristic of simple random sampling. As will be shown below, there are sampling methods where every member of the population has an equal chance of being selected, but some samples (i.e. certain combinations of population members) can never be selected.

The statistical methods in this book are based upon the assumption of simple random sampling from the population. It leads to the most straightforward formulae for estimation of the population parameters. Although many statistical surveys are not based upon simple random sampling, the use of statistical tests based on simple random sampling is justified since the sampling process is often hypothetical in many problems. For example, if one were to compare annual growth rates of two countries over a 30-year period, a z-test on the difference of two sample means (i.e. the average annual growth rate in each country) would be conducted. In a sense the data is not a sample since it is the only possible data for those two countries over that time period. Why not therefore, just regard the data as constituting the whole population? Then it would just be a case of finding which country had the higher growth rate; there would be no uncertainty about it.

The alternative way of looking at the data would be to suppose that there exists some hypothetical population of annual growth rates and that the data

159

for the two countries were drawn by (simple) random sampling from this population. Is this story consistent with the data available? In other words, could the data we have simply arise by chance? If the answer to this is no (i.e. the z-score exceeds the critical value) then there *is* something causing a difference between the two countries (it is not yet known what that something is, but this will be dealt with in later chapters). In this case it is reasonable to assume that all probable samples have an equal chance of selection, i.e. that simple random sampling takes place. Since the population is hypothetical, one might as well suppose it to have an infinite number of members, again required by sampling theory.

Stratified sampling

Returning to the practical business of sampling, one problem with simple random sampling is that it is possible to collect 'bad' samples, i.e. those that are unrepresentative of the population. An example of this is the 'basketball player problem', i.e. in trying to estimate the average height of the population, the sample (by sheer bad luck) contains a lot of basketball players. One way round this problem is to ensure that the proportion of basketball players in the sample accurately reflects the proportion of basketball players in the population (i.e. very small!). The way to do this is to divide up the population into 'strata' and then to ensure that each stratum is properly represented in the sample. This is best illustrated by means of an example.

A survey of newspaper readership, which is thought to be associated with social class, is to be carried out. People higher up the social scale are more likely to read a newspaper and to read different newspapers from those at the bottom of the social scale. Suppose the population is made up of three social classes, A (highest), B and C as follows:

Percentage of population in social class:

A	B	C
20%	50%	30%

Suppose a sample of size 100 is taken. With luck it would contain 20 people from class A, 50 from B and 30 from C, and thus would be representative of the population as a whole. But if, by bad luck (or bad sampling), all 100 people in the sample were from class A, poor results would be obtained since newspaper readership differs between social classes.

To avoid this type of problem a stratified sample is taken, which ensures that all social classes are represented in the sample. This means that the survey would have to ask people about their social class as well as their reading habits. The simplest form of stratified sampling is *equiproportionate* sampling, whereby a stratum which constitutes (say) 20% of the population also makes up 20% of the sample. For the example above the sample would be made up as follows:

	Class			
	A	B	C	Total
No. in sample	20	50	30	100

It should be clear why stratified sampling constitutes an improvement over simple random sampling, since it rules out 'bad' samples, i.e. those not representative of the population. It is simply impossible to get a sample consisting completely of social class A, or B, or C. In fact, it is impossible to get a sample in anything but the proportions 20:50:30, as in the population; this is ensured by the method of collecting the sample.

It is easy to see when stratification leads to large improvements over simple random sampling. If there were no difference between strata (social classes) in reading habits, then there would be no gain from stratification. If reading habits were the same regardless of social class, there would be no point in dividing up the population by social class. On the other hand, if there were large differences *between* strata (income classes), but *within* strata reading habits were similiar, then the gains to stratification would be large.

Stratification is therefore beneficial when

(a) the *between*-strata differences are large and
(b) the *within*-strata differences are small.

These benefits take the form of greater precision of the estates, i.e. narrower confidence intervals.* The greater precision arises because stratified sampling makes use of supplementary information — i.e. the proportion of the population in each social class. Simple random sampling does not make use of this. Obviously, therefore, if those proportions of the population are unknown, stratified sampling cannot be carried out. However, even if the proportions are only known approximately there could be a gain in precision.

In this example social class is a *stratification factor*, i.e. a variable which is used to divide the population into strata. Other factors could of course be used, such as income or even height. A good stratification factor is one which is related to the subject of investigation. Income would therefore probably be a good stratification factor since it is related to reading habits, but height is not since there is probably little difference between tall and short people in the newspaper they read. What is a good stratification factor obviously depends upon the subject of study. A bed manufacturer might well find height to be a good stratification factor if conducting an enquiry into preferences about the size of beds. Although good stratification factors improve the precision of estimates, bad factors do not make them worse: there will merely be no gain over simple random sampling. If would be as if there were no differences between the social classes in reading habits, so that ensuring the right proportions in the sample is irrelevant, but it has no detrimental effects.

Proportional allocation of sample observations to the different strata (as done above) is the simplest method but is not necessarily the best. For the optimal allocation there should generally be a divergence from proportional allocation, and the sample should have more observations in a particular stratum (relative to proportional allocation)

---

* The formulae for calculating confidence intervals with stratified sampling are not given here, since they merit a whole book to themselves. The interested reader should consult C.A. Moser and G. Kalton, *Survey Methods in Social Investigation*, Heineman, London, 1971.

(a) the more heterogeneous the stratum, and
(b) the cheaper it is to sample the stratum.

Starting from the 20:50:30 proportional allocation derived earlier, suppose that members of class A all read the same newspaper, but those of class C read a variety of titles. Then the representation of class C in the sample should be increased, and that of A reduced. If it really were true that everyone in class A read the same paper, then one observation from that class would be sufficient to yield all there is to know about it. Furthermore, if it is cheaper to sample class C, perhaps because they are geographically more concentrated than class A, then again the representation of class C in the sample should be increased. This is because, for a given budget, it will allow a larger total sample size.

Cluster sampling

A third form of sampling is cluster sampling which, although intrinsically inefficient, can be much cheaper than other forms of sampling, allowing a larger sample size to be collected. Drawing a simple, or stratified, random sample of size 100 from the whole of Britain would be very expensive to collect since the sample observations would be geographically very spread out. Interviewers would have to make many long and expensive journeys simply to collect one or two observations. To avoid this, the population can be divided into 'clusters' (for example, regions or local authorities) and one or more of these clusters are then randomly chosen. Sampling takes place only within the selected clusters, is therefore geographically concentrated, and the cost of sampling falls, allowing a larger sample to be collected.

Within each cluster one can either have a 100% sample or a lower sampling fraction, which is called *multi-stage sampling* (this is explained further below). Cluster sampling gives unbiased estimates of population parameters but, for a given sample size, these are less precise than the results from simple or stratified sampling. This arises in particular when the clusters are very different from each other, but fairly homogeneous within themselves. In this case, once a cluster is chosen, if it is unrepresentative of the population, poor (inaccurate) estimate of the population parameter is inevitable. The ideal circumstances for cluster sampling are when all clusters are identical, since in that case examining one cluster is as good as examining the whole population.

Dividing up the population into clusters or into strata are similar procedures, but the difference is that sampling is from one or at most a few clusters, but from all strata. This is reflected in the characteristics which make for good sampling. In the case of stratified sampling, it is beneficial if the between-strata differences are large and the within-strata differences small. For cluster sampling this is reversed: it is desirable to have small between-cluster differences but heterogeneity within clusters. Cluster sampling is less efficient (precise) for a given sample size, but is cheaper so can offset this disadvantage with a larger sample size. In general, cluster sampling needs a much larger sample to be effective, so is only worthwhile where there are significant gains in cost.

Multi-stage sampling

Multi-stage sampling was referred to in the previous section and is commonly found in practice. It may consist of a mixture of simple, stratified and cluster sampling at the various stages of sampling. Consider the problem of selecting a random sample of 1,000 people from a population of 25 m. to find out about voting intentions. A simple random sample would be extremely expensive to collect, for the reasons given above, so an alternative method must be found. Suppose further that it is suspected that voting intentions differ according to whether one lives in the north or south of the country and whether one is a home-owner or renter. How is the sample to be selected? The following would be one appropriate method.

First the country is divided up into clusters of counties or regions, and a random sample of these is taken, say one in five. This would be the first way of reducing the cost of selection, since only one-fifth of all counties now need to be visited. This one in five sample would be stratified to ensure that north and south were both appropriately represented. To ensure that each voter has an equal chance of being in the sample, the probability of a county's being drawn should be proportional to its adult population. Thus a county with twice the population of another should have twice the probability of being in the sample.

Having selected the counties, the second stage would be to select a random sample of local authorities within each selected county. This might be a one in ten sample from each county and would be a simple random sample within each cluster. Finally, a selection of voters from within each local authority would be taken, stratified according to tenure. This might be a one in 500 sample. The sampling fractions would therefore be

$$\frac{1}{5} \times \frac{1}{10} \times \frac{1}{500}$$
$$= 1/25{,}000$$

So from the population of 25 m. voters a sample of 1,000 would be collected. For different population sizes the sampling fractions could be adjusted so as to achieve the goal of a sample size of 1,000.

The sampling procedure is a mixture of simple, stratified and cluster sampling. The two stages of cluster sampling allow the selection of 50 local authorities for study and so costs are reduced. The north and south of the country are both adequately represented and housing tenures are also correctly represented in the sample by the stratification at the final stage. The resulting confidence intervals will be difficult to calculate but should give an improvement over the method of simple random sampling.

Quota sampling

Quota sampling is a non-random method of sampling and therefore it is impossible to use sampling theory to calculate confidence intervals from the sample data, or to find whether or not the sample will give biased results. However, it is by far the cheapest method of sampling and so allows much larger sample sizes. As shown above, large sample sizes can still give biased results if sampling is non-random; but in some cases the budget is too small to afford even the smallest properly conducted random sample, so a quota sample is the only alternative.

Even with quota sampling, where the interviewer is simply told to go out and obtain (say) 1,000 observations, it is worth making some crude attempt at stratification. The problem with human interviewers is that they are notoriously non-random, so that when they are instructed to interview every tenth person they see (a reasonably random method), if that person turns out to be a shabbily dressed tramp slightly the worse for drink, they are quite likely to select the eleventh person instead. Shabbily dressed tramps slightly the worse for drink, are therefore under-represented in the sample. To combat this sort of problem the interviewers are given quotas to fulfil, e.g. 20 men and 20 women, ten old age pensioners, etc., so that the sample will at least broadly reflect the population under study and give reasonable results.

It is difficult to know how accurate quota samples are, since it is rare for their results to be checked against proper random samples or against the population itself. Probably the most common quota samples relate to voting intentions and so can be checked against actual election results. These opinion polls have had mixed success. Between elections they seem to yield a wide variety of results which could be the result of either

(a) good sampling of a volatile electorate, or
(b) bad sampling of a fairly stable electorate.

It is difficult to tell which is the case but the sometimes widely varying results from different polls within a few days of each other would tend to favour the latter explanation. On the other hand, the success and accuracy of 'exit' polls (i.e. sampling those coming out of polling stations) is an argument in their favour. (It also makes election night broadcasts much less exciting since the overall result is often known very early before the counting of votes even starts.) Just to complicate the argument, it is sometimes suggested that opinion polls themselves influence the results of elections.

Collecting the sample

The sampling frame

We now move on to the fine detail of how to select the individual observations which make up the sample. In order to do this it is necessary to have some sort of *sampling frame*, i.e. a list of all the members of the population from which the sample is to be drawn. This can be a problem if the population is extremely large, for example the population of a country, since it is difficult to manipulate so much information (cutting up 50 million pieces of paper to put into a hat for a random draw is a tedious business). Alternatively the list might not even exist or, if it does, might not be in one place convenient for consultation and use. In this case there is often an advantage to multi-stage sampling, for the selection of regions or even local authorities is fairly straightforward and not too time consuming. Once at this lower level the sampling frame is more manipulable (each local authority has an electoral register, for example) and individual observations can be relatively easily chosen. Thus it is not always necessary to have a complete sampling frame for the entire population.

Choosing from the sampling frame

There are a variety of methods available for selecting a sample of (say) 1,000 observations from a sampling frame of (say) 25,000 names, varying from the manual to the electronic. The oldest method is to cut up 25,000 pieces of paper, put them in a (large) hat, shake it (to randomise) and pick out 1,000. This is fairly time consuming, however, and has some pitfalls: if the pieces are not all cut to the same size, is the probability of selection the same? It is much better if the population in the sampling frame is numbered in some way, for then one only has to select random numbers. This can be done by using a table of random numbers (see Table A1). Starting at any point in the table and moving in any direction enables one to read off a series of random numbers. Digits can be taken either singly or in groups of two, three, four, etc. according to the size of the numbers required. The use of random number tables is an important feature of statistics, and in 1955 the Rand Corporation produced a book entitled *A Million Random Numbers with One Hundred Thousand Normal Deviates to Help Researchers*. This book, as the title suggests, contained nothing but pages of random numbers which allowed researchers to collect random samples. Interestingly, the authors did not bother to proof-read the text fully, since a few (random) errors here and there wouldn't matter! These numbers were calculated electronically, and nowadays every computer has a facility for rapidly choosing a set of random numbers. (It is an interesting question how a computer, which follows rigid rules of behaviour, can select random numbers which, by definition, are unpredictable by any rule.)

A further alternative, if a one in 25 sample is required, is to select a random starting point between one and 25 and then select every subsequent 25th observation (e.g. the 3rd, 28th, 53rd, etc.). This is a satisfactory procedure if the sampling frame is randomly sorted to start with, but otherwise there can be problems. For example, if the list is sorted by income (poorest first), a low starting value will almost certainly give an underestimate of the population mean. If *all* the numbers were randomly selected, this 'error' in the starting value will not be important.

Interviewing techniques

Good training of interviewers is vitally important to the results of a survey. It is very easy to lead an interviewee into a particular answer to a question. Consider the following two sets of questions:

A.
(1) Do you know how many people were killed by the atomic bomb at Hiroshima?
(2) Do you think nuclear weapons should be banned?

B.
(1) Do you believe in nuclear deterrence?
(2) Do you think nuclear weapons should be banned?

A2 is almost certain to get a higher 'yes' response than B2. Even a different ordering of the questions can have an effect upon the answers (considering asking A2 before A1). The construction of the questionnaire therefore has to be done with care. The manner in which the questions are asked is also important, since it can often suggest the answer. Good interviewers are trained to avoid these problems by sticking precisely to the wording of the question, and not to suggest an expected answer.

Even when these procedures are adhered to there can be various types of response bias. The first problem is of non-response, due to the subject not being at home when the interviewer calls. There might be a temptation to remove that person from the sample and call on someone else, but this should be resisted. There could well be important differences between those who are at home all day and those who are not, especially if the survey concerns employment or spending patterns, for example. Continued efforts should be made to contact the subject. One should be wary of surveys which have low response rates, particularly where it is suspected that the non-response is in some way systematic and related to the goal of the survey.

A second problem is that subjects may not answer the question truthfully for one reason or another, sometimes inadvertently. This commonly occurs in the case of income, where people often overstate their true income (for reasons of self-aggrandisement) or, if they think the interviewer represents the tax authorities, understate it! Break (1957), in a study of the effects of taxation upon labour supply, found one respondent who professed to the disincentive effects of taxation on his own labour supply. Further questioning revealed that he worked an average of 80 hours per week! Similar problems arise with drinking and smoking habits, which both tend to be understated (these can be cross-checked by examining figures for total sales kept by retailers or wholesalers). In some cases, the interviewer could ask for evidence, such as a salary slip, though obviously many people might object to revealing this. Furthermore, the salary might include exceptional overtime payments in that week, and so would not give an accurate picture of normal income. On the expenditure side it is unwise to ask people to recall what they spent on various items since memory is fallible and selective.

Case study: The Family Expenditure Survey

Introduction

The Family Expenditure Survey (FES) is an example of a large government survey which examines households' expenditure patterns and income receipts. It is therefore worthwhile having a brief look at it to see how the principles of sampling techniques outlined in this chapter are put into practice. The FES is used for many different purposes, including the calculation of weights to be used in the UK Retail Price Index and the assessment of the effects of changes in taxes and state benefits upon different households.

Choosing the sample

The sample design is known as a three-stage, rotating, stratified, random sample. This is obviously quite complex so will be examined stage by stage.

Stage 1: the country is first divided into 168 strata, each stratum made up of a number of local authorities sharing similar characteristics. The characteristics used as stratification factors are

(a) geographic area
(b) urban or rural character (based on a measure of population density)
(c) prosperity (based on a measure of property values).

A stratum might therefore be made up of local authorities in the south-west region, of medium population density and high prosperity.

In each quarter of the year, one local authority from each stratum is chosen at random, the probability of selection being proportional to population. Once an authority has been chosen, it remains in the sample for one year (four quarters) before being replaced. Only a quarter of the authorities in the sample are replaced in any quarter, which gives the sample its 'rotating' characteristic. Each quarter some authorities are discarded, some are kept and some new ones are brought in.

Stage 2: from each local authority selected, four wards (smaller administrative units) are selected, one to be used in each of the four quarters for which the local authority appears in the sample.

Stage 3: finally, within each ward, 16 addresses are chosen at random, and these constitute the sample.

Altogether this means that 10,752 ($168 \times 4 \times 16$) households are chosen each year to make up the sample.

The sampling frame

The register of electors in each ward is used as the sampling frame, which contains the names and addresses of everyone living in the ward. It is reasonably accurate and up to date, but is under-representative of those who have no permanent home or who move frequently (e.g. tramps, students, etc). The addresses are chosen from the register by interval sampling from a random starting point.

Response rate

The response rate is usually about 70%, meaning that the actual sample consists of about 7,000 households each year. Given the complexity of the information gathered, this is a remarkably good figure.

167

Collection of information

The data is collected by interview, and by asking participants to keep a diary in which they record *everything* they purchase over a two-week period. Highly skilled interviewers are required to ensure accuracy and compliance with the survey, and each participating family is visited several times. As a small inducement to co-operate, each member of the family is paid £5 (it is to be hoped that the anticipation of this does not distort their expenditure patterns!).

Sampling errors

Given the complicated survey design it is difficult to calculate sampling errors exactly. The multi-stage design of the sample actually tends to increase the sampling error relative to a simple random sample, but of course this is offset by cost savings which allow a greatly increased sample size. Overall, the results of the survey are of good quality, and can be verified by comparison with other statistics, such as retail sales, for example.

References

G.F. Break, (1957), 'Income tax and incentives to work: an empirical study', *American Economic Review*, **47**, 529–549.

W.F.F. Kemsley, R.U. Redpath and M. Holmes (1980) *The Family Expenditure Survey Handbook*, Office of Population Censuses and Surveys, Social Survey Division, HMSO, London.

Rand Corporation (1955) *A Million Random Digits with One Hundred Thousand Normal Deviates to Help Researchers*. The Glencoe Free Press, Glencoe.

8 The chi-squared and F distributions

Introduction

The final two distributions to be studied are the χ^2 (chi-squared) and F distributions. The former distribution is used in situations where an empirical distribution (e.g. the outcome of a series of experiments) is to be compared with a theoretical distribution. For example, if a die is rolled many times and the numbers of ones, twos, etc. appearing are counted, then these results can be compared with the expected outcomes (assuming a fair die) using the chi-squared distribution. In this way it is a generalisation of the Binomial distribution examined in Chapter 3 on probability. Instead of just two possible outcomes (success/failure, six/not-six, boy/girl) the χ^2 distribution allows many possible outcomes (1, 2 . . . 6 on a die) to be dealt with. The χ^2 distribution is thus useful when the results of an experiment fall into different categories which are difficult to handle numerically (e.g. unskilled manual worker/skilled manual worker/non-manual worker/professional). This leads on to the second use of the distribution, for contingency tables. An example of a contingency table is the following, relating level of educational attainment to type of job held. Table 8.1 shows the number of people in a sample holding different types of job and the level of education received.

Table 8.1 Educational attainment and type of job

	School	College	University
Professional	6	13	24
Managerial	16	25	29
Skilled manual	35	27	3
Unskilled manual	77	12	0

The data in Table 8.1 do seem to exhibit a relationship between education and job held, but this is only a sample of 266 people. Whether this implies a similar relationship for the population as a whole can be tested using the χ^2 distribution.

The F distribution has many uses in statistics, but here it will be used to construct a hypothesis test of the equality of two variances. This is the same in spirit as testing for the equality of two means, except that instead of using the Normal or t distribution, the F distribution must be used. The test for the equality of two variances can be performed as a precursor to testing the difference of two means using the t distribution, as set out in Chapter 5 on hypothesis testing.

The shapes of the χ^2 and F distributions

Like the other distributions encountered, the χ^2 and F distributions are actually families of distributions, and their shapes depend upon the parameters of the distributions. In both of these cases the only parameter is the number of degrees of freedom. The χ^2 distribution is drawn in Fig. 8.1 for different values of v, the number of degrees of freedom. It should be noted that the χ^2 distribution:

(1) is always non-negative;
(2) is skewed to the right;
(3) becomes more symmetric as v increases.

Figure 8.1 The χ^2 distribution

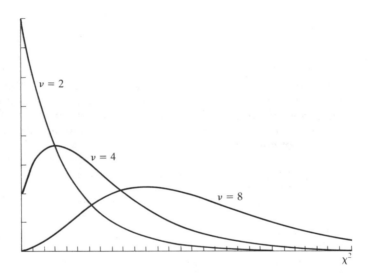

The F distribution depends upon two sets of degrees of freedom and typically looks like the example in Fig. 8.2. The F distribution

(1) is always non-negative;
(2) is skewed to the right.

The use of these distributions is the same in principle as the Normal and t distributions. From the data a test statistic is calculated which is then compared with a designated rejection region of the χ^2 or F distribution (whichever is appropriate to the problem). A test statistic falling into the rejection region implies that the null hypothesis being tested is rejected.

Figure 8.2 The F distribution

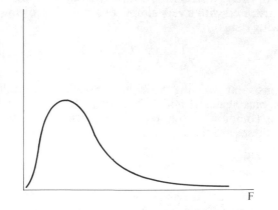

Relationships with other distributions

The χ^2 distribution is actually derived from the Normal distribution. A chi-squared variable with k degrees of freedom is the sum of k independent, squared, standardised Normal variables. Suppose a Normally distributed random variable is taken. The variable is then standardised (i.e. the z-score is calculated) and squared. Call this result z_1^2. Take a second random variable, independent of the first, and perform the same manipulation, to give z_2^2. Repeat this k times to obtain k of these variables, all distributed independently of each other. If these z^2 are all added together, the result is a χ^2 variable with $v = k$ degrees of freedom (the number of degrees of freedom is equal to the number of *independent* z^2 variables), i.e.

$$z_1^2 + z_2^2 + \ldots + z_k^2 \sim \chi_k^2 \qquad \text{if all } z^2 \text{ variables are independently distributed.}$$

$$[8.1]$$

This will become much clearer when some examples are looked at below.

The F distribution is derived from two independent χ^2 distributions. In fact it is the ratio of them, each divided by their degrees of freedom. That is,

$$\frac{\chi_1^2/k_1}{\chi_2^2/k_2} \sim F_{k1,k2} \qquad\qquad [8.2]$$

where χ_1^2 and χ_2^2 are two independently distributed chi-squared variables with $v_1 = k_1$ and $v_2 = k_2$ degrees of freedom, respectively. The F distribution therefore inherits two degrees of freedom, k_1 in the numerator and k_2 in the denominator.

Use of the χ^2 distribution

The χ^2 distribution compares *observed* values with *expected* values, calculated on the basis of some null hypothesis to be tested. If the observed and expected

171

values differ significantly, as judged by the χ^2 test (the test statistic falls into the rejection region of the χ^2 distribution), then the null hypothesis is rejected.

This can be illustrated with a very simple example. Throwing a die 72 times yields the following data

Number showing	1	2	3	4	5	6
Frequency	6	15	15	7	15	14

Are the data consistent with the die being unbiased? A crude examination suggests a slight bias against 1 and 4, but is this truly bias or just a random fluctuation quite common in this type of experiment? First the null and alternative hypotheses are set up:

H_0: the die is unbiased
H_1: the die is biased.

Notice that the hypotheses are not so neat and concise as in previous cases (H_0: $\mu = 0$ for example). This is commonly the case in χ^2 tests, but is not of great concern. The important point is that the null hypothesis should be constructed in such a way as to permit the calculation of the *expected* outcome of the experiment. Thus the null and alternative hypotheses could not be reversed in this case, since 'the die is biased' is a very vague statement (exactly *how* biased, for example?) and would not permit the calculation of the expected outcome of the experiment. On the basis of the null hypothesis, the expected values are constructed, which are 12 for each possible outcome if the die is unbiased. The data are now as in Table 8.2 (ignore columns 4–6 for the moment).

The χ^2 test statistic is now constructed using the formula*

$$\chi_v^2 = \sum \frac{(O - E)^2}{E}$$ [8.3]

which has a χ^2 distribution with $v = k - 1$ degrees of freedom (k is the number of classes, here six). The calculation of the test statistic is shown in columns (4) to (6) of Table 8.2, and is quite straightforward, yielding a value of $\chi_s^2 = 7.66$ to be compared with the critical value.

Large values of this test statistic mean that observed and expected values do not match very well, and therefore lead to rejection of the null hypothesis upon which the expected values were calculated. Thus if the calculated test statistic exceeds the critical value of the χ^2 distribution, then the null hypothesis is rejected. This is illustrated in Fig. 8.3.

The diagram shows the distribution of the test statistic under H_0, which is a χ^2 distribution with $v = 5$ degrees of freedom. Note that the rejection region lies entirely in the right-hand tail of the distribution, despite the fact that the

* The number of degrees of freedom is $k - 1$, not k, because not all of the terms $(O - E)^2/E$ are independent. Once the first $k - 1$ expected values have been calculated, the final value is determined by the condition that the sums of the observed and expected values must be equal. Since only $k - 1$ terms are independent, this is the number of degrees of freedom for the χ^2 statistic.

Table 8.2 Data for 72 rolls of a die

(1) Number	(2) Observed frequency (O)	(3) Expected frequency (E)	(4) $(O-E)$	(5) $(O-E)^2$	(6) $\dfrac{(O-E)^2}{E}$
1	6	12	-6	36	3.00
2	15	12	3	9	0.75
3	15	12	3	9	0.75
4	7	12	-5	25	2.08
5	15	12	3	9	0.75
6	14	12	2	4	0.33
					7.66

Figure 8.3 Test procedure using χ^2

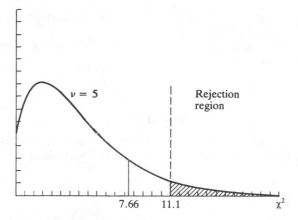

alternative hypothesis ('the die is biased') appears to be of the two tail variety encountered previously. However, the difference now is that whatever the direction of the bias it always leads to a large value of the test statistic, and therefore falls into the right-hand tail of the distribution. The left-hand tail represents close agreement between observed and expected values and is thus associated with the null hypothesis.

The critical value of the χ^2 distribution in this case ($v = 5$, 5% significance level) is 11.1, found from Table A4,* and since the test statistic is less than this the null hypothesis is not rejected. The differences between scores are due to sampling error rather than to bias in the die.

An important point to note is that the value of the test statistic is sensitive to the total frequency (72 in this case). The test should not be carried out on the

---

* See the appendix to this chapter for the use of the χ^2 and F distribution tables.

proportion of times each number comes up (the expected values would all be 1/6, and the observed values 8/72, 13/72, etc.) since information about the 'sample size' (number of rolls of the die) would be lost. As with all sampling experiments, the inferences that can be drawn depend upon the sample size, with large sample sizes giving more reliable results, so care must be taken to retain information about sample size in the calculations. If the test *had* been incorrectly conducted in terms of proportions, all O and E values would have been divided by 72, and this would have reduced the test statistic by a factor of 72 (check the formula to confirm this), reducing it to 0.14, nowhere near significance. It would be surprising if *any* data would yield significance given this degree of maltreatment!

A second, more realistic, example will be examined to reinforce the message about the use of the chi-squared distribution. This examines road accident figures to see if there is any variation through the year. Quarterly data on the number of people killed on British roads are used, and the null hypothesis is that the number does not vary seasonally.

H_0: no difference in fatal accidents between quarters
H_1: some difference in fatal accidents between quarters

Such a study might be carried out by government, for example, to try to find the best means of reducing road accidents.

In *Key Data 86*, Table 8.4 (published by the Central Statistical Office), the following figures are found

Quarter	I	II	III	IV
No. killed	1,082	1,219	1,373	1,535

(These figures are for the year 1985, in billions.)

Under the null hypothesis the total number of deaths (5,209) would be evenly split between the four quarters, yielding the following table and calculation:

Quarter	Observed O	Expected E	$\dfrac{(O-E)^2}{E}$
I	1,082	1,302.25	37.25
II	1,219	1,302.25	5.32
III	1,373	1,302.25	3.84
IV	1,535	1,302.25	41.60
			88.02

The calculated value of the test statistic is 88.02. The number of degrees of freedom is $v = k - 1 = 3$, so the critical value at the 5% significance level is 7.81. Since the test statistic exceeds this, the null hypothesis is rejected; there is a difference between seasons in the accident rate.

The reason for this difference might be the increased hours of darkness during winter months, leading to more accidents. This particular hypothesis can be tested using the same data, but combining quarters I and IV (to represent winter) and quarters II and III (summer). The null hypothesis is of no difference between summer and winter, and the calculation is set out below:

Season	Observed	Expected	$\dfrac{(O - E)^2}{E}$
Summer	2,592	2,604.5	0.06
Winter	2,617	2,604.5	0.06
			0.12

The χ^2 test statistic is much reduced, and is below the critical value ($v = 1$, 5% significance level) of 3.84, so the null hypothesis cannot be rejected. This may seem a surprising conclusion, but looking at the data shows the number of fatal accidents not to vary much between summer and winter. One might object by saying that quarters I and IV do not correspond very closely to winter, which might more appropriately be represented by December, January and February. Unfortunately, the quarterly data as given do not allow this hypothesis to be tested, but the data could be assembled from the monthly figures (which *are* aviailable) and the test could be performed.

Another point which the example brings out is that the data can be examined in a number of ways using the chi-squared technique. Some of the classes were combined to test a slightly different hypothesis from the original one. This is a quite acceptable technique but should be used with caution. In any set of data (even totally random data) there is bound to be *some* way of dividing it up such that there are differences between the divisions. The point is, however, whether there is any meaning to the division. In the above example the division of the quarters into summer and winter has some intuitive meaning and we have some good reason to believe that there might be differences between them. Driving during the hours of darkness might be more dangerous and might have had some relevance to accident prevention policy (e.g. an advertising campaign to persuade people to check that their lights work correctly). The fact that this hypothesis was rejected by the data (i.e. the null hypothesis was *not* rejected!) suggests that this type of policy is not worth pursuing. If quarters I and III were combined, and II and IV combined, the χ^2 test statistic might be significant (it is) but does this signify anything? An advertising campaign to tell people to drive more carefully in quarters II and IV is likely to leave motorists somewhat bemused, and is unlikely to be successful. The point, as usual, is that it is no good looking at data in a vacuum and simply hoping that it will 'tell you something'.

There is one further point to make about combining classes when carrying out a χ^2 test, and this involves circumstances where classes *must* be combined. The theoretical χ^2 distribution from which the critical value is obtained is a continuous distribution, yet the calculation of the test statistic comes from data which are divided up into a discrete number of classes. The calculated test statistic is therefore only an approximation to the true χ^2 variable, but this approximation is good enough as long as each expected (not observed) value is

175

greater than or equal to five. It does not matter what the observed values are. In these circumstances, the class (or classes) with expected values less than five must be combined with other classes until all expected values are at least five. A later example discusses this in more detail.

In all cases of χ^2 testing the most important part of the analysis is the calculation of the expected values (the rest of the analysis is mechanical). It is therefore always worthwhile devoting most of the time to this part of the exercise. The expected values are of course calculated on the basis of the null hypothesis being true, so different null hypotheses will give different expected values. Consider again the case of road fatalities. Although the null hypothesis ('no differences in fatal accidents between quarters') seems clear enough, it could mean different things. Here it was taken to mean an equal number of deaths in each quarter; but another interpretation is an equal number of deaths *per car mile* in each quarter; in other words accidents might be higher in a given quarter simply because there are more journeys in that quarter (during the holiday periods, for example). Table 8.8 of *Key Data 86* gives an index of vehicle kilometres travelled on British roads, the relevant figures for 1985 being:

Quarter	I	II	III	IV	Total
Vehicle kilometres	126	124	124	132	506

The high number of fatalities in the fourth quarter might therefore be due to the higher vehicle mileage in that quarter. If this is true, there is little point in a campaign aimed at road safety in that quarter alone. A campaign throughout the year would be more appropriate. How is this to be tested? The expected values should be adjusted so that the 5,209 annual fatalities are distributed over the quarters in proportion to the index of vehicle kilometres.

In QI, 24.9% (= 126/506) of vehicle kilometres are travelled, so one would expect 1,297.1 (24.9% of 5,209) fatal accidents. For QII a similar calculation (124/506 × 5,209) yields 1,276.5 fatalities, and the expected values for QIII and QIV are 1,276.5 and 1,358.9, respectively. The χ^2 test statistic comes out as 68.4, which is still significant (the calculation is left as an exercise for the reader). It can therefore be concluded that there are still differences between quarters, even when distance travelled is taken into account.

The interested reader can also check to see if this has made any difference to the winter/summer distinction (or lack of it).

Contingency tables

It is common to have data presented in the form set out in Table 8.3, where the observations fall into several categories according to a two-way classification. Table 8.3 presents a breakdown of people's voting intentions according to their social class. Such a presentation of data is called a *contingency table* and is a convenient way of summarising information. The natural question to ask is whether there is any *association* between social class and voting behaviour. Are manual workers more likely to vote for the Labour Party than for the Conservative Party? The table would appear to indicate support for this view, but is this truly the case for the whole population or is this just an unrepresentative sample?

Table 8.3   Data on voting intention by social class

	Voting intention			
Social class	Labour	Conservative	Alliance	Total
A	10	15	15	40
B	40	35	25	100
C	30	20	10	60
	80	70	50	200

This sort of problem is also amenable to analysis by the χ^2 test. The data presented in the table represent the *observed* values, so *expected* values need to be calculated and then compared with them using the χ^2 test. The first task is to formulate a null hypothesis, on which to base the calculation of the expected values, and an alternative. These are

H_0: no association between class and voting behaviour
H_1: some association between social class and voting behaviour

As always, the null hypothesis has to be precise, so that expected values can be calculated.

Constructing the expected values

If H_0 is true and there is no association, we would expect the proportions voting Labour, Conservative and Alliance to be the same in each social class. Further, the parties would be identical in the proportions of their support coming from social classes A, B and C. This means that, since the whole sample of 200 splits 80:70:50 for the Labour, Conservative and Alliance parties, each social class should split the same way. Thus of the 40 people of class A, 80/200 of them should vote Labour, 70/200 Conservative and 50/200 Alliance. This yields

Split of social class A:
Labour $40 \times 80/200 = 16$
Conservative $40 \times 70/200 = 14$
Alliance $40 \times 50/200 = 10$

For class B
Labour $100 \times 80/200 = 40$
Conservative $100 \times 70/200 = 35$
Alliance $100 \times 50/200 = 25$

And for C the 60 votes are split Labour 24, Conservative 21 and Alliance 15. Both observed and expected values are presented in Table 8.4 (expected values are in brackets).

Notice that both the observed and expected values sum to the appropriate row and column totals. It can be seen that, compared with the 'no association'

Table 8.4 Observed and expected values

social class	Labour	Conservative	Alliance	Total
		Voting intention		
A	10(16)	15(14)	15(10)	40
B	40(40)	35(35)	25(25)	100
C	30(24)	20(21)	10(15)	60
	80	70	50	200

Source: *Key Data*, 1986

position, Labour gets too few votes from class A and the Alliance too many. However, Labour gets disproportionately too many class C votes, the Alliance too few. The Conservatives' observed and expected values are identical, indicating that the propensities to vote Conservative are the same in all social classes.

A quick way to calculate the expected value in any cell is to multiply the appropriate row total by column total and divide through by the grand total (200). For example, to get the expected value for the class A/Labour cell:

$$\frac{40 \times 80}{200} = 16$$

In carrying out the analysis care should again be taken to ensure that information is retained about sample size, i.e. the numbers in the table should be actual numbers and not percentages or proportions. This can be checked by ensuring that the grand total is always the same as the sample size.

As was the case before, the χ^2 test is only valid if the expected value in each cell is not less than five. In the event of one of the expected values being less than five, some of the rows or columns have to be combined. How to do this is a matter of choice and depends upon the aims of the research. Suppose, for example, that the expected value of class C voting Alliance were less than five. There are four options open:

(a) combine the Alliance column with the Labour column;
(b) combine the Alliance column with the Conservative column;
(c) combine the class C row with the class A row;
(d) combine the class C row with the class B row.

Whether rows or columns are combined depends upon whether interest centres upon differences between parties or differences between classes. If the main interest is the difference between class A and the others, option (d) should be chosen. If it is felt that the Alliance and Conservative parties are similar, option (b) would be preferred, and so on. If there are several expected values less than five, rows and columns must be combined until all are eliminated.

The χ^2 test on a contingency table is similar to the one carried out before, the formula being the same:

178

$$\chi_v^2 = \sum \frac{(O - E)^2}{E}$$

This test statistic follows a χ^2 distribution with the number of degrees of freedom given by

$$v = (r - 1) \times (c - 1)$$

where r is the number of rows in the table and c is the number of columns. In this case $r = 3$ and $c = 3$, so

$$v = (3 - 1) \times (3 - 1) = 4$$

The reason why there are only four degrees of freedom is that once any four cells of the contingency table have been filled, the other five are constrained by the row and column totals. The number of 'free' cells can always be calculated as the number of rows less one, times the number of columns less one, as given above.

Calculation of the test statistic

The evaluation of the test statistic proceeds, then, as follows, cell by cell.

$$\frac{(10 - 16)^2}{16} + \frac{(15 - 14)^2}{14} + \frac{(15 - 10)^2}{10} +$$

$$\frac{(40 - 40)^2}{40} + \frac{(35 - 35)^2}{35} + \frac{(25 - 25)^2}{25} +$$

$$\frac{(30 - 24)^2}{24} + \frac{(20 - 21)^2}{21} + \frac{(10 - 15)^2}{15}$$

$$= 2.25 + 0.07 + 2.50 +$$
$$0 + \quad 0 + \quad 0 +$$
$$1.5 + 0.05 + 1.67$$
$$= 8.04$$

This must be compared with the test statistic from the χ^2 distribution with four degrees of freedom. At the 5% significance level this is (from Table A4) 9.50.

Since the $8.04 < 9.50$, the test statistic is smaller than the critical value, so the null hypothesis cannot be rejected. The evidence is not strong enough to support an association between social class and voting intention. We can be 95% confident of the lack of any association between the two.

Use of the F distribution

The F distribution has a number of uses in statistics but in this chapter it will be used to perform a hypothesis test on the equality of two sample variances (it will be used again in Chapter 9 on correlation and regression). A test of the equality of two variances might be carried out because of some intrinsic interest

179

in those variances, or as a prelude to a test on the equality of two means, as set out in Chapter 6.

Testing the equality of two population variances

Suppose the following data are available regarding the weight of loaves of bread produced by two factories:

	Factory 1	Factory 2
No. of loaves in sample	20	18
Average weight	780 g	760 g
Standard deviation	40 g	35 g

To test whether the average weight of loaves produced by the two factories are equal or not, a two-sample *t*-test (as in Chapter 6) would be performed since the samples are small and the population variances are unknown. The test statistic is

$$t_{n1 + n2 - 2} = \frac{(\bar{x}_1 - \bar{x}_2) - (\mu_1 - \mu_2)}{\sqrt{\dfrac{S^2}{n_1} + \dfrac{S^2}{n_2}}}$$

where

$$S^2 = \frac{(n_1 - 1) s_1^2 + (n_2 - 1) s_2^2}{n_1 + n_2 - 2}$$

This test is strictly only valid if $\sigma_1^2 = \sigma_2^2$, the two population variances are equal. In the examples in Chapter 6 this was taken for granted, but now this assumption can be tested.

The need to test for equality of the population variances can often occur in quality control. A large variance in weight indicates that the machines producing the loaves are not providing consistent results. This may cost the firm money, for if the law requires that a loaf claiming to weigh (say) 750 g must weigh *at least* 745 g, then an inconsistent machine would have to be set to give a higher average weight, at a cost to the firm's profits.

A hypothesis test of the equality of two variances is set up as follows:

Two tail test

$H_0: \sigma_1^2 = \sigma_2^2$ (or $H_0: \sigma_1^2/\sigma_2^2 = 1$
$H_1: \sigma_1^2 \neq \sigma_2^2$ $H_1: \sigma_1^2/\sigma_2^2 \neq 1$)

One tail test

$H_0: \sigma_1^2 = \sigma_2^2$ (or $H_0: \sigma_1^2/\sigma_2^2 = 1$
$H_1: \sigma_1^2 > \sigma_2^2$ $H_1: \sigma_1^2/\sigma_2^2 > 1$)

In the above problem there is no information to suggest which variance is expected to be the larger, so a two-tail test is appropriate.

Derivation of a random variable with an F distribution

It can be proven that the random variable

$$\frac{s^2 (n - 1)}{\sigma^2}$$

follows a χ^2 distribution with $n - 1$ degrees of freedom. From the two samples two such random variables can be constructed:

$$\frac{s_1^2 (n_1 - 1)}{\sigma_1^2} \quad \text{and} \quad \frac{s_2^2 (n_2 - 1)}{\sigma_2^2}$$

It was stated at the beginning of the chapter that the ratio of two independent χ^2 variables, each divided by their degrees of freedom, forms a random variable which follows an F distribution with $n_1 - 1$, $n_2 - 1$ degrees of freedom (the degrees of freedom associated with each χ^2 variable). Thus the ratio of the above two variables is formed, each divided by their degrees of freedom.

$$\frac{s_1^2 (n_1 - 1)}{\sigma_1^2 (n_1 - 1)} \bigg/ \frac{s_2^2 (n_2 - 1)}{\sigma_2^2 (n_2 - 1)}$$

$$= \frac{s_1^2 / \sigma_1^2}{s_2^2 / \sigma_2^2}$$

But, under the null hypothesis, $\sigma_1^2 = \sigma_2^2$ so these terms cancel in the formula, leaving simply

$$\frac{s^2_1}{s^2_2}$$

Thus the ratio of the two sample variances follows an F distribution with $n_1 - 1, n_2 - 1$ degrees of freedom. Note that the reciprocal of the calculated F statistic (s_2^2/s_1^2) is also an F statistic, with $n_2 - 1, n_1 - 1$ degrees of freedom.

Calculation of the test statistic

From the above, the test statistic is very easy to calculate. It is easier (and avoids confusion) if the larger of the two variances is made the numerator of the test statistic, which will therefore always be greater than one. As will be shown below, this makes consulting tables of the F distribution more straightforward. For the above problem, the test statistic is:

$$\frac{1,600}{1,225} = 1.31$$

This must be compared with the critical value of the F distribution for 19, 17 degrees of freedom (remember that the order of these is important). For a two tail test at the 5% significance level, the rejection region comprises 2.5% in each tail of the F distribution. Since the larger variance was put in the numerator of the F statistic, the calculated value is compared with the critical

181

Figure 8.4

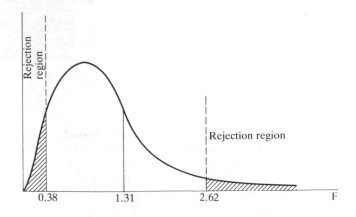

value cutting off the 2.5% *right-hand tail* of the distribution. From Table A5(b) this critical value is 2.62, and since the calculated test statistic is less than this, the null hypothesis is not rejected. Figure 8.4 illustrates the situation. The test statistic falls into the acceptance region. The calculation of the left-hand critical value is set out in the appendix to this chapter. The advantage of putting the large variance in the numerator of the test statistic is that this guarantees that it will not fall into the left-hand critical region. The test statistic therefore need only be compared with the right-hand critical value, and the left-hand one can be ignored for practical purposes.

For the case of a one tail test at the 5% significance level, the critical region comprises the 5% right-hand tail of the distribution. For 19, 17 degrees of freedom, this critical value is 2.23. Again, it is the fact of putting the larger variance into the numerator which ensures that the right-hand tail critical value is relevant.

Problems

8.1 A survey of 100 firms found the following evidence regarding profitability and market share:

Profitability	Market share		
	< 15%	15–30%	> 30%
Low	18	7	8
Medium	13	11	8
High	8	12	15

Is there evidence that market share and profitability are associated?

182

8.2 A company wishes to see whether there are any differences between its departments in staff turnover. Looking at their records for the past year the company finds the following data:

Department	Personnel	Marketing	Administration	Accounts
Number in post at year start	23	16	108	57
Number leaving	3	4	20	13

Does the data provide evidence of a difference in staff turnover between the various departments?

8.3 From Table A1 of random numbers draw a sample of 100 single digits and set them out in a frequency table. Use a chi-squared test to check that there is no bias towards any digit. Combine the five digits with the largest frequencies into one group, the other five digits into another. Again use a chi-squared test to see if there is any difference between the two groups. What does this tell you about the use of the chi-squared test?

8.4 In Chapter 3 the Binomial distribution was applied to families with five children. Given the data (repeated below) for a sample of 500 families, test whether the Binomial distribution is a good fit to the data.

Number of boys	0	1	2	3	4	5
Number of families	20	75	145	140	85	35

8.5 Four different holiday firms, who all carried equal numbers of holiday-makers, reported the following numbers who expressed satisfaction with their holiday:

Firm	A	B	C	D
Number	576	558	580	546

Is there any significant difference between the firms? If told that the four firms carried 2,400 holidaymakers between them, would you modify your conclusion? What do you conclude about your first answer?

8.6 An example in Chapter 6 compared R & D expenditure in Britain and Germany. The sample data were

$$\bar{x}_1 = 3.7 \qquad \bar{x}_2 = 4.2$$
$$s_1 = 0.6 \qquad s_2 = 0.9$$
$$n_1 = 20 \qquad n_2 = 15$$

Is there evidence, at the 5% significance level, of difference in the variances of R & D expenditure between the two countries? What are the implications, if any, for the test carried out on the difference of the two means, in Chapter 6?

8.7 A manufacturer is considering buying a machine tool from one of two suppliers A or B. To test the consistency of the machines, samples of bearings of nominal diameter 5 mm were made on each make of machine. The results were

	A	B
Average diameter	5.0006 mm	4.9998 mm
Standard deviation	0.00002 mm	0.0001 mm
Sample size	25	20

Comment upon the performance of the two machines.

Appendix: Use of χ^2 (Table A4) and F (Table A5) distribution tables

χ^2 distribution

Table A4 presents critical values of the chi-squared distribution for a selection of significance levels and for different degrees of freedom. As an example, to find the critical value of the χ^2 distribution at the 5% significance level for $v = 20$ degrees of freedom, the cell entry in the column labelled '0.05' and the row labelled '20' is consulted. The critical value is 31.41. A test statistic greater than this value implies rejection of the null hypothesis at the 5% significance level.

F distribution

Table A5 presents critical values of the F distribution. Since there are two sets of degrees of freedom to be taken into account, a separate table is required for each significance level. Four sets of tables are provided, giving critical values cutting off the top 5%, 2.5%, 1% and 0.5% of the distribution (Tables A5(a), A5(b), A5(c) and A5(d), respectively). These allow both one and two tail tests at the 5% and 1% significance levels to be conducted. Its use is illustrated by example.

Two tail test: To find the critical values of the F distribution at the 5% significance level of degrees of freedom v_1 (numerator) $= 10$, $v_2 = 20$. The critical values in this case cut off the extreme 2.5% of the distribution in each tail, and are found in Table A5(b).

Right-hand critical value: this is found from the cell of Table A5(b) corresponding to the column $v_1 = 10$ and row $v_2 = 20$. Its value is 2.77.

Left-hand critical value: this cannot be obtained directly from the table, which only gives right-hand values. However, it is obtained indirectly as follows:

(a) find the right-hand critical value for $v_1 = 20$, $v_2 = 10$ (note reversal of degrees of freedom). This gives 3.42.

184

(b) take the reciprocal to obtain the desired left-hand critical value. This gives $1/3.42 = 0.29$.

The rejection region thus consists of values of the test statistic less than 0.29 and greater than 2.77.

One tail test: To find the critical value at the 5% significance level for $v_1 = 15$, $v_2 = 25$. As long as the test statistic has been calculated with the larger variance in the numerator, the critical value is in the right-hand tail of the distribution and can be obtained directly from Table A.5(a). For $v_1 = 15$, $v_2 = 25$, the value is 2.09. The null hypothesis is therefore rejected if the test statistic is greater than 2.09.

9   Correlation and regression

Introduction

In the previous chapter a test for association between two variables was presented, using the chi-squared distribution. The data are presented in the form of a contingency table, and the variables are measured according to some classiification of the data, such as whether profits are low, medium or high. This is quite a crude classification and it would be better if profits were directly measured, rather than assigned to different categories. When the data are directly measured in this way, the more powerful techniques of correlation and regression can be used. These methods have the advantage that the extent of the association between the variables is measured.

Correlation and regression are the techniques most often used by economists and forecasters. They can be used to answer such questions as

(a) Is there a link between the money supply and the price level?
(b) How does the consumption of housing vary with income?
(c) Does instability in a country's export performance hinder its growth?

Each of these questions is about economics or business as much as about statistics. The statistical analysis is part of a wider investigation into the problem; it cannot provide a complete answer to the problem but, used sensibly, it is a vital input.

Correlation and regression techniques may be applied to time-series or cross-section data. Time-series data, as the name suggests, provide observations of the variables over a period of time; to answer the first question above, data on the money supply and the price level over a period of years could be collected. Cross-section data is collected at a point in time; an example would be data on housing consumption and income for a number of different households in 1986, to help answer the second question. Sometimes the data may be a mixture of the two types, as in the third question. Export instability and growth could be measured for a number of different countries, to provide evidence for the association between the two variables. However, the variables would obviously have to be measured over a period of time, making the data a mixture of time-series and cross-section. The methods of analysis of the different types of data are basically the same, although more advanced techniques do recognise the differences in data type. There are also differences in the interpretation of the results depending upon the type of data employed; these will be explained later on.

This chapter deals first of all with the topic of correlation and rank correlation. Regression techniques have been developed by economists and statisticians to a very high level; this chapter explains simple (i.e. two-variable) regression in detail, providing all the necessary formulae and a worked example. Multiple regression, which involves the analysis of three or more variables, is presented in less detail. The formulae are complex and time consuming to evaluate, so that nowadays computers are invariably used for calculation. This chapter sets out the principles of multiple regression analysis and shows how results may be interpreted, but detailed calculations are omitted. This will allow the reader to undertake this kind of analysis with the aid of a suitable computer package (e.g. TSP or MINITAB), and to interpret the results obtained and published by other researchers. Some general advice is given about how to make the best use of regression techniques, along with some warnings of the problems that can arise.

Correlation

The statistical methods which are the subject of this chapter will be illustrated by data relating to the demand for, and price of, bus travel in the UK. The data are presented below in Table 9.1 (data from *Transport Statistics, Great Britain, 1975–85*).

Table 9.1 Data on bus travel and fares, Great Britain, 1975–85

Year	Vehicle kilometres (millions)	Fare index	Retail price index (1980 = 100)	Real fare index
1975	261	44.9	51.1	87.9
1976	259	57.0	59.6	95.6
1977	250	66.5	69.0	96.4
1978	246	73.0	74.7	97.7
1979	242	80.6	84.8	91.8
1980	241	100.0	100.0	100.0
1981	233	119.8	111.9	107.1
1982	232	134.3	121.5	110.5
1983	231	144.4	127.1	113.6
1984	235	155.3	133.4	116.4
1985	232	161.6	141.5	114.2

Source: *Transport Statistics, Great Britain 1975–85*

There are a number of preliminary points to be made about the data. The first is that the actual levels of fares are not given; only an index of fares is available. As will be shown subsequently, this does not affect the methods or results of the analysis. Secondly, the fare index has been deflated to real terms by the use of the retail price index. Economic theory (and common sense) would suggest that it is real fares which determine demand, i.e. after the effects of inflation have been eliminated. The level of demand, measured in vehicle kilometres travelled, does not need to be deflated. If demand had been measured by expenditure on bus travel (which is the product of price and quantity), then it would have to be deflated to constant prices before the analysis could proceed.

Normally one would expect an inverse relationship between the two variables – higher fares associated with lower demand, and this is confirmed by a graph of the data which is presented as Fig. 9.1.

Figure 9.1 Bus travel demand and fares

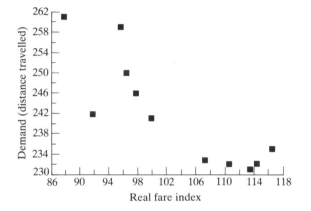

The technique of correlation allows the relationship between two variables, such as that illustrated, to be summarised by a sample statistic, the *correlation coefficient*. This shares the advantages and disadvantages of other descriptive statistics: it provides a quick and convenient summary of the data, but most of the detail is lost. Before going on to calculate the correlation coefficient, its properties and relationship to the data need to be established.

The different types of relationship between two variables, X and Y, may be summarised as follows:

(a) High values of X tend to be associated with low values of Y and vice versa. This is termed *negative* correlation, and appears to be the case for bus travel and fares, graphed in Fig. 9.1.

(b) High (low) values of X tend to be associated with high (low) values of Y. This is *positive* correlation and is likely to represent the relationship between housing consumption and income: the rich tend to live in larger and better houses than the poor.

(c) No relationship between X and Y exists. High (low) values of X are associated about equally with high (low) values of Y. This is zero, or the absence of, correlation. An example of zero correlation is the relationship between bus fares in the UK and sales of rice in Shanghai.

These three cases are illustrated in Fig. 9.2.

188

Figure 9.2 Different degrees of correlation

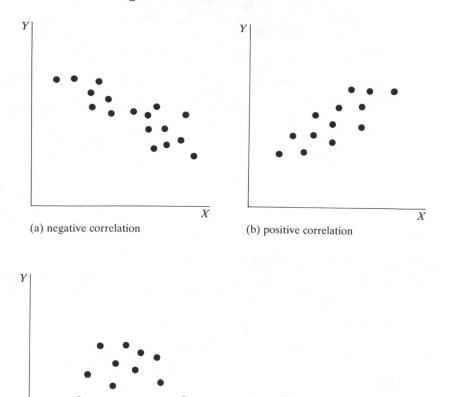

(a) negative correlation

(b) positive correlation

(c) no correlation

It should be noted that positive correlation does not mean that high values of *X* are *always* associated with high values of *Y*, but as a general rule they are.

It is also the case that correlation only represents *linear* relationships between the two variables. Consider the backward-bending labour-supply curve, as suggested by economic theory (higher wages initially encourage extra work effort, but above a certain point the benefit of higher wage rates is taken in the form of more leisure). If data on labour supplied and wage rates were obtained for a sample of workers it would map out the relationship represented in Fig. 9.3 (though the effect is probably less pronounced in practice). Calculating the correlation coefficient for this data would indicate a lack of correlation, though labour supply is obviously influenced by the wage rate. The relationship is too complex to be discovered by the technique of correlation alone. It should

189

Figure 9.3 The backward-bending labour-supply curve

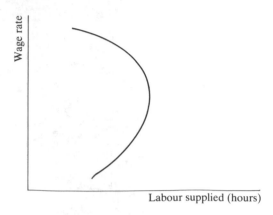

not, therefore, be concluded that no relationship exists between two variables just on the basis of the value of the correlation coefficient. It is always a good idea to graph the data first and inspect them visually.

Calculation of the correlation coefficient

A statistic is required which will differentiate between cases (a), (b) and (c) above. The correlation coefficient is such a statistic, is denoted by the letter r and is given by the formula

$$r = \frac{1}{n-1} \sum \frac{(X - \bar{X})}{S_X} \frac{(Y - \bar{Y})}{S_Y} \qquad [9.1]$$

where

$$S_X = \sqrt{\frac{1}{n-1} \sum (X - \bar{X})^2} \qquad S_Y = \sqrt{\frac{1}{n-1} \sum (Y - \bar{Y})^2}$$

are the sample standard deviations of X and Y.

The correlation coefficient has the following properties:

(a) It lies between -1 and $+1$;
(b) A positive value of r indicates positive correlation, a higher value indicating a stronger correlation between X and Y. $r = 1$ indicates perfect positive correlation and means that all the observations lie on a straight line with positive slope, as Fig. 9.4 illustrates.
(c) A negative value of r indicates negative correlation. Similar to the above, a larger negative value indicates stronger negative correlation and $r = -1$ signifies perfect negative correlation.
(d) A value of $r = 0$ (or close to it) indicates a lack of correlation between X and Y. The precise meaning of 'close to 0' will be explained later.

190

Figure 9.4 Perfect positive correlation

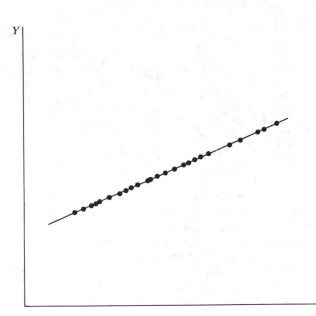

Figure 9.5

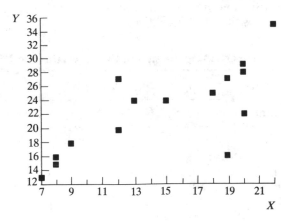

Figure 9.6

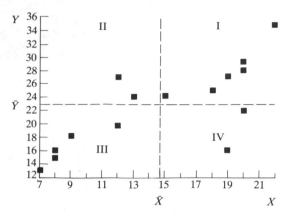

Before evaluating eqn [9.1] for the above data, the properties of the correlation coefficient are examined in more detail. Consider the data graphed in Fig. 9.5. The data indicate positive correlation between X and Y. The diagram may be transformed by drawing a vertical line at the mean of the X values and a horizontal line at the mean of the Y values. This could alternatively be thought of as shifting the axes to the means of the two variables. This divides the figure into four quadrants, as in Fig. 9.6. If the two variables are positively correlated (as here), then most of the observations will fall into quadrants I and III, leaving relatively few in II and IV. The stronger the correlation, the more pronounced this effect will be. For any points in the quadrants I and III the value of the term $(X_i - \overline{X})(Y_i - \overline{Y})$ will be positive. In quadrants II and IV the value of the term will be negative. Table 9.2 illustrates this. Thus if there is positive correlation, eqn [9.1] is made up of mainly positive terms so that r will also be positive (S_X, S_Y and $1/(n - 1)$ must all be positive so cannot turn r into a negative number). For negative correlation most of the observations lie in quadrants II and IV so that r contains mainly negative terms and is thus itself negative.

Table 9.2   Determining the sign of the correlation co-efficient

Observation in	Value of		
quadrant	$(X_i - \overline{X})$	$(Y_i - \overline{Y})$	$(X_i - \overline{X})(Y_i - \overline{Y})$
I	>0	>0	>0
II	<0	>0	<0
III	<0	<0	>0
IV	>0	<0	<0

Why are the other terms included in the formula for r? The S_X and S_Y terms are included to make the value of r independent of the units of measurement. If demand were measured in thousands (not millions) of vehicle kilometres, and fares measured by an index with 1975 = 100, nothing fundamental would be altered, certainly not the relationship between fares and demand. Dividing through by S_X and S_Y in eqn [9.1] ensures that the calculated value of r is not affected by the units in which X or Y is measured. The factor $1/(n-1)$ ensures that r remains within the limits of -1 to $+1$; otherwise it could increase (either positively or negatively) without limit, making interpretation difficult.

To calculate the value of r a variant of eqn [9.1] is used which is more convenient for calculation, even though it looks more complex. The two formulae are equivalent and either one may be derived from the other (there are in fact a number of different ways of writing the formula). The formula is

$$r = \frac{n\Sigma XY - \Sigma X \Sigma Y}{\sqrt{(n\Sigma X^2 - (\Sigma X)^2)(n\Sigma Y^2 - (\Sigma Y)^2)}} \qquad [9.2]$$

The calculation of r for the data on demand for bus travel and fares is performed in Table 9.3.

Table 9.3 Calculation of the correlation coefficient

	Y	X	Y^2	X^2	XY
1975	261	87.9	68,121	7,726.4	22,941.9
1976	259	95.6	67,081	9,139.4	24,760.4
1977	250	96.4	62,500	9,293.0	24,100.0
1978	246	97.7	60,516	9,545.3	24,034.2
1979	242	91.8	58,564	8,427.2	22,215.6
1980	241	100.0	58,081	10,000.0	24,100.0
1981	233	107.1	54,289	11,470.4	24,954.3
1982	232	110.5	53,824	12,210.3	25,636.0
1983	231	113.6	53,361	12,905.0	26,241.6
1984	235	116.4	55,225	13,549.0	27,354.0
1985	232	114.2	53,824	13,041.6	26,499.4
	2,662	1,131.2	645,386	117,307.48	272,832.4

Hence

$$r = \frac{11 \times 272,832.4 - 1,131.2 \times 2,662.0}{\sqrt{(11 \times 117,307.48 - 1,131.2^2)(11 \times 645,386 - 2,662^2)}}$$

$$= -0.8534$$

The result indicates a substantial negative correlation between demand and fares, as might be expected; higher fares lead to a lower level of demand for bus services.

Interpreting the result

The calculated value of the correlation coefficient shows a substantial negative relationship between the two variables, as was expected. Remember that it is the real value of the fare, rather than an index of the fare in current prices (see Chapter 2, Index numbers), that is used in this relationship. A correlation of bus demand with a *nominal* fare index yields a result of $r = -0.92$. Although this appears to show a stronger correlation, economic theory would suggest that the former result is the more relevant.

Testing the significance of the result

The data is of course only a sample of the data that could have been collected. If data for the period 1964–74 had been collected instead, a slightly different result for the correlation coefficient would have been obtained. How then does this result compare with the results of other samples that could have been obtained? The usual question in statistical inference can be asked: what can be inferred about the population from the sample evidence?

It is best to think of the data as being a random sample drawn from a (hypothetical) population of bus fares and levels of demand. This may strain credulity a little, for it implies that the 'experiment' could be repeated and a new set of data for 1975–85 collected! Moreover, the observations should be independent of each other for the theory of statistical inference to be legitimately applied, though in fact it is quite likely that fares in one year are not independent of those in the previous year (high fares in one year may lead to larger profits, allowing lower fares in the following year, for example). There are methods which are available for dealing with these problems, but for the moment these will be ignored.

Since the data may be considered a random sample, the (sample) correlation coefficient r is a random variable with some probability distribution, just like the sample mean. Thus a hypothesis test can be performed on different values of the population correlation coefficient (which is denoted by ρ, the Greek letter rho). Almost invariably, the hypothesis test is that ρ is equal to zero, since this implies no correlation at all between X and Y. It is not easy to think of circumstances where one would want to test the hypothesis $\rho = 0.5$, for example. Thus the null and alternative hypotheses are

H_0: $\rho = 0$
H_1: $\rho < 0$

A one tail test has been chosen because economic theory suggests that demand curves always slope down. The test statistic is

$$t_{n-2} = \frac{r\sqrt{n-2}}{\sqrt{1-r^2}} \qquad [9.3]$$

which follows a t distribution with $n - 2$ degrees of freedom. This test statistic is only valid when testing the null hypothesis that ρ is zero.

The calculated test statistic is therefore

$$t_9 = \frac{-0.8534\sqrt{11 - 2}}{\sqrt{1 - (-0.8534)^2}}$$

$$= -4.91$$

The critical value of the t distribution for a one tail test with nine degrees of freedom at the 5% significance level is 1.83. Since the test statistic exceeds this in absolute value, the null hypothesis is rejected. There does appear to be significant negative correlation between demand and fares.

Correlation and causality

It is important to test the significance of the result because almost every pair of variables will have a non-zero correlation coefficient, even if they are totally unconnected (the chance of the sample correlation coefficient being *exactly* zero is very, very small). Therefore it is important to distinguish between correlation coefficients which are significant and those which are not, using the t-test just outlined. But even when the result is significant one should beware of the danger of 'spurious' correlation. Many variables which clearly cannot be related turn out to be significantly correlated with each other. One now famous example is between the price level and cumulative rainfall over a period of years. Since they both rise year after year it is easy to see why they are correlated, yet it is hard to think of a plausible reason why they should be causally related to each other.

This type of problem tends to arise quite often with time-series data since many variables are trended, particularly when there are high rates of inflation. All prices tend to rise together, and since the output of most goods and services increases over time as the economy expands (bus travel is probably an inferior good and hence falls), many prices and quantities are positively correlated even though one would expect a negative correlation. Here again it is useful to have some theory as a guide. Economic theory suggests that results indicating positively sloped demand curves should be treated with caution. The problem of spurious correlation can sometimes be cured by detrending the variables. Take the example above of the price level and cumulative rainfall. If there really is some causal connection between the two (as opposed to their both just being trended over time), then one might expect the rate of change of the price level to be correlated with the rate of change of cumulative rainfall. This would imply a correlation between the rate of inflation and the annual amount of rainfall. The correlation coefficient between these two variables is much lower, which is a fairer reflection of the true state of affairs.

The presence of correlation is often taken to imply causality, but this is mistaken. Suppose that two variables are correlated. Apart from spurious correlation there are four possibilities:

(a) X influences Y;
(b) Y influences X;
(c) X and Y jointly influence each other;
(d) another variable, Z, influences both X and Y.

Correlation alone does not allow one to distinguish between these alternatives. As an example, let X be wages and Y prices. Some people believe in the cost–push theory of inflation, i.e. that wage rises lead to price rises. This is (a) above. Others believe that wages rise to keep up with the cost of living (i.e. rising prices), which is (b) above. A more convincing explanation is (c), a wage–price spiral where each feeds upon the other. Still others would suggest that it is the growth of the money supply, Z, which allows both wages and prices to rise. To distinguish between these alternatives is important for the control of inflation, but correlation alone does not allow that distinction to be made.

Correlation is therefore best used as a suggestive piece of analysis, rather than a technique which gives definitive answers. It is often a preparatory piece of analysis, which gives some clues to what the data might yield, to be followed by more sophisticated techniques such as regression.

Coefficient of rank correlation

If the data is presented in the form of *ranks*, instead of the actual values, the technique of *rank correlation* can be used. Table 9.4 gives data of countries ranked according to their investment and their growth record (data from *United Nations Statistical Yearbook, 1982*). Thus Japan is top of both the investment league (highest investment per capita) and has the highest growth rate. Note that, when ranking the countries, if two countries have the same investment ratio or growth rate, they are given the same rank, which is the average of the relevant ranking values. Thus West Germany and Canada both have an investment ratio of 23.0% and are each given the rank 3.5, which is the average of third and fourth places.

Table 9.4 Investment and growth in nine countries, 1970–80

Country	Investment (% of GDP)	Rank	Growth (% p.a.)	Rank
USA	18.4	8	2.6	5.5
UK	18.0	9	1.4	9
Germany	23.0	3.5	2.4	8
Japan	32.6	1	4.3	1
France	22.0	5	3.0	4
Italy	20.0	7	2.6	5.5
Belgium	20.4	6	2.5	7
Canada	23.0	3.5	3.7	3
Norway	28.2	2	4.0	2

Source: Adapted from data from *United Nations Statistical Yearbook 1982*

The original data is assumed unavailable or unsuitable so the analysis has to proceed in terms of the ranks alone. Looking at the rankings, there does appear to be some relationship between investment and growth. Spearman's coefficient of rank correlation (named after its discoverer) is calculated using the formula:

$$r_S = 1 - \frac{6 \, \Sigma d^2}{n \, (n^2 - 1)} \qquad\qquad [9.4]$$

where d is the difference in the ranks. Table 9.5 illustrates the calculation.

Table 9.5 Calculation of Spearman's coefficient of rank correlation

Country	Investment rank	Growth rank	Rank difference (d)	(d^2)
USA	8	5.5	2.5	6.25
UK	9	9	0	0
Germany	3.5	8	−4.5	20.25
Japan	1	1	0	0
France	5	4	1	1
Italy	7	5.5	1.5	2.25
Belgium	6	7	−1	1
Canada	3.5	3	0.5	0.25
Norway	2	2	0	0
				31.00

Hence

$$r_S = 1 - \frac{6 \times 31}{9 \, (81 - 1)}$$

$$= 0.742$$

Thus a positive correlation between the ranks of X and Y appears, suggesting a positive connection between investment and growth.

To test the significance of the result a hypothesis test can be performed on the value of ρ_S, the corresponding population parameter.

H_0: $\rho_S = 0$
H_1: $\rho_S > 0$

This time the t distribution cannot be used, but prepared tables of the critical values of ρ_S may be consulted, which are given as Table A6. These show that the critical value at the 5% significance level is 0.643 for a sample size of eight, for a one tail test. The result is therefore significant and the data supports the hypothesis of a relationship between investment and growth.

Regression analysis

The major differences that exist between correlation and regression are the following:

(a) Regression can incorporate the relationships between two or more variables.
(b) Some direction of causality is asserted, from the *explanatory* variable (or variables) to the *dependent* variable.
(c) The influence of each explanatory variable upon the dependent variable is measured.

Thus regression permits answers to the following questions:

(a) If bus fares rise by 10%, by how much will demand fall?
(b) If the money supply is increased, by how much can the price level be expected to increase?
(c) Which variables influence firms' investment decisions?

None of these questions could be answered by the use of correlation analysis. The data on bus fares and demand will again be used to illustrate the use of regression analysis. Using correlation there was found to be a significant negative relationship between the two variables. We shall now assert a causal link between the two, running from fares to demand, in accordance with economic theory. The reason that bus travel has fallen over the period is therefore because fares have risen in real terms (a more sophisticated analysis might also account for the possibility of the level of demand influencing costs and hence fares, if there were economies of scale in bus services, for example).

Figure 9.7 The line of best fit

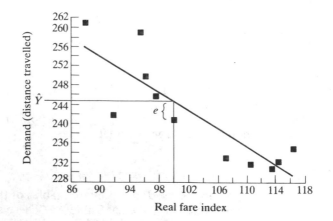

Regression analysis summarises this causal relationship by a straight line drawn through the data, which best summarises the data. It is sometimes called 'the line of best fit' for this reason. These points are illustrated in Fig. 9.7. Note that the explanatory variable is placed on the horizontal axis, the explained variable on the vertical. This is the convention. The regression line is shown downward sloping (its derivation will be explained shortly), for the same reason that the correlation coefficient is negative, i.e. high values of Y are generally associated with low values of X and vice versa.

Since the regression line summarises knowledge of the relationship between X and Y, it can be used to predict the value of Y given any particular value of X. In Fig. 9.7 the value of $X = 100$ (the fare index in 1980) is related via the regression line to a value of Y (denoted by $\hat{Y}$) of 244.7, close to the actual value of Y in that year of 241. $\hat{Y}$ is the predicted demand for bus travel at a fare index level of 100.

The difference between the actual value, Y, and the predicted value, $\hat{Y}$, is called the *error* or *residual*. In Fig. 9.7 this is the distance labelled 'e'. Why should these errors occur? The relationship between fares and demand is never going to be an exact (deterministic) one for a variety of reasons. There are bound to be other factors besides fare levels which affect demand (e.g. income, weather, prices of other means of transport) and these effects are all subsumed in the error term. Later on (in the section on multiple regression) one of these, income, will be taken out of the error term and included explicitly in the regression. There might additionally be measurement error (of Y) and of course people do act in a somewhat random fashion rather than follow rigid rules of behaviour. All of these factors are put into the error term and it means that the observations lie around the regression line rather than all being on it. If there are many of these factors, none of which is predominant, and they are independent of each other, then these errors may be assumed to be Normally distributed about the regression line.

Since it is possible to include nearly all of these factors explicitly, rather than just making them part of the error, why not do so? On the face of it this would seem to be an improvement, making the model more realistic. However the costs of doing this are that the model becomes more complex, calculation becomes more difficult (not so important now with computers) and it is generally more difficult for the reader (or researcher) to interpret what is going on. If the main interest is the relationship between fares and demand, why complicate the model unduly? There is a virtue in simplicity. In the later section on multiple regression, the trade-off between simplicity and realism will be discussed further, particularly with reference to the problems that can arise if relevant explanatory variables are omitted from the analysis.

Calculation of the regression line

The regression line equation may be written

$$\hat{Y}_i = a + bX_i \tag{9.5}$$

where

199

$\hat{Y}_i$ = predicted value of Y (demand for bus travel) in year i
X_i = fare in year i
a, b = fixed coefficients to be estimated. a measures the intercept on the Y axis, b measures the slope of the regression line.

This is illustrated in Fig. 9.8.

Figure 9.8 Intercept and slope of the regression line

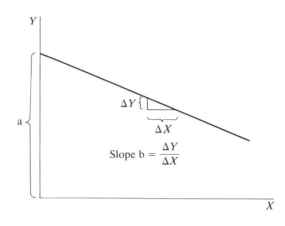

The difference between the actual value of Y, Y_i, and its predicted value, $\hat{Y}_i$, is e_i, the error. Thus

$$Y_i = \hat{Y}_i + e_i \qquad [9.6]$$

Substituting eqn [9.6] into eqn [9.5] the regression equation can be written

$$Y_i = a + bX_i + e_i \qquad [9.7]$$

Equation [9.7] shows that observed levels of demand are made up of two components:

(i) that part explained by the fare level, $a + bX_i$, and
(ii) an error component, e_i

The best position for the regression line is found by maximising (i), the explained part and minimising (ii) the error part. This is achieved by finding the values of a and b which *minimise the sum of squared errors* from the regression line. A fuller justification for this will be given later, but it can be said in passing that the sum of errors is not minimised because that would not lead to a unique answer for the values a and b. In fact there is an infinite number of possible regression lines which all yield a sum of errors equal to zero. Minimising the sum of squared errors does yield a unique answer.

The task is therefore to:

Minimise Σe_i^2 $\qquad [9.8]$

by choice of a and b.

From eqn [9.7] the error is given by

$$e_i = Y_i - a - bX_i \qquad\qquad [9.9]$$

so eqn [9.8] is equivalent to

$$\text{Minimise } \Sigma(Y_i - a - bX_i)^2 \qquad\qquad [9.10]$$

by choice of a and b.

Finding the solution to [9.10] requires the use of differential calculus, and is not given here. The formulae for a and b are

$$b = \frac{n\Sigma XY - \Sigma X \Sigma Y}{n\Sigma X^2 - (\Sigma X)^2} \qquad\qquad [9.11]$$

$$a = \overline{Y} - b\overline{X} \qquad\qquad [9.12]$$

where $\overline{Y}$ and $\overline{X}$ are the mean values of Y and X, respectively. The values necessary to evaluate eqns [9.11] and [9.12] can be obtained from Table 9.3 which was used to calculate the correlation coefficient. These are repeated for convenience:

$$\begin{aligned}
\Sigma Y &= 2{,}662 & \Sigma X &= 1{,}131.2 \\
\Sigma Y^2 &= 645{,}386 & \Sigma X^2 &= 117{,}307.48 \\
\Sigma XY &= 272{,}832.4 &&
\end{aligned}$$

Hence

$$\begin{aligned}
b &= \frac{11 \times 272{,}832.4 - 1{,}131.2 \times 2{,}662.0}{11 \times 117{,}307.48 - 1{,}131.2^2} \\[2mm]
&= \frac{10{,}098.00}{10{,}768.84} \\[2mm]
&= -0.937705 \\[2mm]
a &= 242.00 - (-0.937705) \times 102.836 \\[2mm]
&= 338.430219
\end{aligned}$$

Thus the regression equation can be written, to two decimal places for clarity, as

$$Y_i = 338.43 - 0.94X_i + e_i \qquad\qquad [9.13]$$

Interpretation of the result

The most important result is the coefficient $b = -0.94$. This indicates that if the fare index were to rise by one unit, demand would fall by 0.94 units. Since demand is measured in millions of vehicle kilometres, this implies a fall of 940,000 vehicle kilometres. A rise of two units in the fare index would lead to a fall of $2 \times 940{,}000 = 1{,}880{,}000$ vehicle kilometres in demand. The negative value of b indicates a downward sloping demand curve, as expected based on *a priori* knowledge of economic behaviour, and upon the results of the correlation analysis.

A firm might use this knowledge to evaluate the effect of a rise in fares on profit. The fare index is currently (1985) at 114.2 and demand at 232 million vehicle kilometres. The firm is contemplating a rise in the real fare (i.e. above the rate of inflation) of 5 units, to 119.2. It would expect demand to fall by 5 × 0.94 = 4.7 units, i.e. from 232 to 227.3. The effect on revenue is

Old revenue: 232 × 114.2 = 26,494.40
New revenue: 227.3 × 119.2 = 27,094.16

There is thus a rise in revenue of

$$\frac{27{,}094.16 - 26{,}494.40}{26{,}494.40} = 0.0226$$

i.e. 2.26%

The fall in demand has not quite offset the rise in price so revenue has risen. Suppose current revenue is £45m. Then a 2.26% rise represents £1.017m. extra in revenue.

So much for revenue, what about cost? Suppose that the running costs of bus services are £0.1m. per million vehicle kilometres. A reduction of 4,700,000 vehicle kilometres therefore saves £470,000. The overall gain in profit would therefore be £1.487m. It would obviously be beneficial for the firm (though not the consumer!) to raise its fares.

Note two things about this result. First, since the regression used the real fare as explanatory variable, the effect on profit of a real fare increase has to be calculated, i.e. above the increase necessary simply to keep pace with inflation. Secondly, it would probably be unwise to extend the analysis to a rise of 10, 20

Figure 9.9 The danger of prediction outside the range of sample data

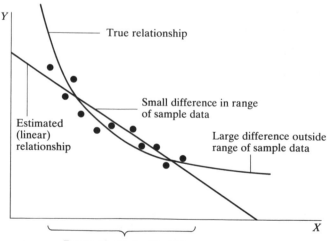

or more in the fare index, since this would be going well outside the range of the sample data. The problem arises because it is *assumed* that the relationship is a straight line when in fact it might be curvilinear. The difference is unlikely to be great within the range of the sample values, but might get worse outside it. Figure 9.9 illustrates.

Inference in the regression model

The relationship calculated above is in fact a *sample* regression line, based upon data collected over the period 1975–85. Other data could have been collected, e.g. from 1970 to 1980, which would have constituted a different sample and would have yielded a slightly different sample regression line. The usual question can be asked in the context of statistical inference, namely how representative is this sample of the population as a whole?

The question is best approached by writing down a 'true' or population regression equation, of a form similiar to the sample regression equation:

$$Y_i = \alpha + \beta X_i + \varepsilon_i \qquad [9.14]$$

α and β are the population parameters, of which a and b are (point) estimates. ε_i is the population error term. This population regression equation may be considered as some sort of machine, or 'data generation process'. A value of X_i is chosen and fed into the 'machine'. Back comes a value of Y_i, which is calculated from the values of α and β and a random error component, ε_i. Of course, the values of α, β and ε_i are unknown; we only observe the value of Y_i calculated from the X_i input. Further values of X_i are fed into the data generation process, yielding Y_i in return each time. Thus a sample of values of X_i and Y_i is built up from the population.

The purpose of regression is to find estimates of α and β from the sample data. In the previous section sample regression coefficients a and b were calculated which were used as estimates of α and β to work out the effects of the bus company's altering fares. The situation is analogous to the earlier discussion of estimation (Chapter 6). There the sample mean was used to estimate the population mean. Here the sample regression coefficients are used to estimate the population regression coefficients.

In practice we do not always have the luxury of being able to feed values of X_i to the data generation process to see what comes back. Very often there is no possibility of influencing the sample data, i.e. of choosing values of X_i. For example, if estimating a consumption function (the relation of consumption to national outcome), one cannot choose different values of income to see what values of consumption come back. (One American economist has warned against this type of experiment: 'Empirical experiments in economics are best admired from a distance.') The data have to be accepted as presented in the official (and unofficial) statistics, which are often not ideal from the point of view of statistical analysis. It is strictly the case therefore that the inferences drawn about α and β are *conditional* upon the values of X_i in the sample. In practice, this consideration is usually ignored as the practical consequences are not profound.

Test of the goodness of fit of the regression line

However good or bad the relationship between X and Y, a regression line can always be calculated, so by itself the regression line does not reveal a great deal. Some way of differentiating between 'good' and 'bad' regressions is therefore needed. Consider the cases illustrated in Fig. 9.10. In both cases the calculated regression line is the same, yet it is obvious that there is a much more precise relationship between X and Y in (a) than in (b).

Figure 9.10 Two data sets yielding the same regression line

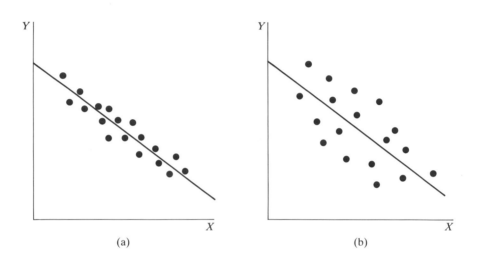

(a)   (b)

A useful way of differentiating between these two cases is on the basis of 'goodness of fit' of the line, measured by the coefficient of determination and denoted R^2 (it is usually referred to as 'R squared'). This turns out (in two-variable regression) to be the square of the correlation coefficient calculated earlier. Figure 9.11 illustrates the principle behind the calculation of R^2.

Figure 9.11 shows the mean value of Y, the calculated sample regression line and an arbitrarily chosen sample observation (X_i, Y_i). The difference between Y_i and $\overline{Y}$ (length AC) can be divided up into

(a) that part 'explained' by the regression line, $\hat{Y}_i - \overline{Y}$ (i.e. due to the value of X_i). This is length AB.
(b) the error term $e_i = Y_i - \hat{Y}_i$, length BC.

It is obvious that

$$(Y_i - \overline{Y}) = (\hat{Y}_i - \overline{Y}) + (Y_i - \hat{Y}_i) \qquad [9.15]$$

A good regression line should 'explain' a large part of the difference between Y_i and Y, i.e. the length $(\hat{Y}_i - \overline{Y})$ should be large relative to $(Y_i - \hat{Y}_i)$.

204

Figure 9.11 The principle for calculating R^2

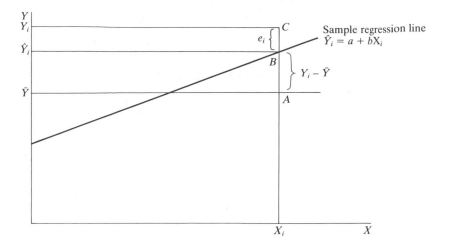

If each of the terms in [9.15] is squared and then summed over all the sample observations, we obtain

$\Sigma(Y_i - \overline{Y})^2$, termed the total sum of squares (TSS)
$\Sigma(\hat{Y}_i - \overline{Y})^2$, the regression sum of squares (RSS)   [9.16]
$\Sigma(Y_i - \hat{Y}_i)^2$, the error sum of squares (ESS)

Further, it is the case that

$$\text{TSS} = \text{RSS} + \text{ESS}$$ [9.17]

The measure of goodness of fit, R^2, is then defined as

$$R^2 = \frac{\text{RSS}}{\text{TSS}}$$

Alternatively, using eqn [9.17]

$$R^2 = \frac{\text{TSS} - \text{ESS}}{\text{TSS}}$$ [9.18]

The greater the divergences between Y_i and $\overline{Y}$ are explained by the regression line, the better the goodness of fit, and the higher the calculated value of R^2. From eqns [9.17] and [9.18] it should be obvious that R^2 must lie between 0 and 1 (note that since each term in eqn [9.17] is a sum of *squares*, none of them can be negative). Thus

$$0 \leq R^2 \leq 1$$

A value of $R^2 = 1$ indicates that all the sample observations lie exactly on the regression line (this is an extremely rare occurrence and is more likely to indicate an error than a wonderful empirical regularity). If $R^2 = 0$, then the

205

regression line is of no use at all – X does not influence Y (linearly) at all, and to try to predict a value of Y_i one might as well use the mean $\overline{Y}$ as use X_i and the sample regression coefficients.

To calculate R^2, alternative formulae to those in eqn [9.16] make the task easier.

TSS: $\Sigma(Y_i - \overline{Y})^2 = \Sigma Y_i^2 - n\overline{Y}^2$
ESS: $\Sigma(Y_i - \hat{Y}_i)^2 = \Sigma Y_i^2 - a\Sigma Y_i - b\Sigma X_i Y_i$
RSS: TSS – ESS

Thus the following results are obtained:

TSS $= 645,386 - 11 \times 242.0^2 = 1,182.00$

ESS $= 645,386 - 338.430219 \times 2,662.0 - \dfrac{-10,098}{10,768.84} \times 272,832.4$

$= 321.1865$

RSS $= 1,182.00 - 321.1865 = 860.8135$

Hence

$$R^2 = \frac{\text{RSS}}{\text{TSS}} = \frac{860.8135}{1,182.00} = 0.728$$

This is interpreted as 72.8% of the variation in demand (measured by TSS) being explained by variation in fares (as measured by RSS). This is quite a respectable figure to obtain, leaving only 27.2% of the variation in demand left to be explained by other factors. The regression would seem to make a worthwhile contribution to explaining why the demand for bus travel has changed over time.

A brief note on rounding errors: Rounding errors can be a considerable nuisance in regression because they can easily accumulate. Suppose, for example, that the error sum of squares (ESS) above had been calculated using – 0.94 as the slope coefficient instead of the correct value (presented above in ratio form –10098.00/10768.84 to ensure accuracy). This would have resulted in a calculated value of 947.796, almost three times the correct answer! The value of R^2 would then have been 19.8%, a highly misleading figure. The large error arises here because the error sum of squares is the small (we hope!) difference between two large numbers. In this sense it is like the balance of payments problem mentioned in Chapter 1.

The answer to this problem is *never* to round intermediate answers, but to keep them to as many decimal places as possible (most conveniently in the memory of a calculator). In the above calculations the intermediate answers are reported to six significant figures, though they were held to nine significant figures in a calculator memory (and were also checked on a computer). These problems only arise when doing calculations by hand; use of a computer statistical package should rule out the possibility of rounding errors. The final answers may be rounded to clarify the presentation of the results.

Figure 9.12(a)

Figure 9.12(b)

Figure 9.12(c)

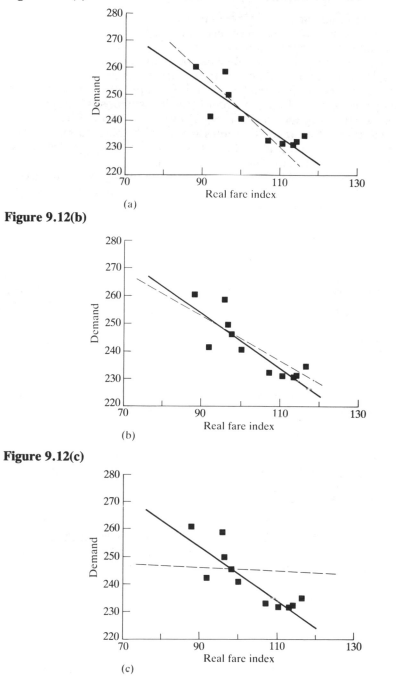

Confidence interval estimates of α and β

The sample coefficients a and b will serve as point estimates of α and β. It can be shown that, under plausible assumptions, the least squares estimates are *unbiased* estimates of the population parameters α and β. This is one justification for using the least squares rule. Because these are the results of just one random sample of the data, confidence interval estimates for α and β may be constructed around the point estimates a and b. First, Fig. 9.12 presents some diagrams showing the data, the sample regression line and possible population regression lines (shown by the dotted lines). Figures 9.12(a) and 9.12(b) show fairly plausible population regression lines from which the data might have been drawn, while the example in 9.12(c) seems rather implausible. This slope is unlikely to appear in the confidence interval for β.

In order to find confidence interval estimates the sampling distributions of a and b are needed, and in particular their standard errors. It turns out that both a and b follow t distributions with their standard errors given by

$$\text{Standard error } (b) = S_b = \sqrt{\frac{S_e^2}{\Sigma(X_i - \overline{X})^2}} \tag{9.19}$$

$$\text{Standard error } (a) = S_a = \sqrt{\frac{S_e^2}{n} + \frac{\overline{X}^2 S_e^2}{\Sigma(X_i - \overline{X})^2}} \tag{9.20}$$

where

$$S_e^2 = \frac{\Sigma e_i^2}{n - 2}$$

(this is an unbiased estimate of the variance of ε_i, the population error term).

The 95% confidence interval estimate for β is therefore

$$[b - t_\nu^{5\%} s_b, b + t_\nu^{5\%} s_b]$$

where $t_\nu^{5\%}$ is the (two tail) critical value of the t distribution at the 5% significance level, with $n - 2$ degrees of freedom ($\nu = 9$ in this case). Similarly for a, the confidence interval is

$$[a - t_\nu^{5\%} s_a, a + t_\nu^{5\%} s_a]$$

We proceed by first calculating S_e^2, then s_b and s_a, and finally constructing the confidence intervals. Most of the calculations have already been performed when deriving a and b. It is just a question of assembling the pieces in the right order.

Σe_i^2 is just the error sum of squares, ESS, already calculated. Hence

$$S_e^2 = \frac{\text{ESS}}{n - 2} = \frac{321.1865}{9} = 35.6874$$

For s_b, $\Sigma(X_i - \overline{X})^2$ is better calculated as $\Sigma X_i^2 - (\Sigma X_i)^2/n$, which gives $117307.48 - (1131.2)^2/11 = 978.9855$. Hence

$$s_b = \sqrt{\frac{35.6874}{978.9855}}$$

$$= 0.1909$$

is the standard error for b. For a the standard error is, using eqn [9.20]

$$S_a = \sqrt{\frac{35.6874}{11} + \frac{102.836 \times 35.6874}{978.9855}}$$

$$= 19.7167$$

The 95% confidence intervals are therefore:

for β
$$[-0.94 - 2.26 \times 0.1909 , -0.94 + 2.26 \times 0.1909]$$
$$= [-1.37 , -0.51]$$
for α
$$[338.43 - 2.26 \times 19.7167 , 338.43 + 2.26 \times 19.7167]$$
$$= [293.87 , 382.99]$$

Thus we can be 95% confident that the true value of β lies in the range [-1.37, -0.51]. Note that all of these values are negative: there is little danger of the true demand curve sloping up!

It is useful (and customary) to write the regression equation with the standard errors written below the appropriate coefficient, and also with the value of R^2, as follows:

$$Y_i = 338.43 - 0.94\,X_i + e_i$$
s.e. (19.72) (0.19)
$$R^2 = 0.728 \qquad n = 11$$

This conveys all the necessary information to the reader at a glance, who can then draw the inferences deemed appropriate. Any desired confidence interval (not just the 95% one) can be quickly calculated with the aid of a set of t tables.

Hypothesis tests of the coefficients

These tests are quickly and easily conducted given the information above. Consider the following hypothesis

$H_0: \beta = 0$
$H_1: \beta < 0$

This null hypothesis is interesting because it implies no influence of X upon Y at all (i.e. the slope of the true regression line is flat and Y_i can be equally well predicted by $\bar{Y}$). The alternative hypothesis is one-sided because demand curves are normally expected to be downward sloping. The procedure is the same as in Chapter 6 on hypothesis testing. The critical value of the t distribution at the 5% significance level, $v = 9$, for a one tail test is $t^* = 1.83$. The test statistic is

$$t_v = \frac{b - \beta}{s_b}$$

[9.21]

$$= \frac{-0.9377 - 0}{0.1909}$$

$$= -4.91$$

Since $t > t^*$ in absolute value, the null hypothesis is rejected. X does have some (negative) influence on Y. A similar test can be carried out on α.

Sometimes the regression results are presented with the t statistic (as calculated above), rather than the standard errors, below the coefficient. This is not to be preferred because $H_0: \beta = 0$ as the null hypothesis might be inappropriate (in the consumption function a test for the marginal propensity to consume being equal to one might be appropriate, for example).

Testing the significance of the regression as a whole

The hypotheses tests on α and β test each coefficient separately for significance, but there is also a test for the significance of the regression as a whole. This is an F-test, and the test statistic is

$$F_{1,n-2} = \frac{RSS/1}{ESS/(n - 2)}$$

[9.22]

The F statistic is the ratio of the regression sum of squares to the error sum of squares, each divided by their degrees of freedom. Hence

$$F_{1,n-2} = \frac{860.8135}{321.1865/9} = 24.12$$

The critical value of the F distribution at the 5% significance level, with $v_1 = 1$ and $v_2 = n - 2 = 9$, is $F^* = 5.12$. The test statistic exceeds this, so the regression as a whole is significant i.e. the regression line is a better predictor of demand than the average demand.

In the case of simple regression, with only one explanatory variable, the F-test is equivalent to a t-test of the hypothesis $H_0: \beta = 0$. The F-test statistic is the square of the t statistic calculated earlier. This just reflects another of the relationships between different statistical distributions, for

$$F_{1, n-2} = t^2_{n-2}$$

so a superfluous test has been conducted. However, in multiple regression with more than one explanatory variable, the relationship no longer holds and the tests do perform different functions.

Prediction

As well as predicting values of Y_i within the sample range of X_i, values outside the sample range can also be predicted. Suppose the bus company wanted to know what would happen if fares rose by 10% to 125. How would the level of Y_i be predicted at this level of fares? A simple (unbiased) point estimate is obtained by use of the regression line. The predicted value, which will be denoted by Y_P, is:

$$Y_P = 338.430 - 0.937705 \times 125$$
$$= 221.22$$

The use of the sample regression line for prediction is illustrated in Fig. 9.13.

Figure 9.13 Using the sample regression line for prediction

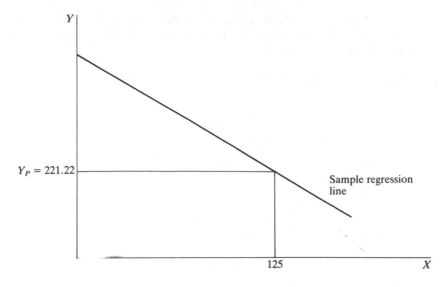

Since there is some uncertainty about the true values of the coefficients, there will also be some uncertainty about prediction. A confidence interval around Y_P needs to be calculated. The 95% confidence interval is given by

$$\left[Y_P - t_{n-2}{}^{5\%} \times s_e \sqrt{\frac{1}{n} + \frac{(X_P - \overline{X})^2}{\Sigma(X_i - \overline{X})^2}} \right. , \qquad\qquad [9.23]$$

$$\left. Y_P + t_{n-2}{}^{5\%} \times s_e \sqrt{\frac{1}{n} + \frac{(X_P - \overline{X})^2}{\Sigma(X_i - \overline{X})^2}} \right]$$

where X_P is the value of X_i for which the prediction is made. The interval estimate is therefore

$$\left[221.22 - 2.26 \times 5.97 \sqrt{\frac{1}{11} + \frac{(125 - 102.836)^2}{978.9855}} \right. ,$$

$$\left. 221.22 + 2.26 \times 5.9739 \sqrt{\frac{1}{11} + \frac{(125 - 102.836)^2}{978.9855}} \right]$$

211

which gives [210.83, 231.61] as the 95% confidence interval. This gives the confidence interval for the *regression line* at $X_P = 125$, but the observations themselves rarely lie on the line itself. The confidence interval for the value of Y_i itself at $X_P = 125$ is therefore somewhat wider, given by the formula

$$\left[Y_P - t_{n-2}{}^{5\%} \times s_e \sqrt{1 + \frac{1}{n} + \frac{(X_P - \overline{X})^2}{\Sigma(X_i - \overline{X})^2}} \right., \tag{9.24}$$

$$\left. Y_P + t_{n-2}{}^{5\%} \times s_e \sqrt{1 + \frac{1}{n} + \frac{(X_P - \overline{X})^2}{\Sigma(X_i - \overline{X})^2}} \right]$$

This when evaluated gives a 95% confidence interval of [204.18, 238.26] which is the answer to the bus company's original problem. The two confidence intervals are illustrated in Fig. 9.14.

Figure 9.14 Confidence interval prediction for $X_P = 125$

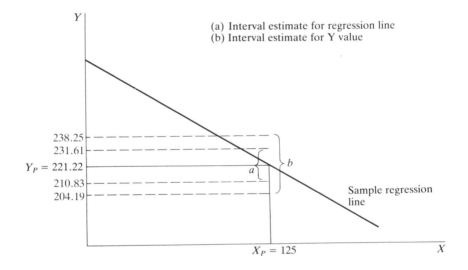

Non-linear transformations

So far only *linear* regression has been dealt with, that is, fitting a straight line to the data. This can sometimes be restrictive, especially when there is good reason to believe that the true relationship is non-linear (e.g. that between inflation and unemployment – the Phillips curve). Poor results would be obtained by fitting a straight line through the data in Fig. 9.15, yet the relationship is obvious from a glance.

Fortunately this problem can be reduced by transforming the data, so that when graphed it shows a linear relationship between the two variables. Then a straight line can be fitted to this transformed data. This is equivalent to fitting a curved line to the original data. All that is needed is to find a suitable

212

Figure 9.15

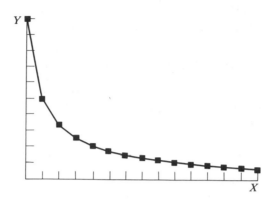

transformation to 'straighten out' the data. Given the data represented in Fig. 9.15, if Y were graphed against $1/X$ the relationship shown in Fig. 9.16 would appear. Thus if the regression line

$$Y_i = a + b \frac{1}{X_i} + e_i \qquad [9.25]$$

were fitted, this would provide a good representation of the data in Fig. 9.15. The procedure is quite straightforward. Simply calculate the reciprocal of each of the X values and use these (together with the original data for Y), employing exactly the same methods as above. A brief example of how to transform the data is given below.

Figure 9.16

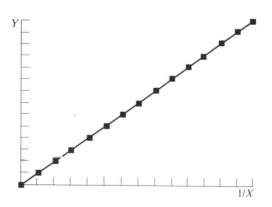

Original data:

Y_i	5	8	7	10...
X_i	15	14	12	8...

Transforming the X variable, the new data become

Y_i	5	8	7	10...
$1/X_i$	0.067	0.071	0.083	0.125...

The new data are used for the purposes of calculation. Most computer statistical packages have facilities to transform the data so that this tedious task need not be done by hand.

Table 9.6 Data transformations

Name	Graph of relationship	Original relationship	Transformed relationship	Regression
Double log		$Y=aX^b e$	$\ln Y = \ln a + b \ln X + \ln e$	$\ln Y$ on $\ln X$
Reciprocal		$Y=a+b/X+e$	$Y=a+b\dfrac{1}{X}+e$	Y on $\dfrac{1}{X}$
Semi-log		$e^Y=aX^b e$	$Y=\ln a+bX+\ln e$	Y on $\ln X$
Exponential		$Y=e^{a+bX+e}$	$\ln Y = a+bX+e$	$\ln Y$ on X

Table 9.6 presents a number of possible shapes for the data, with suggested data transformations which will allow the relationship to be estimated using linear regression. In each case, once the data have been transformed, the methods used above can be applied.

It is sometimes difficult to know which transformation (if any) to apply. Economic theory rarely suggests the *form* which a relationship should follow, and there are no simple statistical tests for choosing alternative formulations. The choice can sometimes be made after simple visual inspection of the data, or sometimes it can be made on the basis of convenience. The first transformation (the 'double log') in Table 9.6 will be examined in this light. It turns out that using this type of estimating equation allows a very convenient interpretation of the coefficients.

Table 9.7 Transformed data

	In Y	In X
1975	5.564	4.476
1976	5.557	4.560
1977	5.521	4.569
1978	5.505	4.582
1979	5.489	4.520
1980	5.485	4.605
1981	5.451	4.674
1982	5.447	4.705
1983	5.442	4.733
1984	5.460	4.757
1985	5.447	4.738

Each of the variables used in the bus study above is transformed by taking natural (to the base e) logarithms of the observations, yielding the data as in Table 9.7. The sums of squares and cross-products of the data are

$\Sigma X_i = 50.919 \qquad \Sigma Y_i = 60.368$
$\Sigma X_i^2 = 235.797 \qquad \Sigma Y_i^2 = 331.319$
$\Sigma X_i Y_i = 279.407$

Feeding these values into the formlae (eqns [9.11] and [9.12]) for the sample regression coefficients, for R^2 (eqn [9.18]) and for the standard errors (eqns [9.19] and [9.20]) the following results are obtained:

$\ln \hat{Y}_i = 7.31 - 0.39 \text{ in } X_i$
s.e.   (0.36) (0.08)

$R^2 = 0.743$
$F_{1,9} = 26.08$

The coefficient $b = -0.39$ can be interpreted as the *elasticity of demand*, i.e. the proportionate change in demand divided by the proportionate change in price.* Thus a 1% rise in price is predicted to lead to a 0.39% fall in demand, for example. This is a more useful way of presenting the results than using the untransformed data, and is why demand curves are usually estimated in logarithmic form. The elasticity is the same at all points on the demand curve, unlike the linear case, where it changes as one moves along it.

Elasticity measures can be obtained with a little more effort from the linear demand curve, as follows. Since the elasticity is different at different points along the linear demand curve, the elasticity will be estimated at the mean of X and Y, at $\bar{X} = 102.84$, $\bar{Y} = 242.0$. The formula for the demand elasticity is

$$e = \frac{dQ}{dP} \cdot \frac{P}{Q}$$

$$= \frac{dY}{dX} \cdot \frac{X}{Y} \quad \text{in the notation used in this chapter.}$$

$dY/dX = b = -0.94$, from the linear regression equation.

Hence

$$e = -0.94 \cdot \frac{102.84}{242.00}$$

$$= -0.40$$

This is a similar value to the logarithmic result, but cannot be read off directly from the regression coefficients. Another advantage of the logarithmic form is that it is obvious that demand is *inelastic* ($e > -1$), so it is immediately clear that raising prices will increase revenue.

Units of measurement

If the units of measurement of one or both of the variables are changed, what happens to the results? As in the case of descriptive statistics, nothing *fundamental* alters, but superficially some calculated values will alter. Suppose that demand is measured not on millions of vehicle kilometres but in thousands of vehicle kilometres. Clearly neither fares nor demand *per se* change, but the dependent variable is multiplied by 1,000. Y_i becomes 261,000, 259,000, etc.

Once again it is best to think of this in graphical terms. A graph of the data will look exactly the same, except that the scale on the Y axis will change; it will be multiplied by 1,000. The intercept of the regression line will therefore change to 338,430 and the slope to –937.7705 Thus the regression equation becomes

$Y_i = 338,430 - 937 \, X_i + e_i'$
$(e_i' = 1,000 \, e_i)$.

* If $\ln Y = a + b \ln X$, then $b = d(\ln Y)/d(\ln X) = dY/Y \times X/dX$, which is the demand elasticity.

Since nothing fundamental has altered, any hypothesis tests must yield the same test statistics. Thus neither t nor F statistic is altered by changes in the units of measurement, nor is R^2. However, standard errors will be multiplied by 1,000 (they have to be to preserve the t statistics, see eqn [9.21]). Table 9.8 sets out the effects of changes in the units of measurement upon the coefficients and standard errors. In the table it is assumed that the variables have been multiplied by a constant, k; in the above case $k = 1,000$ was used.

Table 9.8 The effects of data transformations

Factor (k) multiplying ...		Effect upon			
Y	X	a	s_a	b	s_b
k	1	—— all multiplied by k ——			
1	k	unchanged		divided by k	
k	k	multiplied by k		unchanged	

The results in Table 9.8 apply to a regression using *untransformed* data. If the double log transformation is used, changing the units of measurement has no effect upon the coefficients (since elasticity is independent of the units of measurement, changing them cannot have any effect). This is another advantage of the logarithmic formulation for demand curves.

Using a computer to find the regression line

Regression calculations are most often (and most easily) performed using a computer statistical package. There is an enormous variety of such packages now available; Fig 17(a) shows how two of these packages present the results for the example of bus fares and demand. Fig. 9.17(a) shows the output from MINITAB, a widely used statistical package on mainframes and microcomputers, while Fig. 9.17(b), shows the output from LOTUS 123, the most popular spreadsheet program for microcomputers such as the IBM PC.

The MINITAB output gives the regression coefficients and their standard errors, and the results of the hypothesis tests on the values of the coefficients being equal to zero (under the columns headed 'Coef', 'Stdev' and 't-ratio' respectively). The standard deviation of the error term is given as 's = 5.974', which has been labelled s_e in this book. R^2 is given as 72.8% and a further statistic, $\overline{R}^2$ (or adjusted R^2), is also presented. Discussion of this latter statistic is left to the section on multiple regression below.

The section labelled 'Analysis of variance' allows calculation of the F statistic although this is not given explicitly. The regression (RSS), error (ESS) and total (TSS) sums of squares are all given under the 'SS' column. The 'MS' (for mean square) column divides the sums of squares by their respective degrees of freedom (given under the 'DF' column); one degree of freedom for RSS, 9 ($n-2$) for ESS. The figure 35.69 is therefore equal to ESS/($n-2$), or s_e^2. The F statistic is thus calculated as the ratio of the two numbers in the MS column, $860.81/35.69 = 24.12$.

Turning to LOTUS 123, the output provides less information and in a slightly different format. The standard error of the constant is assumed to be of little interest to the user and is not given; nor are the various sums of squares. s_e is given, labelled 'Std err of Y est'. With a little manipulation however, the sums of squares can be derived. The error sum of squares can be obtained as ESS $= S_e^2.(n-2) = 5.973891^2. 9 = 321.1864$. R^2 may be written (see eqn 9.18)

$$R^2 = 1 - \frac{\text{ESS}}{\text{TSS}}$$

so, rearranging

$$\text{TSS} = \frac{\text{ESS}}{1 - R^2}$$

$$= \frac{321.1864}{1 - 0.728}$$

$$= 1180.83$$

(the discrepancy with the correct value is due to a slight rounding error in the above calculation, not due to computer inaccuracy). From knowledge of these sums of squares the F statistic may be calculated and the significance of the regression equation tested.

Figure 9.17 Computer output for regression

(a) Minitab output

```
MTB > regr 'vkms' 1 'realfare'

The regression equation is
vkms = 338 − 0.938 realfare

Predictor          Coef        Stdev        t-ratio
Constant          338.43       19.72         17.16
realfare         −0.9377       0.1909        −4.91

s = 5.974      R-sq = 72.8%        R-sq(adj) = 69.8%

Analysis of variance

SOURCE            DF          SS           MS
Regression         1        860.81       860.81
Error              9        321.19        35.69
Total             10       1182.00
```

(b) Lotus 1.2.3 output

Regression output:	
Constant	338.4302
Std err of Y est	5.973891
R squared	0.728268
No. of observations	11
Degrees of freedom	9
X coefficient(s)	−0.93770
Std err of coef	0.190927

Multiple regression

This section examines the case where there are several explanatory variables, though still only one dependent variable. The formulae for calculating regression coefficients, standard errors, and hypothesis tests become more complicated (unless matrix algebra is used) and very time consuming to evaluate. For these reasons, these calculations are nowadays almost invariably performed by computer. This section does not therefore give these formulae nor perform the calculations, but describes the principles of multiple regression. This allows multiple regression equations to be estimated (with the aid of a computer) and understood, as well as the results published by other researchers.

Principles of multiple regression

There is still one dependent variable, Y_i, but several explanatory variables, labelled X_{1i}, X_{2i}, ..., X_{ki}. For the demand for bus travel, these explanatory variables might be the fare level, income, the weather, etc. Each of these factors now influences demand, so will be included explicitly in the regression equation and will no longer form part of the error term. For simplicity only the fare and income are used as explanatory variables.

Y_i : demand for bus travel in year i
X_{1i} : fare level in year i
X_{2i} : income level in year i

The sample regression equation now becomes

$$Y_i = a + bX_{1i} + cX_{2i} + e_i \qquad [9.26]$$

with an extra coefficient, c, for income. It should be noted that the errors e_i will be different from those in the simple regression, due to the presence of the extra explanatory variable.

Rather than fitting a line through the data, the task is now to fit a plane to the data, which is now in three dimensions as shown in Fig. 9.18. The plane is drawn sloping down in the direction of X_1 and up in the direction of X_2. The observations are now points dotted about in three-dimensional space and the task of regression analysis is to find the plane which minimises the sum of

Figure 9.18 The regression plane in three dimensions

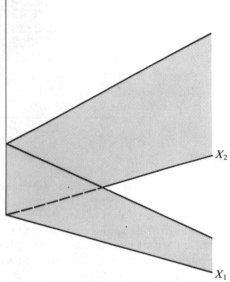

squares of vertical distances from each point to the plane. The principle is the same as in simple regression and the regression plane is the one that best summarises the data.

When there are more than two explanatory variables, more than three dimensions are needed to represent the data and a *hyperplane* has to be fitted to the data. The reader will understand that it is difficult to give a visual interpretation of this case.

Table 9.9 Index of real income, 1975–85
(1980 = 100)

1975	88.9	1979	98.7	1983	100.1
1976	88.4	1980	100.0	1984	102.2
1977	87.4	1981	97.6	1985	105.0
1978	93.5	1982	97.8		

Source: Adapted from *Economic Trends, Oct. 1986*

The data for income that will be used for the example is given in Table 9.9 (from *Economic Trends*, October 1986 edn). The regression equation which results from this data is:

$$\hat{Y}_i = 385.54 - 0.52X_{1i} - 0.94X_{2i} \qquad [9.27]$$
$$\text{s.e.} \quad (24.98) \quad (.23) \qquad (.38)$$

220

$$R^2 = 0.844$$
$$F_{2,8} = 21.67$$

The coefficient $b = -0.52$ now shows the effect upon Y of a unit change in X_1, *as long as X_2 remains constant*. Similarly, $c = -0.94$ shows the response of Y to a unit change in X_2 if X_1 remains constant. If both X_1 and X_2 rose by one unit simultaneously, then the effect upon Y would be $-0.52 + (-0.94) = -1.46$, a fall of 1.46 units.

This equation still finds a negative relationship between price and demand (holding income constant) and also reveals a negative relationship between income and demand, i.e. bus travel is an inferior good. This is not surprising; as people earn more they tend to rely more upon motor cars and reduce their dependence upon buses.

Hypothesis tests on both coefficients can be carried out, just as in the single explanatory variable case, again using a t-test. For the coefficient on price:

H_0: $\beta = 0$
H_1: $\beta < 0$

$$t_{n-k-1} = \frac{b - \beta}{s_b} = \frac{-0.5166 - 0}{0.2309} = -2.24$$

The critical value of the t distribution at the 5% significance level for a one tail test with eight degrees of freedom is $t^* = 1.86$. Note that the number of degrees of freedom for the t test is $n - k - 1$, where k is the number of explanatory variables, here two (note that the constant is not counted as an explanatory variable). The null hypothesis that price has no effect upon demand is rejected in favour of the alternative that higher prices reduce demand.

For the coefficient on income a two tail test is carried out, since bus travel could be a normal (positive coefficient) or inferior (negative coefficient) good.

H_0: $\gamma = 0$
H_1: $\gamma \neq 0$

γ is the population parameter associated with income.

$$t_{n-k-1} = \frac{c - \gamma}{s_c} = \frac{-0.9386 - 0}{0.3848} = -2.44$$

The critical value for a two tail test is 2.31. The coefficient is significantly different from zero, and bus travel turns out to be an inferior good. Both fares and income make a significant contribution to explaining variation in demand.

The value of R^2 has risen and now 84.4% of the variation in Y is explained by the variation in fare *and* income. Adding an extra explanatory variable will always raise the value of R^2, or at worst leave it the same (since 75.2% of the variation was explained by the fare level alone, adding another variable (even if irrelevant) cannot detract from this). One way round this problem is to calculate $\bar{R}^2$ *(called R-bar squared or adjusted R squared)*. This is given by the formula

$$\bar{R}^2 = 1 - \frac{n-1}{n-k-1}(1 - R^2) \qquad\qquad [9.28]$$

$\bar{R}$ therefore takes account of the different number of explanatory variables and so can be used to compare the two regression equations above. For the single variable case

$$\bar{R}^2 = 1 - \frac{11-1}{11-1-1}(1 - 0.728) = 0.698$$

For the two explanatory variables case

$$\bar{R}^2 = 1 - \frac{11-1}{11-2-1}(1 - 0.844) = 0.805$$

so the rise in R^2 is not solely due to the extra explanatory variable. It should be noted that $\bar{R}^2$ can be used only to compare regressions where additional regressors have been added. It is inappropriate to use it to compare completely unrelated regressions.

In multiple regression the F statistic has $v_1 = k$, $v_2 = n - k - 1$ degrees of freedom in numerator and denominator respectively. In this case therefore, the F statistic has $v_1 = 2$, $v_2 = 8$ degrees of freedom. The F statistic is again significant at the 5% significance level (critical value 4.46). In the case of multiple regression the F statistic is not linked in a straightforward way to the t statistics, so one is not performing the same test under a different guise. Indeed it is possible to have none of the t statistics significant, yet the F statistic will indicate the overall regression to be worthwhile. Each explanatory variable on its own is not very important, but *together* they explain a significant part of the variation in Y.

All in all the results appear satisfactory. The coefficients are both significant and of the expected sign; the F test implies that the regression as a whole is significant; and a substantial part of the variation in the dependent variable is explained. Nor is the model too complex, with only two explanatory variables, and adding further explanatory variables would not advance the cause a great deal, with only 15.6% of the variation in Y left to be explained.

Computer output

The multiple regression results are given in Fig. 9.19 as they would be presented by MINITAB and LOTUS 123. The LOTUS output is the same as before except for the addition of the extra coefficient and its standard error. MINITAB also provides this, and in addition gives a more detailed analysis of variance. Regression, error and total sums of squares are given (notice that the total sum of squares is the same as in the simple regression case), and the F statistic can again be calculated as the ratio of the two mean squares, with the degrees of freedom of the F statistic given in the 'DF' column. The regression sum of squares is then further broken down into its two sources, fare and income, in the 'SEQ SS' (sequential sums of squares) column. This shows that

Figure 9.19 Multiple regression results

(a) Minitab output

```
MTB > regr 'vkms' 2 'realfare' 'realinc'
The regression equation is
vkms = 386 − 0.517 realfare − 0.939 realinc

Predictor          Coef         Stdev        t-ratio
Constant          385.54        24.98         15.44
realfare         − 0.5166       0.2309       − 2.24
realinc          − 0.9386       0.3848       − 2.44

s = 4.798      R-sq = 84.4%        R-sq(adj) = 80.5%

Analysis of variance

SOURCE          DF          SS            MS
Regression       2        997.81        498.90
Error            8        184.19         23.02
Total           10       1182.00

SOURCE          DF        SEQ SS
Realfare         1        860.81
Realinc          1        136.99

MTB > outf
```

(b) Lotus 1.2.3 output

```
              Regression output:
Constant                        385.5403
Std err of Y est                4.798363
R squared                       0.844167
No. of observations                   11
Degrees of freedom                     8

X coefficient(s)   − 0.51660   − 0.93861
Std err of coef     0.230913    0.384798
```

the fare level made the greater contribution to RSS, the figure of 860.81 being the RSS of a regression of demand on the fare level alone, found in the simple regression exercise above. The figure of 136.99 shows the addition to RSS when real income is added to the regression equation. Thus the two figures in the SEQ SS column sum to the RSS figure above them.

Some problems in regression

The model set out above is the most straightforward regression model, and a number of problems can arise which affect the interpretation of the results. Many of these difficulties can be surmounted by suitable estimation techniques. Some of these problems are now described.

Omitted variable bias: The simple and multiple regressions do not give the same estimate of the effect of the fare level on demand:

Simple regression: $b = -0.94$
Multiple regression: $b = -0.53$

Which of these is correct, and why does the difference arise? The better estimate is the second one and the difference arises because in the case of simple regression a relevant explanatory variable (income) was left out of the regression equation. Consider what happens over the sample period:

Y_i: falls over time
X_{1i}: rises over time
X_{2i}: rises over time.

The fall in demand can be due to

(a) the rise in the fare, or
(b) the rise in income, or
(c) both of these.

The correct answer was found to be (c) since both explanatory variables were significant. But if the rising fare level is the only explanatory variable included in the regression, it has to do the job of rising income as well as its own. Part of the fall in demand is due to rising income, but it is (incorrectly) attributed to rising fares, increasing the coefficient on fares in the sample regression. This is called omitted variable bias.

Table 9.10 Omitted variable bias

Sign of X_1	Correlation between X_1 and X_2	Direction of bias	Example values	
			True	Estimated
> 0	> 0	upwards	0.5	0.9
			−0.5	−0.1
> 0	< 0	downwards	0.5	0.1
			−0.5	−0.9
< 0	> 0	downwards	0.5	0.1
			−0.5	−0.9
< 0	< 0	upwards	0.5	0.9
			−0.5	−0.1

The remedy is to include all relevant explanatory variables in the regression equation. It doesn't matter if irrelevant (i.e. insignificant) variables are included since they will cause no bias. If a relevant explanatory variable cannot be included (the data may be unavailable or too costly to collect), some idea of directions of bias can be obtained. This is shown in Table 9.10. X_{1i} is the included variable, with coefficient b; X_{2i} is the excluded variable with coefficient c.

Multicollinearity: Sometimes some or all of the explanatory variables are highly correlated (in the sample), which means it is difficult to tell which of them is influencing the dependent variable. This is known as multicollinearity. Since all variables are correlated to some degree, multicollinearity is a problem of degree also. In the preceeding example both fares and income rise over time so there might be a problem in establishing the degree to which each affects demand. Fortunately in this problem there is enough independent movement (the correlation coefficient between fares and income is 0.748) for their separate influences to be disentangled.

The symptoms of multicollinearity are

(a) high correlation between two or more of the explanatory variables,
(b) high standard errors on the coefficients leading to insignificant t statistics,
(c) a high value of R^2 in spite of the insignificance of the individual coefficients.

The difficulty of disentangling the separate influences of the explanatory variables means there is uncertainty about their individual importance; it is this which is reflected in the high standard errors. One should therefore be cautious about concluding that variables are not important just because the standard errors are high. It might be due to the presence of multicollinearity.

The best cure for multicollinearity is to obtain more data, which might exhibit more independent movement of the explanatory variables and allow better estimates to be obtained. This is not always possible, however, for example if a sample survey has been completed or if published statistics do not contain more observations. An alternative is to drop one of the collinear variables, though the choice of which one to exclude is somewhat arbitrary. Another procedure is to obtain extraneous estimates of the effects of one of the collinear variables (for example from other studies which have been carried out). These effects can be allowed for when estimates of the remaining coefficients are made.

Simultaneity: It is sometimes difficult to decide which variables are endogenous and which exogenous. In the example used above, demand was taken to be endogenous with price and income exogenous. However, it might be argued that price is also endogenous, since it is determined by the equilibrium of demand and supply. Ignoring this possible simultaneity can lead to biased estimates of the parameters. There are techniques (beyond the scope of this book) for dealing with these sorts of problems. In the present example it could be argued that price is exogenous, since it is determined in part by competition from other means of transport, such as car travel, which are exogenous to the model. Thus there is little feedback from the demand for bus travel on to its price, and the estimates of the coefficients are unlikely to be far wrong.

Measurement error: It is not always possible to measure the variables in a regression equation precisely, so the problem of measurement error exists. Either or both of the endogenous or exogenous variables could be affected. This is mainly a problem for estimation when the measurement error is systematic rather than random (in which case it disappears into the error term). Demand was measured above in vehicle kilometres travelled, but it might be better to use passenger kilometres instead. The difference would not be important if the average number of passengers per bus remained constant over the estimation period. But a switch to smaller buses, for example, would mean that the true fall in demand had been underestimated, and so the estimates of price and income elasticities are too low.

General advice on regression

Regression is a widely used and misused technique. Here are a few pieces of advice.

(a) As always, large samples are better than small. Reasonable results were obtained above with only 11 observations, but this is rather a small sample size on which to base solid conclusions.
(b) Check the data carefully before calculation. This is especially true if a computer is used to analyse the data. If the data is typed in incorrectly, *every* subsequent result will be wrong. A substantial part of any research project should be devoted to verifying the data, checking definitions of variables (is pre-tax or post-tax income being used, for example). The work is tedious, but important.
(c) Don't go fishing. Otherwise known as data-mining, this is searching through the data hoping something will turn up. Some idea of what the data is expected to reveal, and why, allows the search to be conducted more effectively. It is easy to see imaginary patterns in data if an aimless search is being conducted. Try looking at the table of random numbers (Table A1), which will probably soon reveal something 'significant', like your telephone number or your credit card number.
(d) Don't be afraid to start with a fairly simple model or set of techniques. Draw a graph of demand against price to see what it looks like, if it is linear or log linear, if there are any outliers (a data error?), if there are seasonal factors, etc. This will give an overview of the problem which can be kept in mind when more refined techniques are used.

Problems

9.1 The following data (from the *Annual Abstract of Statistics, 1985*, pp. 218 and 323) provides information on cinema admissions, average price of admission and the retail price index for 1973–1983.

Year	Admissions	Admission price	Retail price index
1973	134	43.2	93.5
1974	138	50.1	108.5
1975	116	61.2	134.8
1976	104	73.0	157.1
1977	103	82.6	182.0
1978	126	93.7	197.1
1979	112	113.4	223.5
1980	96	141.3	263.7
1981	84	162.4	295.0
1982	60	177.4	320.4
1983	63	189.8	335.1

(a) Graph the relevant data series and describe the main features of the data.
(b) Calculate a regression of cinema admissions on the real price of admission.
(c) Estimate the elasticity of demand for cinema admission.
(d) Predict the number of admissions in 1984 if the real price is 5% higher than its 1983 level.
(e) Does the regression equation adequately explain cinema admissions? What other explanatory variables might be relevant?

9.2 Dornbusch and Fischer (in R.E. Caves and L.B. Krause, *Britain's Economic Performance*, Brookings, Washington, DC, 1980) report the following equation for predicting the UK balance of payments:

$$B = 0.29 + 0.24U + 0.17\ln Y - 0.004t - 0.10\ln P - 0.24\ln C$$
$$t \quad (0.56) \quad (5.9) \quad (2.5) \quad (3.8) \quad (3.2) \quad (3.9)$$

$R^2 = 0.76$ $s_e = 0.01$ $n = 36$ (quarterly data 1970:1–1978:1) where

B = the current account of the balance of payments as a percentage of gross domestic product (a balance of payments deficit of 3% of GDP would be recorded as –3.0, for example)
U = the rate of unemployment
Y = the OECD index of industrial production
t = a time trend
P = the price of materials relative to the GDP deflator (price index)
C = an index of UK competitiveness (a lower value of the index implies greater competitiveness)
(It indicates the natural logarithm of a variable)

(a) Explain why each variable is included in the regression. Do they all have the expected sign for the coefficient?
(b) Which of the following leads to a higher BOP deficit (relative to GDP): (i) higher unemployment, (ii) higher OECD industrial production, (iii) higher material prices, (iv) greater competitiveness.
(c) What is the implied shape of the relationship between B and (i) U, (ii) Y?
(d) Why cannot a double log equation be estimated for this data? What

227

implications does this have for obtaining elasticity estimates? Why are elasticity estimates not very useful in this context?

(e) Given the following values of the explanatory variables, estimate the state of the current account (point estimate): unemployment rate = 10%, OECD index = 110, time trend = 37, materials price index = 100, competitiveness index = 90.

9.3 A town's ice cream vendors wish to know more about the demand for their product. Data for the last 15 years yield the following regression equation, between weekly ice cream sales (in thousands) during the summer months and the real price of the product (in pence).

$$S_t = 66.0 - 0.8 \, P_t + e_t$$
$$s.e. \quad (6.0) \quad (0.22)$$
$$R^2 = 0.64 \quad n = 15$$

(a) If the average price of ice cream over the sample period was 20 pence, what is the elasticity of demand? Is demand elastic or inelastic?
(b) The vendors are considering raising the price to 30 pence (in real terms) next year. Estimate sales at that price.
(c) Can one be 95% confident that the true demand curve is downward sloping?
(d) The data reveal that ice cream sales have been rising slowly over the sample period. It is known that the number of holidaymakers has fallen over the period. What does this suggest about the estimated demand elasticity?
(e) What other factors might be included in a more comprehensive analysis of the problem?

9.4 A construction company wishes to know the effects of income and the mortage interest rate on the number of new houses started each year. The following data are available from the years 1969–84:

Year	Starts (000)	Real personal disposable income	Mortgage interest rate	Retail price index
1969	166.8	73.3	8.5	51.0
1970	165.1	76.2	8.5	54.2
1971	207.4	77.1	8.0	59.3
1972	228.0	83.7	8.5	63.6
1973	215.7	89.4	11.0	69.4
1974	105.9	88.6	11.0	80.5
1975	149.1	88.9	11.0	100.0
1976	154.7	88.4	12.25	116.5
1977	134.8	87.4	9.5	135.0
1978	157.3	93.5	11.75	146.2
1979	144.0	98.7	15.0	165.8

1980	98.9	100.0	14.0	195.6
1981	116.7	97.6	15.0	218.9
1982	140.5	97.8	10.0	237.7
1983	169.8	100.1	11.25	248.6
1984	154.2	102.2	12.0	260.9

(a) Graph the relevant data series to see if there are any obvious features of the data.

(b) Using the RPI data, calculate the inflation rate (losing the first observation in the process), then use this to obtain the real mortage rate, defined as the difference between the mortgage rate and the inflation rate.

(c) Carry out two regressions as follows:
(i) regress starts on the growth of real PDI and the mortgage rate,
(ii) regress starts on the growth of real PDI and the real mortgage rate.
Compare the two regressions. Which of the two is superior?

(d) Give reasons why both nominal and real mortgage rates could be relevant explanatory variables.

(e) By how much does a rise in the mortgage rate depress housing starts, *ceteris paribus*? Is the *cet. par.* assumption reasonable?

(f) Mortgage interest in the UK attracts tax relief, so that a mortgage rate of 12%, for example is equivalent to 8.76% ($12 \times (1-0.27)$) after tax relief at 27% (the marginal tax rate). How would this affect the parameter estimates?

10 The analysis of time series

Introduction

'The headline total of jobless, including school leavers, rose last month by 12,400 to 3,229,167. But, bucking the seasonal trend, the underlying total fell by 28,400 to 3,116,400 adults.'

The Guardian, 16 January 1987.

One often reads such a statement in the newspapers, which seems to imply unemployment both rising and falling at the same time. What is the meaning of the figures? The answer is that the actual number of people unemployed rose in December; but unemployment always rises in December, and this year's rise isn't as large as it usually is. It is therefore said that the seasonally adjusted figure (i.e. adjusted for the usual rise in December) has fallen. The bad news isn't as bad as expected, so it's really quite good.

Seasonal adjustment is one part of what is known as time-series analysis (since it applies to time-series not cross-section data). Time-series analysis consists of a set of techniques for decomposing time-series data into its constituent parts, which can help in interpreting the data and predicting its future course. There are in fact a wide variety of methods of analysing time-series data; this chapter looks at the more straightforward methods. There is therefore no unique way of decomposing a time series, and a variety of different results can be obtained. However, they will all give similar answers to the problem. Discussion of why variables should vary seasonally is left to a later section.

Decomposing a time series

Unemployment data will be used to illustrate the methods involved in time-series analysis. Exactly the same sort of analysis could be carried out for any time-series data, common examples being monthly sales data for a firm or quarterly data on the money supply.

Table 10.1 presents the monthly unemployment figures for the period January 1982 to December 1984, and Fig. 10.1 shows a plot of the data. For any time series there are two possibilities:

(a) the data varies systematically over time (a trend, for example), or
(b) the data is quite random, i.e. past values of the data are of no help in predicting future values of the data.

230

Table 10.1
Monthly unemployment 1982–4 (000s)

	1982	1983	1984
January	2,769.0	3,087.4	3,082.9
February	2,758.9	3,075.6	3,080.9
March	2,725.9	3,060.2	3,048.0
April	2,731.6	3,035.4	3,022.4
May	2,695.9	2,923.7	2,980.3
June	2,670.6	2,865.0	2,934.5
July	2,753.2	2,905.0	3,008.1
August	2,796.3	2,897.8	3,025.9
September	2,862.3	2,952.8	3,101.7
October	2,874.8	2,925.9	3,074.6
November	2,915.6	2,946.7	3,094.7
December	2,966.4	2,961.3	3,108.1

Source: *Monthly Digest of Statistics, Dec. 1983 and 1985*

Figure 10.1 Monthly unemployment

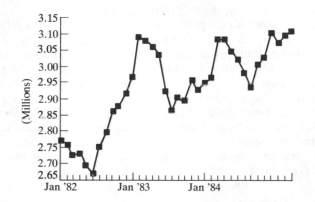

If the data are truly random, then there is no point in carrying out any analysis; no model is going to help in predicting the future. A look at the unemployment data, however, suggests that the series is definitely non-random – there is strong evidence of an upward trend in unemployment and there does appear to be a seasonal component; the peaks of the series are twelve observations (months) apart, with a tendency for there to be a sharp rise in January and a fall in May (a longer data series would show these more clearly). If unemployment in January 1985 had to be predicted, the trend would be projected forwards and account taken of the fact that unemployment tends to be high in January. Time-series analysis provides the quantitative tools for this task.

Any variable can be said to be made up of four components:

(a) a trend: many economic variables are trended over time, for example prices tend to move inexorably upwards.
(b) a cycle: most economies tend to progress unevenly, mixing periods of rapid growth with periods of relative stagnation. This business cycle can vary in length, which makes it difficult to analyse.
(c) a seasonal component: this is a regular, short-term (one-year) cycle. Sales of ice cream vary seasonally, for obvious reasons. Since it is a regular cycle, it is relatively easy to isolate.
(d) have a random component: this is what is left over after the above factors had been taken into account. By definition it cannot be predicted.

Denoting unemployment in year t by X_t we may write

$$X_t = T + C + S + R \qquad [10.1]$$

Unemployment is thus composed *additively* of trend, cycle, seasonal and random components. An alternative model is one where X_t is made up *multiplicatively* of the four components, i.e.

$$X = T \times C \times S \times R \qquad [10.2]$$

There is little to choose between the two alternatives; the multiplicative formulation will be used in the rest of this chapter.

We shall proceed in this chapter as follows. First, the trend is isolated from the original data by the method of moving averages. As stated above, the cyclical component is difficult to analyse because of its irregular nature. Some of it will be removed from the data by the moving average method, along with the trend; otherwise it will be assumed to be absent or unimportant. After isolating the trend, the actual unemployment figures are compared to the trend values to see which months tend to have a level of unemployment above or below trend. These results are then used to seasonally adjust the original data, so that the underlying movement in the figures can be observed, and forecasts made. An alternative method of isolating the trend, using regression techniques, is also explained.

Isolating the trend

There are a variety of methods for isolating the trend from time-series data. The method used here is that of *moving averages*, which is one of several methods of 'smoothing' the data. These smoothing methods iron out the short-term fluctuations in the data by averaging successive observations. For example, to calculate the three-month moving average figure for the month of July, one would take the average of the unemployment figures for June, July and August. The three-month moving average for August would be the average of the July, August and September figures. The figures are therefore as follows (for 1982):

July:

$$\frac{2{,}670.6 + 2{,}753.2 + 2{,}796.3}{3} = 2{,}740.0$$

August:

$$\frac{2{,}753.2 + 2{,}796.3 + 2{,}862.3}{3} = 2{,}803.9$$

The effect of the averaging is to pull the moving average figure for each month towards the unemployment figures for the neighbouring months, and thus smooth the data series.

The choice of the three-month moving average was arbitrary; it could just as easily have been a four-, five- or twelve-month moving average process. How should the appropriate length of the moving average process be chosen? This depends upon the degree of smoothing of the data which is desired, and upon the nature of the fluctuations. The longer the period of the moving average process the greater the smoothing of the data, since the greater is the number of terms in the averaging process. In the case of unemployment data the fluctuations are probably fairly consistent from year to year since, for example, school-leavers arrive on the unemployment register at the same time every year, causing a jump in the figures. A twelve-month moving average process would therefore be appropriate to smooth this data series.

Table 10.2 shows how the moving average series is calculated. Column 1 repeats the raw data from Table 10.1. In column 2 is calculated the successive twelve-month totals. Thus the total of the first twelve observations is 33,520.5 and this is placed in the middle of 1982, between the months of June and July. The sum of observations 2–13 is 33,838.9 and falls between July and August, and so on. Notice that it is impossible to calculate any total before June/July by the moving average process. Values at the beginning and end of the period in question are always lost by this method of smoothing. The greater the length of the moving average process the greater the number of observations lost.

It is inconvenient to have this series falling between the months, so it is centred in column 3. This is done by averaging every two consecutive months' figures, so the June/July and July/August figures are averaged to give the July figure, as follows

$$\frac{33{,}520.5 + 33{,}838.9}{2} = 33{,}679.7$$

This centring problem always arises when the length of the moving average process is an even number. It is merely an inconvenience to have to centre the data; it is not worth choosing an odd-number moving average process simply to avoid it.

Column 4 of Table 10.2 is equal to column 3 divided by 12, and so gives the average of twelve consecutive observations, and this is the moving average series.

Comparison of the original data with the smoothed series shows the latter to

Table 10.2 Calculation of 12 month moving average

		(1)	(2)	(3)	(4)
1982	January	2,769.0	*		
	February	2,758.9	*		
	March	2,725.9	*		
	April	2,731.6	*		
	May	2,695.9	*		
	June	2,670.6			
	July	2,753.2	33,520.5	33,679.7	2,806.6
	August	2,796.3	33,838.9	33,997.3	2,833.1
	September	2,862.3	34,155.6	34,322.8	2,860.2
	October	2,874.8	34,489.9	34,641.8	2,886.8
	November	2,915.6	34,793.7	34,907.6	2,909.0
	December	2,966.4	35,021.5	35,118.7	2,926.6
1983	January	3,087.4	35,215.9	35,291.8	2,941.0
	February	3,075.6	35,367.7	35,418.5	2,951.5
	March	3,060.2	35,469.2	35,514.5	2,959.5
	April	3,035.4	35,559.7	35,585.3	2,965.4
	May	2,923.7	35,610.8	35,626.4	2,968.9
	June	2,865.0	35,641.9	35,639.4	2,969.9
	July	2,905.0	35,636.8	35,634.6	2,969.5
	August	2,897.8	35,632.3	35,635.0	2,969.6
	September	2,952.8	35,637.6	35,631.5	2,969.3
	October	2,925.9	35,625.4	35,618.9	2,968.2
	November	2,946.7	35,612.4	35,640.7	2,970.1
	December	2,961.3	35,669.0	35,703.8	2,975.3
1984	January	3,082.9	35,738.5	35,790.1	2,982.5
	February	3,080.9	35,841.6	35,905.7	2,992.1
	March	3,048.0	35,969.7	36,044.2	3,003.7
	April	3,022.4	36,118.6	36,193.0	3,016.1
	May	2,980.3	36,267.3	36,341.3	3,028.4
	June	2,934.5	36,415.3	36,488.7	3,040.7
	July	3,008.1	36,562.1		
	August	3,025.9	*		
	September	3,101.7	*		
	October	3,074.6	*		
	November	3,094.7	*		
	December	3,108.1	*		

be free of the short-term fluctuations present in the former. The two series are graphed together in Fig. 10.2. The smoothed data reveal a fairly rapid increase during 1982 and a slowing down in 1983 before picking up again in 1984. These features are more difficult to infer from the original data.

Figure 10.2 Smoothed unemployment

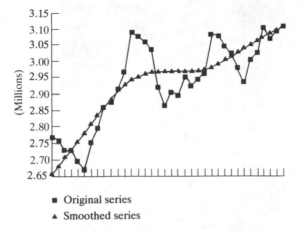

- Original series
- Smoothed series

The trend has thus been disentangled from the raw data. Since the decomposition of the data into its four component parts is never perfect, there is probably some of the cyclical component also left in the moving average series, and possibly also small elements of the seasonal and random components. The trend component is the predominant part, however, and thus the smoothed series will be referred to as the trend.

Isolating seasonal factors

Having obtained the trend, the original data (Table 10.1) may be divided by the trend values (Table 10.2) to leave only the seasonal and random components. The cycle is assumed to be absent or included with the trend. This can best be seen by manipulating eqn [10.2]:

$$X = T \times S \times R$$

Dividing the original data series X by the trend values T therefore gives the seasonal and random components

$$\frac{X}{T} = S \times R \qquad [10.3]$$

Table 10.3 gives the results of this calculation.

Column 3 of the table shows the relationship between the actual observations and the trend values (the trend values for January–June 1982 and July–December 1984 were calculated using data from outside the sample range,

Table 10.3 Isolating seasonal and random components

		Original data (1)	Trend (2)	Ratio (3)
1982	January	2,769.0	2,656.4	1.042
	February	2,758.9	2,682.0	1.029
	March	2,725.9	2,706.5	1.007
	April	2,731.6	2,730.4	1.000
	May	2,695.9	2,754.3	0.979
	June	2,670.6	2,779.9	0.961
	July	2,753.2	2,806.6	0.981
	August	2,796.3	2,833.1	0.987
	September	2,862.3	2,860.2	1.001
	October	2,874.8	2,886.8	0.996
	November	2,915.6	2,909.0	1.002
	December	2,966.4	2,926.6	1.014
1983	January	3,087.4	2,941.0	1.050
	February	3,075.6	2,951.5	1.042
	March	3,060.2	2,959.5	1.034
	April	3,035.4	2,965.4	1.024
	May	2,923.7	2,968.9	0.985
	June	2,865.0	2,969.9	0.965
	July	2,905.0	2,969.5	0.978
	August	2,897.8	2,969.6	0.976
	September	2,952.8	2,969.3	0.994
	October	2,925.9	2,968.2	0.986
	November	2,946.7	2,970.1	0.992
	December	2,961.3	2,975.3	0.995
1984	January	3,082.9	2,982.5	1.034
	February	3,080.9	2,992.1	1.030
	March	3,048.0	3,003.7	1.015
	April	3,022.4	3,016.1	1.002
	May	2,980.3	2,028.4	0.984
	June	2,934.5	3,040.7	0.965
	July	3,008.1	3,053.0	0.985
	August	3,025.9	3,065.3	0.987
	September	3,101.7	3,076.8	1.008
	October	3,074.6	3,089.2	0.995
	November	3,094.7	3,102.5	0.997
	December	3,108.1	3,114.6	0.998

which is not shown). The value for January 1982, 1.042, shows the unemployment level in that month to be 4.2% above the trend. The May 1982 figure of 0.979 shows unemployment 2.1% below trend. Other months' figures can be interpreted in the same way. Closer examination of the table shows unemployment to be above its trend in January to April, below trend in May to August and otherwise to be on or about the trend line. This reflects the seasonal nature of the demand for labour (more jobs are available in the summer months) and the fact that school-leavers who don't immediately get a job come on to the unemployment register around September each year, causing a jump in the figures.

The next task is to disentangle the seasonal and random components which make up data in column 3 of the table. Each month's figure is now made up of a seasonal and a random element. A seasonal factor for each month of the year can be found by averaging over several years; random factors tend to cancel out when an average is taken. This is best illustrated by example. From Table 10.3 the January figures for each year are obtained

January 1982	1.042
January 1983	1.050
January 1984	1.034

To isolate the seasonal factor for January the average of these figures is taken.

$$\frac{1.042 + 1.050 + 1.034}{3} = 1.042$$

(Since this is a multiplicative model, the geometric mean of the figures should be taken. This would mean calculating the cube root of the product of the three numbers, but this makes very little difference to the answer.)

The seasonal component for January each year is therefore 4.2% and there are zero, positive and negative random errors in 1982, 1983 and 1984, respectively. Similar calculations for the other eleven months show the seasonal

**Table 10.4 Monthly
seasonal factors**

January	1.042
February	1.033
March	1.019
April	1.009
May	0.983
June	0.963
July	0.982
August	0.983
September	1.001
October	0.992
November	0.997
December	1.002

Table 10.5 Seasonally adjusted series

		Original data	Seasonal factor	Adjusted series
1982	January	2,769.0	1.042	2,657.5
	February	2,758.9	1.033	2,669.6
	March	2,725.9	1.019	2,676.0
	April	2,731.6	1.009	2,708.0
	May	2,695.9	0.983	2,743.7
	June	2,670.6	0.963	2,771.8
	July	2,753.2	0.982	2,805.1
	August	2,796.3	0.983	2,843.7
	September	2,862.3	1.001	2,859.2
	October	2,874.8	0.992	2,897.2
	November	2,915.6	0.997	2,923.5
	December	2,966.4	1.002	2,959.7
1983	January	3,087.4	1.042	2,963.1
	February	3,075.6	1.033	2,976.0
	March	3,060.2	1.019	3,004.2
	April	3,035.4	1.009	3,009.2
	May	2,923.7	0.983	2,975.6
	June	2,865.0	0.963	2,973.6
	July	2,905.0	0.982	2,959.7
	August	2,897.8	0.983	2,946.9
	September	2,952.8	1.001	2,949.6
	October	2,925.9	0.992	2,948.7
	November	2,946.7	0,997	2,954.7
	December	2,961.3	1.002	2,954.6
1984	January	3,082.9	1.042	2,958.8
	February	3,080.9	1.033	2,981.1
	March	3,048.0	1.019	2,992.2
	April	3,022.4	1.009	2,996.3
	May	2,980.3	0.983	3,033.2
	June	2,934.5	0.963	3,045.7
	July	3,008.1	0.982	3,064.8
	August	3,025.9	0.983	3,077.2
	September	3,101.7	1.001	3.098.3
	October	3,074.6	0.992	3,098.5
	November	3,094.7	0.997	3,103.1
	December	3,108.1	1.002	3,101.1

The analysis of time series

factors given in Table 10.4. The table shows positive seasonal factors for January to April, September and December each year.

Seasonal adjustment

With the foregoing knowledge the original data can now be seasonally adjusted. Table 10.4 provides the seasonal factors, denoted by S in eqn [10.2]. Dividing the original data by these seasonal factors leaves the trend, cyclical and random components.

$$\frac{X}{S} = T \times C \times R$$

This gives the seasonally adjusted data series and the results of this process are shown in Table 10.5.

Some of the effects noted at the beginning of the chapter can now be observed. In February 1982 the unemployment figure fell from the previous month's total, but the seasonally adjusted figure rose. The reason for this can be seen in the seasonal factors. Unemployment is usually lower in February (seasonal factor 1.033) than January (1.042); the fall in February 1982 is smaller than one would normally expect, so the seasonally adjusted figure rises.

An alternative method for finding the trend

Chapter 9 on regression showed how a straight line could be fitted to a set of data as a means of summarising it. This is another means of smoothing data and finding a trend line. The dependent variable in the regression is unemployment, which is regressed on a time trend variable. This is simply measured 1, 2, 3, . . . 36 and is denoted by the letter t. January 1982 is therefore represented by 1, February 1982 by 2, etc. The regression equation is

$$X_t = a + bt + e_t \qquad\qquad [10.4]$$

where e_t is the error term which, in this case, is composed of the cyclical, seasonal and random elements of the cycle. The calculated regression equation is (calculation not shown)

$$X_t = 2,755.90 + 9.77\ t + e_t \qquad\qquad [10.5]$$
s.e. $\qquad\qquad (1.295)$
$R^2 = 62.6\%$

The trend values for each month can easily be calculated from this equation, by inserting the values $t = 1, 2, 3$, etc. as appropriate. January 1982, for example, is found by substituting $t = 1$ into eqn [10.5], giving

$$2,755.90 + 9.77 \times 1 = 2,765.67$$

For July 1982 ($t = 7$) we obtain

$$2,755.90 + 9.77 \times 7 = 2,824.29$$

which compares with the moving average value of 2,806.6. The two methods give slightly different results, possibly because the true trend is non-linear (see Fig. 10.2) and because the regression method contains less of any cyclical element.

It would be possible to incorporate a non-linear trend into the analysis by using one of the non-linear transformations outlined in Chapter 9. One final point to note is that the regression has the advantage of not losing observations at the beginning and end of the sample period. It is also possible to examine the seasonal component within the regression framework. This is done below, in the section on dummy variables.

Forecasting

It is possible to forecast future levels of unemployment using the methods outlined above. Each component of the series is forecast separately and the results are multiplied together. As an example the level of unemployment for April 1985 will be forecast.

The trend can only be forecast using the regression method, since the moving average method requires future values of unemployment, which is what is being forecast! April 1985 corresponds to time period $t = 40$, so the forecast of the trend by the regression method is

$$T = 2,755.90 + 9.77 \times 40 = 3,146.70$$

The seasonal factor for April is 1.009* (Table 10.4) so the trend figure is multiplied by this, giving

$$3,146.70 \times 1.009 = 3,175.02$$

The cyclical component is ignored and the random component set to a value of 1 (in the multiplicative model, zero in the additive model). This leaves 3,175.02 as the forecast for April 1985. In the event the actual figure was 3,188.90, so the forecast is reasonably accurate. The error is only 0.44% of the predicted value.

Some observations on time-series analysis

The above analysis has taken a fairly mechanical approach to the analysis of time series, and has not sought the reasons why data might vary seasonally. The seasonal adjustment factors are therefore a measure of ignorance as much as of knowledge, so further investigation might be worthwhile and help in the business of forecasting. Some examples will bring this out.

Unemployment varies seasonally because of (among other things) greater

---

* If the regression method were used for establishing the trend, slightly different seasonal factors would have been found. The small difference involved is ignored.

employment opportunities in summer (e.g. deckchair attendants) and school-leavers entering the register in September. The availability of summer jobs might be predictable (based on forecasts of number of tourists, weather, etc.), and the number of school-leavers next year can presumably be predicted by the number of pupils at present in their final year. These sorts of considerations should provide better forecasts rather than blindly following the rules set out above.

Another example of seasonality is company behaviour, which can be influenced by accounting periods and tax rules. A large amount of investment might be observed in the last quarter of a tax year as companies bring forward investment plans to take advantage of tax reliefs. This is especially true when changes to the tax system are introduced. For example, the 1984 Budget changed the rules regarding capital allowances, so that companies could no longer write off 100% of capital investment in the first year. Because the allowances were phased out over a period of three years, it was expected that companies would bring forward their investment plans, leading to a rise in the figures for investment. Knowledge of this sort of behaviour can aid interpretation of the statistics and improve forecasting.

Many time series will exhibit monthly variation simply because the months are of different length. Overseas trade statistics, for example, are first adjusted for the number of working days in each month. Otherwise a lot of time might be spent wondering why exports and imports were regularly lower in February! The unemployment figures analysed above should not suffer from this defect, since they measure a stock of unemployed, rather than a flow.

Another important consideration is whether a series should be adjusted as a whole, or different parts of the series adjusted separately. For example, one could either seasonally adjust the balance of trade deficit, or one could adjust exports and imports separately. The seasonally adjusted trade balance would then be the difference between these two adjusted series. One advantage of the latter method is that different trends and seasonal factors might affect exports and imports, so that the balance of trade figure is a mixture of the two effects. In the official UK trade statistics this approach is adopted and extended. Exports are broken down under 27 different commodity categories, each of which is individually seasonally adjusted, before the (now seasonally adjusted) categories are summed to give seasonally adjusted exports. For imports there are 28 categories. Even this does not exhaust the possibilities, for it could be argued that seasonality is related not to commodity category but to the source or destination country. This would imply disaggregating the statistics by area, seasonally adjusting, and then aggregating again. The disaggregation by commodities method is preferred in the official statistics, but this shows that there is a variety of possible methods which need to be considered.

Dummy variables

Seasonal adjustment can also introduce problems into data analysis as well as resolve them. Although seasonal adjustment can help in interpreting figures, if the adjusted data is then used in further statistical analysis it can mislead. It is well known, for example, that seasonal adjustment can introduce a cyclical component into a data series which originally had no cyclical element to it. This occurs because a large (random) deviation from the trend will enter the moving average process for twelve different months (or whatever is the length of the moving average process), and this tends to turn occasional, random disturbances into a cycle. Note also that the adjusted series will start to rise before the random shock in these circumstances.

The question then arises as to whether adjusted or unadjusted data are best used in, say, regression analysis. Use of unadjusted data means that the coefficient estimates will be contaminated by the seasonal effects; using adjusted data runs into the kind of problem outlined above. The problem can be examined in terms of a fictional demand curve for ice cream sales, based on quarterly sales data. The level of demand will be higher (at any price level) when the temperature is higher. Figure 10.3 illustrates the demand curves.

Figure 10.3 The seasonal demand for ice cream

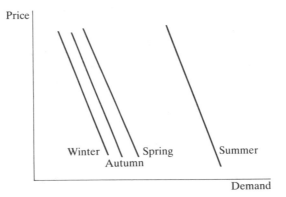

Demand is at its greatest in summer and lowest in winter. One method of estimating the relationship of demand to price would be to use seasonally adjusted sales, which would bring the demand curves closer together. However, this can affect the properties of the regression error term (making the random error terms not independent of each other), which can affect the size of the estimated confidence intervals.

A better method is to use unadjusted data, but to include *dummy variables* into the regression equation, which account for the shifts of the demand curve in different quarters. Suppose quarterly (unadjusted) data for the period 1975:1 to 1985:4 (64 observations) on sales and prices are available. The dummy variable approach would be to estimate the following multiple regressions equation:

$$Y_t = a + bP_t + cZ_{1t} + dZ_{2t} + eZ_{3t} + e_t$$

where

Y_t:	sales in quarter t, in thousands per week
P_t:	price in quarter t

Z_{1t}, Z_{2t}, Z_{3t}: dummy variables
e_t: error term.

The dummy variables take the following form:

Year	Quarter	Z_{1t}	Z_{2t}	Z_{3t}
1975	Spring	1	0	0
	Summer	0	1	0
	Autumn	0	0	1
	Winter	0	0	0
1976	Spring	1	0	0
	Summer	0	1	0
	.	.	.	.
	.	.	.	.
1978	.	.	.	.
	Autumn	0	0	1
	Winter	0	0	0

Thus Z_{1t}, the 'spring' dummy, consists of a one in each spring quarter, zero otherwise. Z_{2t} is the 'summer' dummy, taking the value one in summer, zero otherwise, and Z_{3t} is the autumn dummy. Note that there is no winter dummy: for four quarters only three dummies are required; the number of dummies is always one less than the number of time periods. Thus for monthly data eleven dummies would suffice. The reason for this will become apparent shortly.

Suppose the results of the multiple regression analysis are as follows:

$$Y_t = 10 - 0.2\ P_t + 0.6\ Z_{1t} + 7.2\ Z_{2t} + 0.3\ Z_{3t}$$
$$(\text{s.e.}) \qquad (0.05) \quad (0.4) \qquad (0.3) \qquad (0.5)$$
$$n = 64 \quad R^2 = 0.84$$

How are these results to be interpreted? In the winter quarter, $Z_{1t} = Z_{2t} = Z_{3t} = 0$, so the equation becomes

$$Y_t = 10 - 0.2\ P_t$$

At an average price of 30 pence, predicted sales are 4,000. In the spring quarter, $Z_{1t} = 1$, $Z_{2t} = Z_{3t} = 0$, so the equation is

$$Y_t = 10 - 0.2\ P_t + 0.6$$

which gives predicted sales of 4,600. Similar calculations for summer and autumn give predicted sales of 11,200 and 4,300. Thus the seasonal effects can easily be read off from the dummy variable coefficients. It is also evident why only three dummies were needed, because all seasonal effects are measured *relative* to the winter quarter (the choice of quarter to serve as the basis of comparison is arbitrary).

A further advantage of the regression method is that it allows the significance of the seasonal variance to be established. Apart from price, only the coefficient on the summer dummy, Z_{2t}, is significantly different from zero at the 5% significance level (check this via a hypothesis test). This means that sales in summer are significantly different from sales in winter, but that the autumn and spring sales are much the same as those in winter.

It should be remembered that decomposing a time series is not a clear-cut procedure. It is often difficult to disentangle the separate effects, and different methods will give different results. The seasonally adjusted unemployment figures given in the *Monthly Digest of Statistics* are slightly different from the series calculated here, due to slightly different techniques being applied. The differences are not great and the direction of the seasonal effects is the same even if the sizes are slightly different.

Forecasting the future using time-series techniques is a contentious issue. Much more refined methods than those used above are available, usually relying on techniques of serial correlation (i.e. the correlation between a variable and its own past values). These techniques may be contrasted with the regresssion approach, which tries to predict values of the dependent variable by making use of its relationship to other (explanatory) variables. Thus unemployment would not be forecast without reference to wages, aggregate demand, etc. Simple time-series techniques ignore these relationships, although more advanced techniques would take account of them. The essence of the regression approach is that if economic (or some other) theory suggests some relationship between the variables, and this is not rejected by the data, then this should be incorporated into the forecast. For example, if one time-series analysis forecasts a rise in unemployment and another predicts falling real wages for the same time period, it is unlikely that both forecasts are correct. It would be better to forecast both variables simultaneously, incorporating the constraint that there is a negative relationship between unemployment and real wages.

The debate between the two approaches will no doubt continue. We end here with a warning about extrapolating a trend too far into the future. The time-series forecast (using the data and results obtained above) for unemployment in January 2000 is 5.081 million. We must surely hope that this is wrong . . .

Problems

10.1 The index number series below gives figures for retail sales by electrical and musical goods retailers for the years 1981–5 (data from the *Monthly Digest of Statistics*, various issues).

	1981	1982	1983	1984	1985
Q1	99	105	126	134	141
Q2	86	93	110	113	122
Q3	101	114	125	129	139
Q4	137	159	176	190	207

(a) Use both the regression and moving averages method to decompose the series into its trend, seasonal and random components, using the additive model.

(b) Are there any important seasonal effects? What do you think these might be due to? Do the sizes of these effects differ according to the two types of decomposition?

(c) Predict the level of sales for the first quarter of 1986. You will have to use the regression trend line for this.

10.2 The following data give quarterly figures for energy consumption, 1979:1 to 1982:4, measured in million tons coal equivalent (source: *Economic Trends Annual Supplement*, 1986).

	1979	1980	1981	1982
Q1	107.6	100.1	91.9	92.7
Q2	83.0	75.9	72.0	70.4
Q3	71.3	65.6	63.3	63.0
Q4	93.8	87.1	90.0	85.7

$$\Sigma X = 1{,}313.4 \quad \Sigma t = 136 \quad \Sigma Xt = 10{,}804.9$$
$$\Sigma X^2 = 110{,}618.9 \quad \Sigma t^2 = 1{,}496$$

(a) What trend and/or seasonal effects appear to be present?

(b) Fit a trend line to the data using the regression method (the sums of squares and cross-products are given for this purpose). Is the trend statistically significant? Why might a trend exist?

(c) Use the trend line to calculate seasonal factors (using the additive model). What seasonal factors are present and what reasons for their existence can you think of?

(d) Use the seasonal factors to seasonally adjust the data. Compare the original and adjusted series.

(e) Predict consumption in the first quarter of 1983.

If you have access to a computer statistical package, the following exercise can be attempted.

(f) Fit a regression equation to the data using a time trend and a set of seasonal dummy variables.

(g) Compare the estimate of the trend coefficient (and its standard error) with that found in (b) above. Account for any differences.

(h) Are there any significant seasonal effects?

(i) Predict consumption for the first quarter of 1983. How does this compare with your earlier prediction?

10.3 What trend cycle and seasonal components would you expect to observe in the following data series?

(a) Weekly attendance at league football matches.
(b) A firm's profits over a series of years.
(c) The number of visitors to a museum.
(d) Newspaper readership.

10.4 This problem requires the use of a computer. A consumption function is to be estimated on quarterly data for the period 1980:1 to 1984:4, relating real consumers' expenditure to real personal disposable income. The data are as follows:

Quarter	Consumption	Income
1980:1	33,976	40,095
1980:2	33,178	39,951
1980:3	34,468	40,705
1980:4	35,373	40,434
1981:1	33,219	39,947
1981:2	33,294	39,108
1981:3	34,437	39,214
1981:4	35,648	38,994
1982:1	32,914	39,282
1982:2	33,229	39,006
1982:3	34,856	39,608
1982:4	36,615	39,668
1983:1	34,132	39,181
1983:2	34,581	40,071
1983:3	36,460	40,778
1983:4	37,901	41,289
1984:1	34,896	40,211
1984:2	35,469	40,888
1984:3	36,463	40,954
1984:4	38,627	42,717

(a) Regress consumption expenditure on income. Does the resulting equation seem satisfactory? What is the marginal propensity to consume (i.e. the increase in consumption for a unit increase in income)?
(b) Graph the data to see if there appear to be any seasonal variation to the data. What do you observe?
(c) Regress consumption on income and a set of dummy variables to represent the quarters of the year. Does this seem to be a better model of consumption behaviour? What is the new estimate of the marginal propensity to consume? How has the estimated standard error of this changed, and why?

Appendix: Tables

Table A1 Random number table

This table contains 1000 random numbers within the range 0–99. Each number within the range has an equal probability of occurrence. The range may be extended by combining successive entries in the table. Thus 7,399 becomes the first of 500 random numbers in the range 0–99. To obtain a sample of random numbers, choose an arbitrary starting point in the table and go down the columns collecting successive values until the required sample is obtained. If the population has been numbered, this method can be used to select a random sample from the population. Alternatively, the method can simulate sampling experiments such as the tossing of a coin (an even number representing a head and an odd number a tail).

73	23	41	53	38	87	71	79	3	55	24	7	7	17	19	70
99	13	91	13	90	72	84	15	64	90	56	68	38	40	73	78
97	16	58	2	67	3	92	83	50	53	59	60	33	75	44	95
73	10	29	14	9	92	35	47	21	47	82	25	71	68	87	53
99	79	29	68	44	90	65	33	55	85	7	57	77	84	83	5
71	97	98	60	62	18	49	80	4	51	8	74	81	64	29	45
41	26	41	30	82	38	52	81	89	64	17	10	49	28	72	99
60	87	77	81	91	57	6	1	30	47	93	82	81	67	4	3
95	84	74	92	15	10	37	52	8	10	96	38	69	9	65	41
59	19	2	61	40	67	80	25	31	18	1	36	54	31	100	27
35	3	54	83	62	28	21	23	91	46	73	85	11	63	63	49
66	18	31	17	72	15	8	46	10	3	64	22	100	62	85	16
3	4	42	8	4	6	40	73	97	0	37	34	91	56	48	98
28	20	23	98	86	41	41	13	53	61	16	92	95	31	79	36
74	49	86	5	74	82	12	58	80	14	94	4	88	95	9	32
80	80	2	47	91	100	76	84	0	57	17	69	87	29	52	39
65	67	0	39	11	10	54	80	74	56	55	91	94	52	32	18
67	44	89	50	7	73	70	52	18	28	89	43	54	60	20	10
48	33	61	66	2	71	74	91	31	45	63	2	97	62	30	90
3	18	54	19	17	87	3	91	41	64	78	10	99	24	1	20

Table A1 continued

69	35	12	53	97	30	96	69	59	55	65	64	30	3	100	17
15	0	33	86	93	73	52	57	77	77	83	10	64	54	85	18
87	79	51	68	5	23	50	15	68	67	14	59	42	61	83	2
69	52	34	86	34	34	78	51	48	65	57	91	8	74	72	36
11	1	11	43	51	85	6	47	72	43	34	54	20	56	31	81
59	14	78	32	94	24	19	44	16	49	65	16	30	86	0	65
18	86	62	47	96	46	73	67	79	40	45	82	96	61	34	60
99	63	2	81	58	93	81	37	53	20	64	87	3	27	19	55
34	55	14	29	10	59	7	69	13	8	54	97	56	7	57	16
88	90	6	98	32	55	37	17	35	93	31	66	67	84	15	14
78	30	30	78	41	59	79	77	21	89	76	59	30	9	64	9
67	10	37	14	62	3	85	2	16	74	40	85	30	83	29	5
93	50	83	76	42	86	92	41	27	73	31	70	25	40	11	88
35	68	98	18	67	22	95	34	19	27	21	90	66	20	32	48
32	52	29	78	68	96	94	44	38	95	27	85	53	76	63	78
92	100	75	77	26	39	61	33	88	66	77	76	25	67	90	1
40	73	28	5	50	73	92	32	82	23	78	30	26	52	28	94
57	41	64	50	78	35	12	60	25	4	5	82	82	57	68	43
82	41	67	79	30	43	15	72	98	48	6	22	46	92	43	41
100	11	21	44	43	51	76	89	4	90	48	31	19	89	97	45
94	8	20	67	32	42	39	6	38	25	97	10	18	85	9	60
21	59	27	39	13	81	2	47	83	12	17	54	84	68	56	29
63	62	36	6	57	96	6	36	24	13	70	32	90	92	81	86
91	42	57	99	55	31	58	21	21	65	70	4	37	28	59	9
91	27	61	86	36	57	11	35	92	15	79	30	19	85	39	49
97	39	12	28	35	37	90	93	88	20	99	76	81	61	95	70
64	89	32	80	9	66	73	71	84	69	70	12	10	56	59	56
45	34	1	32	80	99	39	52	25	87	76	91	22	26	46	67
21	65	14	1	78	35	35	63	21	66	34	3	47	51	24	37
85	64	69	93	47	82	55	87	22	56	53	85	43	66	23	66
21	37	62	29	44	39	4	4	99	3	6	82	67	53	14	0
23	8	62	9	19	31	81	92	63	10	65	78	79	96	65	33
84	14	92	85	9	16	51	70	26	60	7	7	55	66	5	51
70	37	11	7	93	63	48	12	35	95	32	5	64	5	63	28
80	27	32	92	81	27	55	98	71	22	66	64	78	79	34	73
66	13	16	48	74	51	78	83	42	31	97	72	25	75	34	40
1	51	47	84	82	27	77	40	99	13	66	52	56	27	2	19
84	26	0	38	55	30	45	80	50	20	17	78	87	4	88	86
95	28	57	33	51	39	18	12	37	100	89	63	22	50	10	22
45	76	48	43	18	24	19	1	65	93	16	48	8	60	32	76

Table A2 The standard Normal distribution

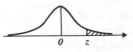

z	0.00	0.01	0.02	0.03	0.04	0.05	0.06	0.07	0.08	0.09
0.0	.5000	.4960	.4920	.4880	.4840	.4801	.4761	.4721	.4681	.4641
0.1	.4602	.4562	.4522	.4483	.4443	.4404	.4364	.4325	.4286	.4247
0.2	.4207	.4168	.4129	.4090	.4052	.4013	.3974	.3936	.3897	.3859
0.3	.3821	.3783	.3745	.3707	.3669	.3632	.3594	.3557	.3520	.3483
0.4	.3446	.3409	.3372	.3336	.3300	.3264	.3228	.3192	.3156	.3121
0.5	.3085	.3050	.3015	.2981	.2946	.2912	.2877	.2843	.2810	.2776
0.6	.2743	.2709	.2676	.2643	.2611	.2578	.2546	.2514	.2483	.2451
0.7	.2420	.2389	.2358	.2327	.2296	.2266	.2236	.2206	.2177	.2148
0.8	.2119	.2090	.2061	.2033	.2005	.1977	.1949	.1922	.1894	.1867
0.9	.1841	.1814	.1788	.1762	.1736	.1711	.1685	.1660	.1635	.1611
1.0	.1587	.1562	.1539	.1515	.1492	.1469	.1446	.1423	.1401	.1379
1.1	.1357	.1335	.1314	.1292	.1271	.1251	.1230	.1210	.1190	.1170
1.2	.1151	.1131	.1112	.1093	.1075	.1056	.1038	.1020	.1003	.0985
1.3	.0968	.0951	.0934	.0918	.0901	.0885	.0869	.0853	.0838	.0823
1.4	.0808	.0793	.0778	.0764	.0749	.0735	.0721	.0708	.0694	.0681
1.5	.0668	.0655	.0643	.0630	.0618	.0606	.0594	.0582	.0571	.0559
1.6	.0548	.0537	.0526	.0516	.0505	.0495	.0485	.0475	.0465	.0455
1.7	.0446	.0436	.0427	.0418	.0409	.0401	.0392	.0384	.0375	.0367
1.8	.0359	.0351	.0344	.0336	.0329	.0322	.0314	.0307	.0301	.0294
1.9	.0287	.0281	.0274	.0268	.0262	.0256	.0250	.0244	.0239	.0233
2.0	.0228	.0222	.0217	.0212	.0207	.0202	.0197	.0192	.0188	.0183
2.1	.0179	.0174	.0170	.0166	.0162	.0158	.0154	.0150	.0146	.0143
2.2	.0139	.0136	.0132	.0129	.0125	.0122	.0119	.0116	.0113	.0110
2.3	.0107	.0104	.0102	.0099	.0096	.0094	.0091	.0089	.0087	.0084
2.4	.0082	.0080	.0078	.0075	.0073	.0071	.0069	.0068	.0066	.0064
2.5	.0062	.0060	.0059	.0057	.0055	.0054	.0052	.0051	.0049	.0048
2.6	.0047	.0045	.0044	.0043	.0041	.0040	.0039	.0038	.0037	.0036
2.7	.0035	.0034	.0033	.0032	.0031	.0030	.0029	.0028	.0027	.0026
2.8	.0026	.0025	.0024	.0023	.0023	.0022	.0021	.0021	.0020	.0019
2.9	.0019	.0018	.0018	.0017	.0016	.0016	.0015	.0015	.0014	.0014
3.0	.0013	.0013	.0013	.0012	.0012	.0011	.0011	.0011	.0010	.0010

Source: *Economic statistics and Econometrics*, 1968

Table A3 Percentage points of the *t* distribution

The table gives critical values of the *t* distribution cutting off an area α in each tail, shown by the top row of the table.

Area (α) in each tail

ν	0.4	0.25	0.1	0.05	0.025	0.01	0.005	0.0025	0.001	0.0005
1	0.325	1.000	3.078	6.314	12.706	31.821	63.657	127.320	318.310	636.620
2	0.289	0.816	1.886	2.920	4.303	6.965	9.925	14.089	22.327	31.598
3	0.277	0.765	1.638	2.353	3.182	4.541	5.841	7.453	10.214	12.924
4	0.271	0.741	1.533	2.132	2.776	3.747	4.604	5.598	7.173	8.610
5	0.267	0.727	1.476	2.015	2.571	3.365	4.032	4.773	5.893	6.869
6	0.265	0.718	1.440	1.943	2.447	3.143	3.707	4.317	5.208	5.959
7	0.263	0.711	1.415	1.895	2.365	2.998	3.499	4.029	4.785	5.408
8	0.262	0.706	1.397	1.860	2.306	2.896	3.355	3.833	4.501	5.041
9	0.261	0.703	1.383	1.833	2.262	2.821	3.250	3.690	4.297	4.781
10	0.260	0.700	1.372	1.812	2.228	2.764	3.169	3.581	4.144	4.587
11	0.260	0.697	1.363	1.796	2.201	2.718	3.106	3.497	4.025	4.437
12	0.259	0.695	1.356	1.782	2.179	2.681	3.055	3.428	3.930	4.318
13	0.259	0.694	1.350	1.771	2.160	2.650	3.012	3.372	3.852	4.221
14	0.258	0.692	1.345	1.761	2.145	2.624	2.977	3.326	3.787	4.140
15	0.258	0.691	1.341	1.753	2.131	2.602	2.947	3.286	3.733	4.073
16	0.258	0.690	1.337	1.746	2.120	2.583	2.921	3.252	3.686	4.015
17	0.257	0.689	1.333	1.740	2.110	2.567	2.898	3.222	3.646	3.965
18	0.257	0.688	1.330	1.734	2.101	2.552	2.878	3.197	3.610	3.922
19	0.257	0.688	1.328	1.729	2.093	2.539	2.861	3.174	3.579	3.883
20	0.257	0.687	1.325	1.725	2.086	2.528	2.845	3.153	3.552	3.850
21	0.257	0.686	1.323	1.721	2.086	2.518	2.831	3.135	3.527	3.819
22	0.256	0.686	1.321	1.717	2.074	2.508	2.819	3.119	3.505	3.792
23	0.256	0.685	1.319	1.714	2.069	2.500	2.807	3.104	3.485	3.767
24	0.256	0.685	1.318	1.711	2.064	2.492	2.797	3.091	3.467	3.745
25	0.256	0.684	1.316	1.708	2.060	2.485	2.787	3.078	3.450	3.725
26	0.256	0.684	1.315	1.706	2.056	2.479	2.779	3.067	3.435	3.707
27	0.256	0.684	1.314	1.703	2.052	2.473	2.771	3.057	3.421	3.690
28	0.256	0.683	1.313	1.701	2.048	2.467	2.763	3.047	3.408	3.674
29	0.256	0.683	1.311	1.699	2.045	2.462	2.756	3.038	3.396	3.659
30	0.256	0.683	1.310	1.697	2.042	2.457	2.750	3.030	3.385	3.646
40	0.255	0.681	1.303	1.684	2.021	2.423	2.704	2.971	3.307	3.551
60	0.254	0.679	1.296	1.671	2.000	2.390	2.660	2.915	3.232	3.460
120	0.254	0.677	1.289	1.658	1.980	2.358	2.617	2.860	3.160	3.373
∞	0.253	0.674	1.282	1.645	1.960	2.326	2.576	2.807	3.090	3.291

Table A4 Critical values of the χ^2 distribution

The values in the table give the critical
values of χ^2 which cut off the area in the
right-hand tail given at the top of the
column.

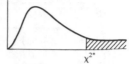

χ^{2*}

Area in right-hand tail

ν	0.995	0.990	0.975	0.950	0.900	0.750	0.500
1	392704.10^{-10}	157088.10^{-9}	982069.10^{-9}	393214.10^{-8}	0.0157908	0.1015308	0.454936
2	0.0100251	0.0201007	0.0506356	0.102587	0.210721	0.575364	1.38629
3	0.0717218	0.114832	0.215795	0.351846	0.584374	1.212534	2.36597
4	0.206989	0.297109	0.484419	0.710723	1.063623	1.92256	3.35669
5	0.411742	0.554298	0.831212	1.145476	1.61031	2.67460	4.35146
6	0.675727	0.872090	1.23734	1.63538	2.20413	3.45460	5.34812
7	0.989256	1.239043	1.68987	2.16735	2.83311	4.25485	6.34581
8	1.34441	1.64650	2.17973	2.73264	3.48954	5.07064	7.34412
9	1.73493	2.08790	2.70039	3.32511	4.16816	5.89883	8.34283
10	2.15586	2.55821	3.24697	3.94030	4.86518	6.73720	9.34182
11	2.60322	3.05348	3.81575	4.57481	5.57778	7.58414	10.3410
12	3.07382	3.57057	4.40379	5.22603	6.30380	8.43842	11.3403
13	3.56503	4.10692	5.00875	5.89186	7.04150	9.29907	12.3398
14	4.07467	4.66043	5.62873	6.57063	7.78953	10.1653	13.3393
15	4.60092	5.22935	6.26214	7.26094	8.54676	11.0365	14.3389
16	5.14221	5.81221	6.90766	7.96165	9.31224	11.9122	15.3385
17	5.69722	6.40776	7.56419	8.67176	10.0852	12.7919	16.3382
18	6.26480	7.01491	8.23075	9.39046	10.8649	13.6753	17.3379
19	6.84397	7.63273	8.90652	10.1170	11.6509	14.5620	18.3377
20	7.43384	8.26040	9.59078	10.8508	12.4426	15.4518	19.3374
21	8.03365	8.89720	10.28293	11.5913	13.2396	16.3444	20.3372
22	8.64272	9.54249	10.9823	12.3380	14.0415	17.2396	21.3370
23	9.26043	10.19567	11.6886	13.0905	14.8480	18.1373	22.3369
24	9.88623	10.8564	12.4012	13.8484	15.6587	19.0373	23.3367
25	10.5197	11.5240	13.1197	14.6114	16.4734	19.9393	24.3266
26	11.1602	12.1981	13.8439	15.3792	17.2919	20.8434	25.3365
27	11.8076	12.8785	14.5734	16.1514	18.1139	21.7494	26.3363
28	12.4613	13.5647	15.3079	16.9279	18.9392	22.6572	27.3362
29	13.1211	14.2565	16.0471	17.7084	19.7677	23.5666	28.3361
30	13.7867	14.9535	16.7908	18.4927	20.5992	24.4776	29.3360
40	20.7065	22.1643	24.4330	26.5093	29.0505	33.6603	39.3353
50	27.9907	29.7067	32.3574	34.7643	37.6886	42.9421	49.3349
60	35.5345	37.4849	40.4817	43.1880	46.4589	52.2938	59.3347
70	43.2752	45.4417	48.7576	51.7393	55.3289	61.6983	69.3345
80	51.1719	53.5401	57.1532	60.3915	64.2778	71.1445	79.3343
90	59.1963	61.7541	65.6466	69.1260	73.2911	80.6247	89.3342
100	67.3276	70.0649	74.2219	77.9295	82.3581	90.1332	99.3341

See p. 184 for a full explanation of the use of this table.

Table A4 continued

ν	.250	0.100	0.050	0.025	0.010	0.005	0.001
1	1.32330	2.70554	3.84146	5.02389	6.63490	7.87944	10.828
2	2.77259	4.60517	5.99146	7.37776	9.21034	10.5966	13.816
3	4.10834	6.25139	7.81473	9.34840	11.3449	12.8382	16.266
4	5.38527	7.77944	9.48773	11.1433	13.2767	14.8603	18.467
5	6.62568	9.23636	11.0705	12.8325	15.0863	16.7496	20.515
6	7.84080	10.6446	12.5916	14.4494	16.8119	18.5476	22.458
7	9.03715	12.0170	14.0671	16.0128	18.4753	20.2777	24.322
8	10.2189	13.3616	15.5073	17.5345	20.0902	21.9550	26.125
9	11.3888	14.6837	16.9190	19.0228	21.6660	23.5894	27.877
10	12.5489	15.9872	18.3070	20.4832	23.2093	25.1882	29.588
11	13.7007	17.2750	19.6751	21.9200	24.7250	26.7568	31.264
12	14.8454	18.5493	21.0261	23.3367	26.2170	28.2995	32.909
13	15.9839	19.8119	22.3620	24.7356	27.6882	29.8195	34.528
14	17.1169	21.0641	23.6848	26.1189	29.1412	31.3194	36.123
15	18.2451	22.3071	24.9958	27.4884	30.5779	32.8013	37.697
16	19.3689	23.5418	26.2962	28.8454	31.9999	34.2672	29.252
17	20.4887	24.7690	27.5871	30.1910	33.4087	35.7185	40.790
18	21.6049	25.9894	28.8693	31.5264	34.8053	37.1565	42.312
19	22.7178	27.2036	30.1435	32.8523	36.1909	38.5823	43.820
20	23.8277	28.4120	31.4104	34.1696	37.5662	39.9968	45.315
21	24.9348	29.6151	32.6706	35.4789	38.9322	41.4011	46.797
22	26–0393	30.8133	33.9244	36.7807	40.2894	42.7957	48.268
23	27.1413	32.0069	35.1725	38.0756	41.6384	44.1813	49.728
24	28.2412	33.1962	36.4150	39.3641	42.9798	45.5585	51.179
25	29.3389	34.3816	37.6525	40.6465	44.3141	46.9279	52.618
26	30.4346	35.5632	38.8851	41.9232	45.6417	48.2899	54.052
27	31.5284	36.7412	40.1133	43.1945	46.9629	49.6449	55.476
28	32.6205	37.9150	41.3371	44.4608	48.2782	50.9934	56.892
29	33.7109	39.0875	42.5570	45.7223	49.5879	52.3356	58.301
30	34.7997	40.2560	43.7730	46.9792	50.8922	53.6720	59.703
40	45.6160	51.8051	55.7585	59.3417	63.6907	66.7660	73.402
50	56.3336	63.1671	67.5048	71.4202	76.1539	79.4900	86.661
60	66.9815	74.3970	79.0819	83.2977	88.3794	91.9517	99.607
70	77.5767	85.5270	90.5312	95.0232	100.425	104.215	112.317
80	88.1303	96.5782	101.879	106.629	112.329	116.321	124.839
90	98.6499	107.565	113.145	118.136	124.116	128.299	137.208
100	109.141	118.498	124.342	129.561	135.807	140.169	149.449

Table A5(a) Critical values of the *F* distribution (upper 5% points)

The entries in the table give the critical
values of *F* cutting off 5% in the right-hand
tail of the distribution. v_1 gives the degrees
of freedom in the numerator, v_2 those in the
denominator.

v_2 \ v_1	1	2	3	4	5	6	7	8	9
1	161.45	199.50	215.71	224.58	230.16	230.99	236.77	238.88	240.54
2	18.513	19.000	19.164	19.247	19.296	19.330	19.353	19.371	19.385
3	10.128	9.5521	9.2766	9.1172	9.0135	8.9406	8.8867	8.8452	8.8123
4	7.7086	6.9443	6.5914	6.3882	6.2561	6.1631	6.0942	6.0410	5.9988
5	6.6079	5.7861	5.4095	5.1922	5.0503	4.9503	4.8759	4.8183	4.7725
6	5.9874	5.1433	4.7571	4.5337	4.3874	4.2839	4.2067	4.1468	4.0990
7	5.5914	4.7374	4.3468	4.1203	3.9715	3.8660	3.7870	3.7257	3.6767
8	5.3177	4.4590	4.0662	3.8379	3.6875	3.5806	3.5005	3.4381	3.3881
9	5.1174	4.2565	3.8625	3.6331	3.4817	3.3738	3.2927	3.2296	3.1789
10	4.9646	4.1028	3.7083	3.4780	3.3258	3.2172	3.1355	3.0717	3.0204
11	4.8443	3.9823	3.5874	3.3567	3.2039	3.0946	3.0123	2.9480	2.8962
12	4.7472	3.8853	3.4903	3.2592	3.1059	2.9961	2.9134	2.8486	2.7964
13	4.6672	3.8056	3.4105	3.1791	3.0254	2.9153	2.8321	2.7669	2.7144
14	4.6001	3.7389	3.3439	3.1122	2.9582	2.8477	2.7642	2.6987	2.6458
15	4.5431	3.6823	3.2874	3.0556	2.9013	2.7905	2.7066	2.6408	2.5876
16	4.4940	3.6337	3.2389	3.0069	2.8524	2.7413	2.6572	2.5911	2.5377
17	4.4513	3.5915	3.1968	2.9647	2.8100	2.6987	2.6143	2.5480	2.4943
18	4.4139	3.5546	3.1599	2.9277	2.7729	2.6613	2.5767	2.5102	2.4563
19	4.3807	3.5219	3.1274	2.8951	2.7401	2.6283	2.5435	2.4768	2.4227
20	4.3512	3.4928	2.0984	2.8661	2.7109	2.5990	2.5140	2.4471	2.3928
21	4.3248	3.4668	3.0725	2.8401	2.6848	2.5727	2.4876	2.4205	2.3660
22	4.3009	3.4434	3.0491	2.8167	2.6613	2.5491	2.4638	2.3965	2.3419
23	4.2793	3.4221	3.0280	2.7955	2.6400	2.5277	2.4422	2.3748	2.3201
24	4.2597	3.4028	3.0088	2.7763	2.6307	2.5082	2.4226	2.3551	2.3002
25	4.2417	3.3852	2.9912	2.7587	2.6030	2.4904	2.4047	2.3371	2.2821
26	4.2252	3.3690	2.9752	2.7426	2.5868	2.4741	2.3883	2.3205	2.2655
27	4.2100	3.3541	2.9604	2.7278	2.5719	2.4591	2.3732	2.3053	2.2501
28	4.1960	3.3404	2.9467	2.7141	2.5581	2.4453	2.3593	2.2913	2.2360
29	4.1830	3.3277	2.9340	2.7014	2.5454	2.4324	2.3463	2.2783	2.2229
30	4.1709	3.3158	2.9223	2.6896	2.5336	2.4205	2.3343	2.2662	2.2107
40	4.0847	3.2317	2.8387	2.6060	2.4495	2.3359	2.2490	2.1802	2.1240
60	4.0012	3.1504	2.7581	2.5252	2.3683	2.2541	2.1665	2.0970	2.0401
120	3.9201	3.0718	2.6802	2.4472	2.2899	2.1750	2.0868	2.0164	1.9588
∞	3.8415	2.9957	2.6049	2.3719	2.2141	2.0986	2.0096	1.9384	1.8799

253

Table A5(a) continued

v_1 / v_2	10	12	15	20	24	30	40	60	120	∞
1	241.88	243.91	245.95	248.01	249.05	250.10	251.14	252.20	253.25	254.31
2	19.396	19.413	19.429	19.446	19.454	19.462	19.471	19.479	19.487	19.496
3	8.7855	8.7446	8.7029	8.6602	8.6385	8.6166	8.5944	8.5720	8.5494	8.5264
4	5.9644	5.9117	5.8578	5.8025	5.7744	5.7459	5.7170	5.6877	5.6581	5.6281
5	4.7351	4.6777	4.6188	4.5581	4.5272	4.4957	4.4638	4.4314	4.3985	4.3650
6	4.0600	3.9999	3.9381	3.8742	3.8415	3.8082	3.7743	3.7398	3.7047	3.6689
7	3.6365	3.5747	3.5107	3.4445	3.4105	3.3758	3.3404	3.3043	3.2674	3.2298
8	3.3472	3.2839	3.2184	3.1503	3.1152	3.0794	3.0428	3.0053	2.9669	2.9276
9	3.1373	3.0729	3.0061	2.9365	2.9005	2.8637	2.8259	2.7872	2.7475	2.7067
10	2.9782	2.9130	2.8450	2.7740	2.7372	2.6996	2.6609	2.6211	2.5801	2.5379
11	2.8536	2.7876	2.7186	2.6464	2.6090	2.5705	2.5309	2.4901	2.4480	2.4045
12	2.7534	2.6866	2.6169	2.5436	2.5055	2.4663	2.4259	2.3842	2.3410	2.2962
13	2.6710	2.6037	2.5331	2.4589	2.4202	2.3803	2.3392	2.2966	2.2524	2.2064
14	2.6022	2.5342	2.4630	2.3879	2.3487	2.3082	2.2664	2.2229	2.1778	2.1307
15	2.5437	2.4753	2.4034	2.3275	2.2878	2.2468	2.2043	2.1601	2.1141	2.0658
16	2.4935	2.4247	2.3522	2.2756	2.2354	2.1938	2.1507	2.1058	2.0589	2.0096
17	2.4499	2.3807	2.3077	2.2304	2.1898	2.1477	2.1040	2.0584	2.0107	1.9604
18	2.4117	2.3421	2.2686	2.1906	2.1497	2.1071	2.0629	2.0166	1.9681	1.9168
19	2.3779	2.3080	2.2341	2.1555	2.1141	2.0712	2.0264	1.9795	1.9302	1.8780
20	2.3479	2.2776	2.2033	2.1242	2.0825	2.0391	1.9938	1.9464	1.8963	1.8432
21	2.3210	2.2504	2.1757	2.0960	2.0540	2.0102	1.9645	1.9165	1.8657	1.8117
22	2.2967	2.2258	2.1508	2.0707	2.0283	1.9842	1.9380	1.8894	1.8380	1.7831
23	2.2747	2.2036	2.1282	2.0476	2.0050	1.9605	1.9139	1.8648	1.8128	1.7570
24	2.2547	2.1834	2.1077	2.0267	1.9838	1.9390	1.8920	1.8424	1.7896	1.7330
25	2.2365	2.1649	2.0889	2.0075	1.9643	1.9192	1.8718	1.8217	1.7684	1.7110
26	2.2197	2.1479	2.0716	1.9898	1.9464	1.9010	1.8533	1.8027	1.7488	1.6906
27	2.2043	2.1323	2.0558	1.9736	1.9299	1.8842	1.8361	1.7851	1.7306	1.6717
28	2.1900	2.1179	2.0411	1.9586	1.9147	1.8687	1.8203	1.7689	1.7138	1.6541
29	2.1768	2.1045	2.0275	1.9446	1.9005	1.8543	1.8055	1.7537	1.6981	1.6376
30	2.1646	2.0921	2.0148	1.9317	1.8874	1.8409	1.7918	1.7396	1.6835	1.6223
40	2.0772	2.0035	1.9245	1.8389	1.7929	1.7444	1.6928	1.6373	1.5766	1.5089
60	1.9926	1.9174	1.8364	1.7480	1.7001	1.6491	1.5943	1.5343	1.4673	1.3893
120	1.9105	1.8337	1.7505	1.6587	1.6084	1.5543	1.4952	1.4290	1.3519	1.2539
∞	1.8307	1.7522	1.6664	1.5705	1.5173	1.4591	1.3940	1.3180	1.2214	1.0000

Table A5(b) Critical values of the *F* distribution (upper 2.5% points)

The entries in the table give the critical values of *F* cutting off 2.5% in the right-hand tail of the distribution. v_1 gives the degrees of freedom in the numerator, v_2 in the denominator.

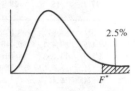

v_1 v_2	1	2	3	4	5	6	7	8	9
1	647.79	799.50	864.16	899.58	921.85	937.11	948.22	956.66	963.28
2	38.506	39.000	39.165	39.248	39.298	39.331	39.355	39.373	39.387
3	17.443	16.044	15.439	15.101	14.885	14.735	14.624	14.540	14.473
4	12.218	10.649	9.9792	9.6045	9.3645	9.1973	9.0741	8.9796	8.9047
5	10.007	8.4336	7.7636	7.3879	7.1464	6.9777	6.8531	6.7572	6.6811
6	8.8131	7.2599	6.5988	6.2272	5.9876	5.8198	5.6955	5.5996	5.5234
7	8.0727	6.5415	5.8898	5.5226	5.2852	5.1186	4.9949	4.8993	4.8232
8	7.5709	6.0595	5.4160	5.0526	4.8173	4.6517	4.5286	4.4333	4.3572
9	7.2093	5.7147	5.0781	4.7181	4.4844	4.3197	4.1970	4.1020	4.0260
10	6.9367	5.4564	4.8256	4.4683	4.2361	4.0721	3.9498	3.8549	3.7790
11	6.7241	5.2559	4.6300	4.2751	4.0440	3.8807	3.7586	3.6638	3.5879
12	6.5538	5.0959	4.4742	4.1212	3.8911	3.7283	3.6065	3.5118	3.4358
13	6.4143	4.9653	4.3472	3.9959	3.7667	3.6043	3.4827	3.3880	3.3120
14	6.2979	4.8567	4.2417	3.8919	3.6634	3.5014	3.3799	3.2853	3.2093
15	6.1995	4.7650	4.1528	3.8043	3.5764	3.4147	3.2934	3.1987	3.1227
16	6.1151	4.6867	4.0768	3.7294	3.5021	3.3406	3.2194	3.1248	3.0488
17	6.0420	4.6189	4.0112	3.6648	3.4379	3.2767	3.1556	3.0610	2.9849
18	5.9781	4.5597	3.9539	3.6083	3.3820	3.2209	3.0999	3.0053	2.9219
19	5.9216	4.5075	3.9034	3.5587	3.3327	3.1718	3.0509	2.9563	2.8801
20	5.8715	4.4613	3.8587	3.5147	3.2891	3.1283	3.0074	2.9128	2.8365
21	5.8266	4.4199	3.8188	3.4754	3.2501	3.0895	2.9686	2.8740	2.7977
22	5.7863	4.3828	3.7829	3.4401	3.2151	3.0546	2.9338	2.8392	2.7628
23	5.7498	4.3492	3.7505	3.4083	3.1835	3.0232	2.9023	2.8077	2.7313
24	5.7166	4.3187	3.7211	3.3794	3.1548	2.9946	2.8738	2.7791	2.7027
25	5.6864	4.2909	3.6943	3.3530	3.1287	2.9685	2.8478	2.7531	2.6766
26	5.6586	4.2655	3.6697	3.3289	3.1048	2.9447	2.8240	2.7293	2.6528
27	5.6331	4.2421	3.6472	3.3067	3.0828	2.9228	2.8021	2.7074	2.6309
28	5.6096	4.2205	3.6264	3.2863	3.0626	2.9027	2.7820	2.6872	2.6106
29	5.5878	4.2006	3.6072	3.2674	3.0438	2.8840	2.7633	2.6686	2.5919
30	5.5675	4.1821	3.5894	3.2499	3.0265	2.8667	2.7460	2.6513	2.5746
40	5.4239	4.0510	3.4633	3.1261	2.9037	2.7444	2.6238	2.5289	2.4519
60	5.2856	3.9253	3.3425	3.0077	2.7863	2.6274	2.5068	2.4117	2.3344
120	5.1523	3.8046	3.2269	2.8943	2.6740	2.5154	2.3948	2.2994	2.2217
∞	5.0239	3.6889	3.1161	2.7858	2.5665	2.4082	2.2875	2.1918	2.1136

Table A5(b) continued

ν_1 / ν_2	10	12	15	20	24	30	40	60	120	∞
1	968.63	976.71	984.87	993.10	997.25	1001.4	1005.6	1009.8	1014.0	1018.3
2	39.398	39.415	39.431	39.448	39.456	39.465	39.473	39.481	39.400	39.498
3	14.419	14.337	14.253	14.167	14.124	14.081	14.037	13.992	13.947	13.902
4	8.8439	8.7512	8.6565	8.5599	8.5109	8.4613	8.4111	8.3604	8.3092	8.2573
5	6.6192	6.5245	6.4277	6.3286	6.2780	6.2269	6.1750	6.1225	6.069?	6.0153
6	5.4613	5.3662	5.2687	5.1684	5.1172	5.0652	5.0125	4.9589	4.9044	4.8491
7	4.7611	4.6658	4.5678	4.4667	4.4150	4.3624	4.3089	4.2544	4.1989	4.1423
8	4.2951	4.1997	4.1012	3.9995	3.9472	3.8940	3.8398	3.7844	3.7279	3.6702
9	3.9639	3.8682	3.7694	3.6669	3.6142	3.5604	3.5055	3.4493	3.3918	3.3329
10	3.7168	3.6209	3.5217	3.4185	3.3654	3.3110	3.2554	3.1984	3.1399	3.0798
11	3.5257	3.4296	3.3299	3.2261	3.1725	3.1176	3.0613	3.0035	2.9441	2.8828
12	3.3736	3.2773	3.1772	3.0728	3.0187	2.9633	2.9063	2.8478	2.7874	2.7249
13	3.2497	3.1532	3.0527	2.9477	2.8932	2.8372	2.7797	2.7204	2.6590	2.5955
14	3.1469	3.0502	2.9493	2.8437	2.7888	2.7324	2.6742	2.6142	2.5519	2.4872
15	3.0602	2.9633	2.8621	2.7559	2.7006	2.6437	2.5850	2.5242	2.4611	2.3953
16	2.9862	2.8890	2.7875	2.6808	2.6252	2.5678	2.5085	2.4471	2.3831	2.3163
17	2.9222	2.8249	2.7230	2.6158	2.5598	2.5020	2.4422	2.3801	2.3153	2.2474
18	2.8664	2.7689	2.6667	2.5590	2.5027	2.4445	2.3842	2.3214	2.2558	2.1869
19	2.8172	2.7196	2.6171	2.5089	2.4523	2.3937	2.3329	2.2696	2.2032	2.1333
20	2.7737	2.6758	2.5731	2.4645	2.4076	2.3486	2.2873	2.2234	2.1562	2.0853
21	2.7348	2.6368	2.5338	2.4247	2.3675	2.3082	2.2465	2.1819	2.1141	2.0422
22	2.6998	2.6017	2.4984	2.3890	2.3315	2.2718	2.2097	2.1446	2.0760	2.0032
23	2.6682	2.5699	2.4665	2.3567	2.2989	2.2389	2.1763	2.1107	2.0415	1.9677
24	2.6396	2.5411	2.4374	2.3273	2.2693	2.2090	2.1460	2.0799	2.0099	1.9353
25	2.6135	2.5149	2.4110	2.3005	2.2422	2.1816	2.1183	2.0516	1.9811	1.9055
26	2.5896	2.4908	2.3867	2.2759	2.2174	2.1565	2.0928	2.0257	1.9545	1.8781
27	2.5676	2.4688	2.3644	2.2533	2.1946	2.1334	2.0693	2.0018	1.9299	1.8527
28	2.5473	2.4484	2.3438	2.2324	2.1735	2.1121	2.0477	1.9797	1.9072	1.8291
29	2.5286	2.4295	2.3248	2.2131	2.1540	2.0923	2.0276	1.9591	1.8861	1.8072
30	2.5112	2.4120	2.3072	2.1952	2.1359	2.0739	2.0089	1.9400	1.8664	1.7867
40	2.3882	2.2882	2.1819	2.0677	2.0069	1.9429	1.8752	1.8028	1.7242	1.6371
60	2.2702	2.1692	2.0613	1.9445	1.8817	1.8152	1.7440	1.6668	1.5810	1.4821
120	2.1570	2.0548	1.9450	1.8249	1.7597	1.6899	1.6141	1.5299	1.4327	1.3104
∞	2.0483	1.9447	1.8326	1.7085	1.6402	1.5660	1.4835	1.3883	1.2684	1.0000

Table A5(c) Critical values of the *F* distribution (upper 1% points)

The entries in the table give the critical values of *F* cutting off 1% in the right-hand tail of the distribution. v_1 gives the degrees of freedom in the numerator, v_2 in the denominator.

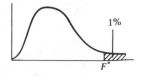

v_1 / v_2	1	2	3	4	5	6	7	8	9
1	4052.2	4999.5	5403.4	5624.6	5763.6	5859.0	5928.4	5981.1	6022.5
2	98.503	99.000	99.166	99.249	99.299	99.333	99.356	99.374	99.388
3	34.116	30.817	29.457	28.710	28.237	27.911	27.672	27.489	27.345
4	21.198	18.000	16.694	15.977	15.522	15.207	14.976	14.799	14.659
5	16.258	13.274	12.060	11.392	10.967	10.672	10.456	10.289	10.158
6	13.745	10.925	9.7795	9.1483	8.7459	8.4661	8.2600	8.1017	7.9761
7	12.246	9.5466	8.4513	7.8466	7.4604	7.1914	6.9928	6.8400	6.7188
8	11.259	8.6491	7.5910	7.0061	6.6318	6.3707	6.1776	6.0289	5.9106
9	10.561	8.0215	6.9919	6.4221	6.0569	5.8018	5.6129	5.4671	5.3511
10	10.044	7.5594	6.5523	5.9943	5.6363	5.3858	5.2001	5.0567	4.9424
11	9.6460	7.2057	6.2167	5.6683	5.3160	5.0692	4.8861	4.7445	4.6315
12	9.3302	6.9266	5.9525	5.4120	5.0643	4.8206	4.6395	4.4994	4.3875
13	9.0738	6.7010	5.7394	5.2053	4.8616	4.6204	4.4410	4.3021	4.1911
14	8.8618	6.5149	5.5639	5.0354	4.6950	4.4558	4.2779	4.1399	4.0297
15	8.6831	6.3589	5.4170	4.8932	4.5556	4.3183	4.1415	4.0045	3.8948
16	8.5310	6.2262	5.2922	4.7726	4.4374	4.2016	4.0259	3.8896	3.7804
17	8.3997	6.1121	5.1850	4.6690	4.3359	4.1015	3.9267	3.7910	3.6822
18	8.2854	6.0129	5.0919	4.5790	4.2479	4.0146	3.8406	3.7054	3.5971
19	8.1849	5.9259	5.0103	4.5003	4.1708	3.9386	3.7653	3.6305	3.5225
20	8.0960	5.8489	4.9382	4.4307	4.1027	3.8714	3.6987	3.5644	3.4567
21	8.0166	5.7804	4.8740	4.3688	4.0421	3.8117	3.6396	3.5056	3.3981
22	7.9454	5.7190	4.8166	4.3134	3.9880	3.7583	3.5867	3.4530	3.3458
23	7.8811	5.6637	4.7649	4.2636	3.9392	3.7102	3.5390	3.4057	3.2986
24	7.8229	5.6136	4.7181	4.2184	3.8951	3.6667	3.4959	3.3629	3.2560
25	7.7698	5.5680	4.6755	4.1774	3.8550	3.6272	3.4568	3.3439	3.2172
26	7.7213	5.5263	4.6366	4.1400	3.8183	3.5911	3.4210	3.2884	3.1818
27	7.6767	5.4881	4.6009	4.1056	3.7848	3.5580	3.3882	3.2558	3.1494
28	7.6356	5.4529	4.5681	4.0740	3.7539	3.5276	3.3581	3.2259	3.1195
29	7.5977	5.4204	4.5378	4.0449	3.7254	3.4995	3.3303	3.1982	3.0920
30	7.5625	5.3903	4.5097	4.0179	3.6990	3.4735	3.3045	3.1726	3.0665
40	7.3141	5.1785	4.3126	3.8283	3.5138	3.2910	3.1238	2.9930	2.8876
60	7.0771	4.9774	4.1259	3.6490	3.3389	3.1187	2.9530	2.8233	2.7185
120	6.8509	4.7865	3.9491	3.4795	3.1735	2.9559	2.7918	2.6629	2.5586
∞	6.6349	4.6052	3.7816	3.3192	3.0173	2.8020	2.6393	2.5113	2.4073

Table A5(c) continued

v_1 / v_2	10	12	15	20	24	30	40	60	120	∞
1	6055.8	6106.3	6157.3	6208.7	6234.6	6260.6	6286.8	6313.0	6339.4	6365.9
2	99.399	99.416	99.433	99.449	99.458	99.466	99.474	99.482	99.491	99.499
3	27.229	27.052	26.872	26.690	26.598	26.505	26.411	26.316	26.221	26.125
4	14.546	14.374	14.198	14.020	13.929	13.838	13.745	13.652	13.558	13.463
5	10.051	9.8883	9.7222	9.5526	9.4665	9.3793	9.2912	9.2020	9.1118	9.0204
6	7.8741	7.7183	7.5590	7.3958	7.3127	7.2285	7.1432	7.0567	6.9690	6.8800
7	6.6201	6.4691	6.3143	6.1554	6.0743	5.9920	5.9084	5.8236	5.7373	5.6495
8	5.8143	5.6667	5.5151	5.3591	5.2793	5.1981	5.1156	5.0316	4.9461	4.8588
9	5.2565	5.1114	4.9621	4.8080	4.7290	4.6486	4.5666	4.4831	4.3978	4.3105
10	4.8491	4.7059	4.5581	4.4054	4.3269	4.2469	4.1653	4.0819	3.9965	3.9090
11	4.5393	4.3974	4.2509	4.0990	4.0209	3.9411	3.8596	3.7761	3.6904	3.6024
12	4.2961	4.1553	4.0096	3.8584	3.7805	3.7008	3.6192	3.5355	3.4494	3.3608
13	4.1003	3.9603	3.8154	3.6646	3.5868	3.5070	3.4253	3.3413	3.2548	3.1654
14	3.9394	3.8001	3.6557	3.5052	3.4274	3.3476	3.2656	3.1813	3.0942	3.0040
15	3.8049	3.6662	3.5222	3.3719	3.2940	3.2141	3.1319	3.0471	2.9595	2.8684
16	3.6909	3.5527	3.4089	3.2587	3.1808	3.1007	3.0182	2.9330	2.8447	2.7528
17	3.5931	3.4552	3.3117	3.1615	3.0835	2.0032	2.9205	2.8348	2.7459	2.6530
18	3.5082	3.3706	3.2273	3.0771	2.9990	2.9185	2.8354	2.7493	2.6597	2.5660
19	3.4338	3.2965	3.1533	3.0031	2.9249	2.8442	2.7608	2.6742	2.5839	2.4893
20	3.3682	3.2311	3.0880	2.9377	2.8594	2.7785	2.6947	2.6077	2.5168	2.4212
21	3.3098	3.1730	3.0300	2.8796	2.8010	2.7200	2.6359	2.5484	2.4568	2.3603
22	3.2576	3.1209	2.9779	2.8274	2.7488	2.6675	2.5831	2.4951	2.4029	2.3055
23	3.2106	3.0740	2.9311	2.7805	2.7017	2.6202	2.5355	2.4471	2.3542	2.2558
24	3.1681	3.0316	2.8887	2.7380	2.6591	2.5773	2.4923	2.4035	2.3100	2.2107
25	3.1294	2.9931	2.8502	2.6993	2.6203	2.5383	2.4530	2.3637	2.2696	2.1694
26	3.0941	2.9578	2.8150	2.6640	2.5848	2.5026	2.4170	2.3273	2.2325	2.1315
27	3.0618	2.9256	2.7827	2.6316	2.5522	2.4699	2.3840	2.2938	2.1985	2.0965
28	3.0320	2.8959	2.7530	2.6017	2.5223	2.4397	2.3535	2.2629	2.1670	2.0642
29	3.0045	2.8685	2.7256	2.5742	2.4946	2.4118	2.3253	2.2344	2.1379	2.0342
30	2.9791	2.8431	2.7002	2.5487	2.4689	2.3860	2.2992	2.2079	2.1108	2.0062
40	2.8005	2.6648	2.5216	2.3689	2.2880	2.2034	2.1142	2.0194	1.9172	1.8047
60	2.6318	2.4961	2.3523	2.1978	2.1154	2.0285	1.9360	1.8363	1.7263	1.6006
120	2.4721	2.3363	2.1915	2.0346	1.9500	1.8600	1.7628	1.6557	1.5330	1.3805
∞	2.3209	2.1847	2.0385	1.8783	1.7908	1.6964	1.5923	1.4730	1.3246	1.0000

Table A5(d) Critical values of the *F* distribution (upper 0.5% points)

The entries in the table give the critical
values of *F* cutting off 0.5% in the right
hand tail of the distribution. v_1 gives the
degrees of freedom in the numerator, v_2
in the denominator.

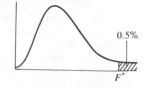

0.5%

F^*

v_1 v_2	1	2	3	4	5	6	7	8	9
1	16211	20000	21615	22500	23056	23437	23715	23925	24091
2	198.50	199.00	199.17	199.25	199.30	199.33	199.36	199.37	199.39
3	55.552	49.799	47.467	46.195	45.392	44.838	44.434	44.126	43.882
4	31.333	26.284	24.259	23.155	22.456	21.975	21.622	21.352	21.139
5	22.785	18.314	16.530	15.556	14.940	14.513	14.200	13.961	13.772
6	18.635	14.544	12.917	12.028	11.464	11.073	10.786	10.566	10.391
7	16.236	12.404	10.882	10.050	9.5221	9.1553	8.8854	8.6781	8.5138
8	14.688	11.042	9.5965	8.8051	9.3018	7.9520	7.6941	7.4959	7.3386
9	13.614	10.107	8.7171	7.9559	7.4712	7.1339	6.8849	6.6933	6.5411
10	12.826	9.4270	8.0807	7.3428	6.8724	6.5446	6.3025	6.1159	5.9676
11	12.226	8.9122	7.6004	6.8809	6.4217	6.1016	5.8648	5.6821	5.5368
12	11.754	8.5096	7.2258	6.5211	6.0711	5.7570	5.5245	5.3451	5.2021
13	11.374	8.1865	6.9258	6.2335	5.7910	5.4819	5.2529	5.0761	4.9351
14	11.060	7.9216	6.6804	5.9984	5.5623	5.2574	5.0313	4.8566	4.7173
15	10.798	7.7008	6.4760	5.8029	5.3721	5.0708	4.8473	4.6744	3.5364
16	10.575	7.5138	6.3034	5.6378	5.2117	4.9134	4.6920	4.5207	4.3838
17	10.384	7.3536	6.1556	5.4967	5.0746	4.7789	4.5594	4.3894	4.2535
18	10.218	7.2148	6.0278	5.3746	3.9560	4.6627	4.4448	3.2759	4.1410
19	10.073	7.0935	5.9161	5.2601	4.8326	4.5614	4.3448	4.1770	4.0428
20	9.9439	6.9865	5.8177	5.1743	4.7616	4.4721	4.2569	4.0900	3.9564
21	9.8295	6.8914	5.7304	5.0911	4.6809	4.3931	4.1789	4.0128	3.8799
22	9.7271	6.8064	5.6524	5.0168	4.6088	4.3225	4.1094	3.9440	3.8116
23	9.6348	6.7300	5.5823	4.9500	3.5441	4.2591	4.0469	3.8822	3.7502
24	9.5513	6.6609	5.5190	4.8898	4.4857	4.2019	3.9905	3.8264	3.6949
25	9.4753	6.5982	5.4615	4.8351	4.4327	4.1500	3.9394	3.7758	3.6447
26	9.4059	6.5409	5.4091	4.7852	4.3844	4.1027	3.8928	3.7297	3.5989
27	9.3423	6.4885	5.3611	4.7396	4.3402	4.0594	3.8501	3.6875	3.5571
28	9.2838	6.4403	5.3170	4.6977	4.2996	4.0197	3.8110	3.6487	3.5186
29	9.2297	6.3958	5.2764	4.6591	4.2622	3.9831	3.7749	3.6131	3.4832
30	9.1797	6.3547	5.2388	4.6234	4.2276	3.9492	3.7416	3.5801	3.4504
40	8.8279	6.0664	4.9758	4.3738	3.9860	3.7129	3.5088	3.3498	3.2220
60	8.4946	5.7950	4.7290	4.1399	3.7599	3.4918	3.2911	3.1344	3.0083
120	8.1788	5.5393	4.4972	3.9207	3.5482	3.2849	3.0874	2.9330	2.8083
∞	7.894	5.2983	4.2794	3.7151	3.3499	3.0913	2.8968	2.7444	2.6210

Table A5(d) continued

v_2 \ v_1	10	12	15	20	24	30	40	60	120	∞
1	24224	24426	24630	24836	24940	25044	25148	25253	25359	25464
2	199.40	199.42	199.43	199.45	199.46	199.47	199.47	199.48	199.49	199.50
3	43.686	43.387	43.085	42.778	42.622	42.466	42.308	42.149	41.989	41.828
4	20.967	20.705	20.438	20.167	20.030	19.892	19.752	19.611	19.468	19.325
5	13.618	13.384	13.146	12.903	12.780	12.656	12.530	12.402	12.274	12.144
6	10.250	10.034	9.8140	9.5888	9.4742	9.3582	9.2408	9.1219	9.0015	8.8793
7	8.3803	8.1764	7.9678	7.7540	7.6450	7.5345	7.4224	7.3088	7.1933	7.0760
8	7.2106	7.0149	6.8143	6.6082	6.5029	6.3961	6.2875	6.1772	6.0649	5.9506
9	6.4172	6.2274	6.0325	5.8318	5.7292	5.6248	5.5186	5.4104	5.3001	5.1875
10	5.8467	5.6613	5.4707	5.2740	5.1732	5.0706	4.9659	4.8592	4.7501	4.6385
11	5.4183	5.2363	5.0489	4.8552	4.7557	4.6543	4.5508	4.4450	4.3367	4.2255
12	5.0855	4.9062	4.7213	4.5299	4.4314	4.3309	4.2282	5.1229	4.0149	3.9039
13	4.8199	4.6429	4.4600	4.2703	4.1726	4.0727	3.9704	3.8655	3.7577	3.6465
14	4.6034	4.4281	4.2468	4.0585	3.9614	3.8619	3.7600	3.6552	3.5473	3.4359
15	4.4235	4.2497	4.0698	3.8826	3.7859	3.6867	3.5850	3.4803	3.3722	3.2602
16	4.2719	4.0994	3.9205	3.7342	3.6378	3.5389	3.4372	3.3324	3.2240	3.1115
17	4.1424	3.9709	3.7929	3.6073	3.5112	3.4124	3.3108	3.2058	3.0971	2.9839
18	4.0305	3.8599	3.6827	3.4977	3.4017	3.3030	3.2014	3.0962	2.9871	2.8732
19	3.9329	3.7631	4.5866	3.4020	3.3062	3.2075	3.1058	3.0004	2.8908	2.7762
20	3.8470	3.6779	3.5020	3.3178	3.2220	3.1234	3.0215	2.9159	2.8058	2.6904
21	3.7709	3.6024	3.4270	3.2431	3.1474	3.0488	2.9467	2.8408	2.7302	2.6140
22	3.7030	3.5350	3.3600	3.1764	3.0807	2.9821	2.8799	2.7736	2.6625	2.5455
23	3.6420	3.4745	3.2999	3.1165	3.0208	2.9221	2.8197	2.7132	2.6015	2.4837
24	3.5870	3.4199	3.2456	3.0624	2.9667	2.8679	2.7654	2.6585	2.5463	2.4276
25	3.5370	3.3704	3.1963	3.0133	2.9176	2.8187	2.7160	2.6088	2.4961	2.3765
26	3.4916	3.3252	3.1515	2.9685	2.8728	2.7738	2.6709	2.5633	2.4501	2.3297
27	3.4499	3.2839	3.1104	2.9275	2.8318	2.7327	2.6296	2.5217	2.4079	2.2867
28	3.4117	3.2460	3.0727	2.8899	2.7941	2.6949	2.5916	2.4834	2.3690	2.2470
29	3.3765	3.2110	3.0379	2.8551	2.7594	2.6600	2.5565	2.4479	2.3331	2.2102
30	3.3440	3.1787	3.0057	2.8230	2.7272	2.6278	2.5241	2.4151	2.2998	2.1760
40	3.1167	2.9531	2.7811	2.5984	2.5020	2.4015	2.2958	2.1838	2.0636	1.9318
60	2.9042	2.7419	2.5705	2.3872	2.2898	2.1874	2.0789	1.9622	1.8341	1.6885
120	2.7052	2.5439	2.3727	2.1881	2.0890	1.9840	1.8709	1.7469	1.6055	1.4311
∞	2.5188	2.3583	2.1868	1.9998	1.8983	1.7891	1.6691	1.5325	1.3637	1.0000

Tables A3, A4, A5(a), (b), (c) and (d) are taken from *Biometrika Tables for Statisticians*, 1966

Table A6 Critical values of Spearman's rank correlation coefficient

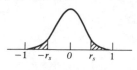

Entries in the table show critical values of Spearman's rank correlation coefficient. The value at the top of each column shows the significance level for a two-tail test. For a one-tail test, the significance level is half that shown.

N	10%	5%	2%	1%
5	0.900	—	—	—
6	0.829	0.886	0.943	—
7	0.714	0.786	0.893	—
8	0.643	0.738	0.833	0.881
9	0.600	0.683	0.783	0.833
10	0.564	0.648	0.745	0.818
11	0.523	0.623	0.763	0.794
12	0.497	0.591	0.703	0.780
13	0.475	0.566	0.673	0.746
14	0.457	0.545	0.646	0.716
15	0.441	0.525	0.623	0.689
16	0.425	0.507	0.601	0.666
17	0.412	0.490	0.582	0.645
18	0.399	0.476	0.564	0.625
19	0.388	0.462	0.549	0.608
20	0.377	0.450	0.534	0.591
21	0.368	0.438	0.521	0.576
22	0.359	0.428	0.508	0.562
23	0.351	0.418	0.496	0.549
24	0.343	0.409	0.485	0.537
25	0.336	0.400	0.475	0.526
26	0.329	0.392	0.465	0.515
27	0.323	0.385	0.456	0.505
28	0.317	0.377	0.448	0.496
29	0.311	0.370	0.440	0.487
30	0.305	0.364	0.432	0.478

Source: *Annals of Statistics*, 1936 and 1949

Answers to problems

Chapter 1

1.1 (c) From the original data $\bar{x} = 42.82$, $s = 13.23$. Similar answers are obtained from grouped data, $\bar{x} = 42.88$, $s = 13.41$

(d) $9/33 = 27\%$ of observations are above 49, while $5/33 = 15\%$ are more than one standard deviation above the mean.

1.2 1900–02: mean 34.01, median 33.52, mode 0–1 age group.
1980–82: mean 69.05, median 71.69, mode 65–74 group.
The 1900–02 distribution is bimodal because of the very high infant mortality. All measures of the average are affected by this. By 1980 infant mortality has declined substantially, so the average figures are more representative. If infant mortality (before 4 years old) is left out, the average age at death is 53.01 in 1900 – 2. Thus, for those who survived infancy, the life expectancy was not too far short of today's. The averages have to be used with caution.

1.3 (b) Using 130 as the mid-point for the >104 category, the averages are: 16–19, 32.68 weeks; 25–34, 65.61 weeks; over 60, 40.18 weeks.

(c) Average unemployment duration seems to rise with age, except for the over 60 category. Many of these retire early or do not register as unemployed. The table indicates that, once unemployed, it is more difficult to find employment the older you are.

(d) The number in each age category unemployed for over a year is as follows (thousands): 16–19, 51.95; 20–24, 162.84; 25–34, 261.45; 35–49, 292.91; 50–59, 237.52; >60, 16.01.

1.4 The figures for all 25 students are: $\Sigma f = 25$; $\Sigma fx = 1540$; $\Sigma fx^2 = 99{,}010$; so the mean is 61.6 and standard deviation 13.14.

1.5 $x_1 = 58.5$; $s_1 = 17.292$; $x_2 = 42.867$; $s_2 = 10.542$.
The marks 86, 59 and 55 (from group 2) have the highest z-scores and should receive the prizes.

1.6 $\bar{x} = 10{,}000$, variance $= 4{,}591{,}836$.

1.7 The problem is comparing non-comparable averages. The average first-time buyer would have an above average mortgage and purchase a below average priced house.

1.8 Multiplying the factors together gives 1.509, so £5,000 would become £7,547.41 at the end of the period. The average rate of interest is 10.843%

Chapter 2

2.1

	1980	1981	1982	1983	1984	1985
Exports	100	107.0	117.3	128.1	148.8	165.4
Imports	100	102.8	114.5	132.8	158.7	170.4
Exports	78.1	83.5	91.6	100	116.2	129.1
Imports	75.3	77.4	86.2	100	119.5	128.3

The actual figure for either exports or imports in at least one year is required to calculate the trade index. It cannot be calculated from the index numbers alone.

2.2

1981	1982	1983	1984	1985
100	106.7	113.0	116.3	123.9

The Paasche index gives the impression of prices growing more slowly so would be preferred by the company.

2.3   Answer in text.

2.4   Answer in text.

2.5

$$P_P = \frac{\Sigma p_n q_n}{\Sigma p_0 q_n} = \frac{\Sigma \dfrac{p_n}{p_n} p_n q_n}{\Sigma \dfrac{p_0}{p_n} p_n q_n} = \frac{\Sigma \dfrac{p_n}{p_n} \dfrac{p_n q_n}{\Sigma p_n q_n}}{\Sigma \dfrac{p_0}{p_n} \dfrac{p_n q_n}{\Sigma p_n q_n}}$$

$$= \frac{1}{\Sigma \dfrac{p_0}{p_n} \dfrac{p_n q_n}{\Sigma p_n q_n}}$$

2.6

	1981	1982	1983	1984
(a) Index	100	144	192	239
(b) Real index	100	108	110.8	112.0

This is a Laspeyres quantity index.
(c) The family is becoming better off as measured by this index. The index

263

Statistics for Economics, Accounting and Business Studies

underestimates the true change in living standards because the family spends proportionately less on housing (the good increasing most rapidly in price) than the RPI weight.

2.7 (a) The Gini coefficients are approximately 56% (1976) and 58% (1984).
  (b) There has been little change in the wealth distribution over the time period. It is really too short a period for much change to take place or be observed.
  (c) It doesn't matter that the data is not inflation adjusted, because the comparison is between the proportions of wealth held by proportions of adults. Inflation has meant, however, that there are few observations at the bottom of the 1976 distribution. If a straight line is drawn from the origin to the first data point, this will tend to underestimate the value of the Gini coefficient, making comparison with 1984 difficult.
  (d) Wealth is less equally distributed because older people have had more time to save, and because of inheritance.
  (e) Wealth could also include non-marketable wealth such as the value of pension rights. The inclusion of these items reduces the inequality in the wealth distribution.

Chapter 3

3.1 4/52, 12/52, 1/2, 4/52×3/51×2/50 = 24/132,600 = 1/5,525, $(1/13)^3$ = 1/2197.

3.2 (a) As proportions unemployed in the various categories they may be interpreted as probabilities according to the frequentist approach. Thus given someone aged 16–19 who is out of work, the probability that they have been unemployed for less than or equal to eight weeks is 27.2%.
  (b) True, false, false, false, true.
  (c) By Bayes theorem,

$$P(A_1|B) = \frac{P(B|A_1)\ P(A_1)}{\Sigma P(B|A_i)\ P(A_i)} = \frac{0.02328}{0.45831} = 0.05079$$

where B is the event 'out of work for over one year', A_i is the event 'a member of age group i out of work' (1 indicating the 16–19 age group).

3.3 (a) 1/15;
  (b) There are 15 ways in which a 4–2 score could be achieved, six of which imply a score of 2–2 at some stage. The probability therefore is 6/ 15.

3.4 P(surviving one year) = 1 − 0.03 = 0.97. Hence P(surviving five years) = 0.97^5 = 0.859. This assumes the probabilities are independent, which is doubtful in practice. A firm builds up stocks, finances, its reputation, etc. in the first year. If it survives, it has an improved chance the second year. The above figure is therefore probably an underestimate.

3.5 (a), (b), (d) are independent.

3.6 P(guessing all six) $= 6/50 \times 5/49 \times 4/48 \times 3/47 \times 2/46 \times 1/45 = 1/15,890,700.$
P(guessing all six from ten guesses) $= 10/50 \times 9/49 \times 8/48 \times 7/47 \times 6/46 \times 5/45 = 151,200/11,441,304,000.$ This is exactly 210 times the first answer, so you don't get a discount for bulk gambling!

3.7 (a) 99.97%;
(b) 99.999603%;
(c) Very small. It is not $1 - 0.99999603$ because there is the possibility of no answer at all being obtained. The probability of any two machines getting the identical *wrong* answer is minute.

3.8 (a) P(answer known or correctly guessed) $= 0.6 + 1/4 \times 0.4 = 0.7.$ Hence
$P(4) + P(5) + P(6) = 0.32 + 0.30 + 0.12 = 0.74$ by the Binomial method.
(b) P(neither knows) $= 0.4 \times 0.5 = 0.2.$ Hence P(answer known) $= 0.8.$ Hence P(answer known or guessed) $= 0.8 + 1/4 \times 0.2 = 0.85.$ Hence $P(4) + P(5) + P(6) = 0.17 + 0.40 + 0.37 = 0.95.$
(c) P(answer known or guessed) $= 0.7.$ Hence $P(3) + P(4) + P(5) = 0.31 + 0.36 + 0.17 = 0.84.$
(d) No. Any probability (short of perfect knowledge) is consistent with getting half marks.

Chapter 4

4.1 13%, 30%, 83%, 17%

4.2 (a) Mean 6, variance 2.4
(b) Mean 5, greater variance. A family is likely to have either a lot of boys or a lot of girls.
(c) Very likely to get an even number of boys and girls.
(d) A preponderance of boys in the family is likely.

4.3 (a) 55%
(b) Taking larger samples or using tighter rejection criteria, e.g. if any defectives are found.
(c) 7%
(d) The assumption of large batches means the probability of a defective component being selected does not alter as the sample is drawn, so the Binomial distribution can be used.

4.4 (a) 5% (b) 30.9% (c) 93.3% (d) 91.0% (e) 22.7% (f) 1.28
(g) -1.04 (h) -0.67 to $+0.67$

4.5 (a) 25.1% (b) 15.9% (c) 70.1% (d) 36.1% (e) zero.

4.6 (a) 6.68% (b) 6.68% (c) 70.78%

4.7 (a) 10.56% (b) 69.15% (c) 10.56%

4.8 (a) 15.87% (b) less than 1%.

4.9 (a) Unknown, since the distribution of income is not Normal.
(b) Unknown again. Sample too small to justify use of Normal distribution.
(c) 88.6%.

4.10 $z = 2.77$, probability $= 0.28\%$. The claim seems unlikely.

4.11 The probability of five or less sales in a week is $P(0) + P(1) + \ldots + P(5) = 0.049 + 0.149 + 0.224 + 0.224 + 0.168 + 0.101 = 0.916$ using the Poisson distribution. The probability of more than five sales (and hence the need to turn away customers) is therefore 8.4%. This can therefore be expected to happen on about four weeks of the year.

4.12 (a) 60 (b) −0.3 (c) 0.7 (d) 360 (e) 144 (f) 0.07 (g) 4.28 if X and Y independent.

4.13 Project A: $E(\text{profit}) = £2.3$ m. Project B: $E(\text{profit}) = £2.6$ m. B has the greater expected profit, but there is some risk of a considerable loss, much more so than with A. This risk can be measured by the variance or standard deviation. The standard deviations are: A £2.61 m. and B £10.44 m.

4.14 (a) Project A: mean $= 1.5$, variance $= 12.25$. Project B: mean $= 2.5$, variance $= 30.25$.
(b) mean $= 4$, variance $= 81$.
(c) mean $= 4$, variance $= 4$.
(d) mean $= 4$, variance $= 42.5$.
(e) $E(X + Y) = E(X) + E(Y)$ and $V(X + Y) = V(X) + V(Y)$ if X and Y are independent. Note that if X and Y are inversely related, this reduces the risk, i.e. the variance. When they are positively related, the risk is increased.

4.15 (a) $E(X/1.1) = 1/1.1\ E(X) = 660{,}000/1.1 = 600{,}000$. $V(X/1.1) = 1/1.1^2\ V(X) = 66{,}550/1.1^2 = 55{,}000$.
(b) $E(X+Y) = E(X) + E(Y) = 500{,}000 + 600{,}000 = 1{,}100{,}000$. $V(X+Y) = V(X) + V(Y) = 40{,}000 + 55{,}000 = 95{,}000$ m. Hence standard deviation $= 308{,}221$.

Chapter 5

5.1 An estimator is a rule which tells you how to find an estimate. A good estimator does not guarantee a good estimate, but on average it will provide a good estimate.

5.2 The biased estimator might be more precise than the unbiased one so a particular estimate might be closer to the true value.

5.3 [35.70, 44.3], [35.23, 44.77]. The second interval is found using the t distribution.

5.4 (a) $z = 1.45$, so the probability of bankruptcy is 7.35%.
(b) $z = 4.58$, so the probability of bankruptcy is virtually zero.
(c) A larger insurance company is less likely to go bankrupt.
(d) In the long run companies of whatever size would have 5% of their clients in accidents each year, so profitability should be the same. However, the large firm has the advantage that the cost of holding reserves to cover bad years is relatively smaller.

5.5 [241.18, 278.82]. The sample size required is approximately 210 for the desired accuracy (at the 95% confidence level).

5.6 [−1.40, 7.40].

5.7 [1545.60, 2454.41]
[53.47, 746.53]
Women earn lower wages because they earn less than men in the same job and because they tend to work in lower wage industries.

5.8 [8.34 m., 10.52 m.] is the interval for 1987.
[0.96 m., 3.90 m.] is the interval estimate of the increase on the previous year.

Chapter 6

6.1 $z = 1$, H_0 not rejected at 95% confidence level.

6.2 (a) False. The sample size could be increased, or a better method of sampling could be used.
(b) True.
(c) False. This ignores the probability of a Type II error.
(d) True.
(e) False. The significance level is the probability of a Type I error.
(f) False. The confidence level is the probability of not rejecting H_0 when it is true.

6.3 P (Type I error) = 2.3%
P (Type II error) = 15.9%, hence power of test is 84.1%

Error probabilities fall and power of test increases as the sample size is increased.

6.4 $z = 2.5$, H_0 rejected at 95% confidence level.

6.5 (a) $z = 5.855$, the drug does seem to be effective.

(b) $z = 1.751$, the drug seems to be not significantly better than the placebo. People want the 'drug' to work, so the effect may be wish fulfilment. This may be particularly true of volunteers. It would be cheaper to prescribe placebos than the drug itself.

6.6 $t_{33} = 2.4$ ($S^2 = 558.9$). This is significant at the 95% confidence level. To use the test it has to be assumed that the variances are equal and that the parent populations are Normally distributed.

6.7 $z = 1.835$, which is significant at 95% for a one tail test. It could be that the storeman is dishonest and pilfering good stock, or that he is checking to higher standards. The two conclusions have very different implications! If the goods were spending less time in stock, this would favour the first conclusion. This statistical evidence would not stand up in a court of law.

6.8   (a) Accept a bad batch or reject a good batch.
(b) $z = 1.41$, so the probability of accepting a bad batch is 8%. For a good batch, $z = 2.13$ and there is a 1.7% chance of rejecting it.
(c) Since the test has become more rigorous (1/30 rejection criteria rather than 2/50) and the sample size has been reduced, there is a greater probability of rejecting a good batch.
(d) (i)   Avoid accepting bad batches.
(ii) Don't worry about rejecting good batches.
(iii) Avoid accepting bad batches.

Chapter 8

8.1 $\chi^2(4) = 8.12$, which is not significant at the 5% level. There is no relationship between size and profitability on this evidence.

8.2   The data has to be altered to give a contingency table of those leaving *and* those not leaving, by department. This then gives $\chi^2(2) = 0.52$, not significant. Note that some cells have to be amalgamated since the expected values are less than five. The obvious choice is to add the personnel and marketing departments columns.

8.3   There should be no bias in a random number table. Once you have combined digits by frequency of occurrence, a significant χ^2 value is quite likely. This shows that even random data can yield 'significant' results if abused.

8.4   The value of chi squared is 28.48, significant at the 5% level. The Binomial distribution does not fit very well, mainly because of the large number of families with five boys relative to the expected numbers.

8.5   Using the data as presented, with expected values of 565, yields $\chi^2(3) = 1.33$, which is not significant. There is no difference in the numbers of satisfied customers. However, when the dissatisfied customers are added (24, 42, 20, 54, respectively) and a contingency table is constructed, then $\chi^2(3) = 22.94$, highly significant. The differences between the small numbers of dissatisfied customers adds most to the test statistic. The additional information allows the null hypothesis to be rejected. The first result should therefore have been treated with suspicion, since it is fairly obvious that there would be a small number of dissatisfied customers.

8.6 $F_{14,19} = 0.9^2/0.6^2 = 2.25$, not significant. Since the hypothesis of equal variances cannot be rejected, the *t*-test conducted in Chapter 6 was valid.

8.7 $F_{19,24} = 10^2/2^2 = 25$, which is highly significant, so the consistency of machine A is much superior to that of machine B. However, machine B is closer on average to the correct nominal length. Adjustment of machine A could presumably improve upon the performance of machine B though.

Chapter 9

9.1 (a) There is a downward trend to admissions, which pick up in 1978. The real price rises over time, especially in 1979–80.

(b) $Y = 346.11 - 486.9\ X$
  s.e.   (53.10)   (106.1)

  t (6.52)   (4.59)
  $R^2 = 0.70$

(c) At the mean values, the demand elasticity is –2.35. A logarithmic regression gives –2.64 as the elasticity.

(d) The point prediction is 56.51, 95% confidence interval for the regression line [31.27, 81.75], for the Y value [14.09, 98.93].

(e) The last two observations are below their predicted values, which may be due to the inroads of video recorders in competition to the cinema.

9.2 (a) Higher unemployment reduces demand (for imports); higher OECD income raises the demand for UK exports; higher materials prices (the UK imports materials) lowers demand, but the effect on expenditure (and hence the balance of payments) depends upon the elasticity. Here, higher P leads to a greater BOP deficit, implying inelastic demand; higher C (lower competitiveness) worsens the BOP.

(b) (iii)

(c) U: linear, Y: non-linear.

(d) Since B is sometimes negative, a logarithmic transformation cannot be performed. This means elasticity estimates cannot be directly obtained. Since B is sometimes positive, sometimes negative, an elasticity estimate would be hard to interpret.

(e) The estimate of B is 1.80, i.e. a surplus.

9.3 (a) Average price is 20 pence so average sales are 50. The demand elasticity is thus $-0.8 \times 20/50 = -0.32$. Demand is inelastic.

(b) At 30 pence, sales are forecast to be $66 - 0.8 \times 30 = 42$.

(c) The 95% confidence interval for the slope coefficient is $[-0.33, -1.28]$.

(d) Fewer holidaymakers should depress sales. This means the effect of price on sales has been underestimated.

(e) The weather would obviously affect sales. This could be measured by the average summer temperature each year, or by the number of sunny days each summer.

9.4 (a) There is a very wide variation in the starts variable, so the effects of other variables should be fairly easy to observe.

(c) Using the nominal mortgage rate is better. There is a higher R^2 and the variable is correctly signed.

(d) The real rate is a better measure of the economic cost of a mortgage; the nominal rate better measures the burden to the mortgagee, especially at high rates of inflation at the start of the repayment period.

(e) Using the 'nominal' equation, a 1% rise in the mortgage rate (equal to a 1% rise in the real rate if the inflation rate is the same) leads to a fall of about 8,400 starts per annum (about 5.0% of starts). Since the mortgage rate responds to changes in the rate of inflation, it is a questionable assumption to assume that the inflation rate is the same. A higher nominal rate might not lead to a higher real rate but simply reflect a higher inflation rate, so that there would be little or no effect on starts.

(f) Leaving out the tax relief variable is like omitting a relevant explanatory variable. If the marginal tax rate is constant (or nearly so) over the period, then omitting it will not be serious and will mainly affect the constant term in the regression.

Chapter 10

10.1 (b) There is an obvious seasonal effect in the fourth quarter of each year, due to increased purchases at Christmas. The size of these effects does differ according to the adjustment method. Using regression to find the trend line, an additive model suggests 1981 Q4 sales to be lower than expected, while the multiplicative model suggests otherwise.

(c) The prediction of the trend for 1986 Q1 is 166.7 using the regression method. The seasonal factor is -4.1 (additive) or 0.97 (multiplicative), giving forecasts of 162.61 and 161.87, respectively.

10.2 (a) A declining trend and pronounced seasonal variation is apparent. Consumption is highest in the winter quarter.

(b) The regression equation is $Y = 91.06 - 1.055\,t$. ($R^2 = 0.14$). The standard error on the trend is 0.71. This is not significant. The trend could be due to conservation measures or lower output.

(c) Seasonal factors are 14.4, −7.29, −15.76, 8.65 for the four quarters, respectively. These obviously follow the seasonal variation in temperature.

(d) The seasonally adjusted series obviously smoothes most of the short-term fluctuations in the original series.

(e) For $t = 17$ the forecast is $91.06 - 1.055 \times 17 + 14.4 = 87.525$ (actual result was 91.2).

(f) $Y = 98.1 - 0.895\,t + 6.24\,Z_{1t} - 15.62\,Z_{2t} - 24.25\,Z_{3t}$
s.e. $\quad\quad (0.15) \quad (1.99) \quad\quad (1.97) \quad\quad (1.95)$
$R^2 = 0.97$. Dummies are for quarters I to III.

(g) The estimate of the trend is much more precise (see standard error) now the seasonal effects are taken care of. It is highly significant.

(h) All the seasonal effects are significant.

(i) The prediction is $98.1 - 0.895 \times 17 + 6.24 = 89.125$.

10.3 (a) There has been a declining trend, possibly as people find other leisure pursuits. Obviously a seasonal effect since it is not played in summer. Attendances also probably respond to temperature.

(b) Probably little trend in real terms (despite what the firm hopes!). Possibly a large random component.

(c) Varies with the tourist season. Possibly a rising trend as people obtain more leisure time. In winter there might be a daily fluctuation with more visitors at the weekends.

(d) Probably an upward trend, with a fluctuation at weekends.

10.4 (a) $C = -15787 + 1.266\,Y$
s.e. $\quad\quad\quad\quad (0.27)$
$R^2 = 0.55 \quad n = 20$

The equation does not appear very satisfactory. The marginal propensity to consume is 1.266, i.e. a £1 increase in income leads to a £1.266 increase in consumption. That is the road to ruin! Despite the significance of the results, the equation does not seem to satisfactorily explain consumption behaviour.

(b) Graphing the data reveals a strong seasonal pattern to the data, especially consumption, with a strong rise in every fourth quarter (guess why).

(c) A regression with seasonal dummies yields:
$Y = 998.92 + 0.88\,Y - 2231.6\,D_1 - 2163.1\,D_2 - 1170.8\,D_3$
s.e. $\quad\quad\quad\quad (0.19) \quad (490.1) \quad\quad (486.1) \quad\quad (465.4)$
$R^2 = 0.83 \quad n = 20$

This appears much better. The marginal propensity to consume now takes on a reasonable value, 0.88, and its standard error is also reduced quite substantially. Effectively, some of the variation in C

has been eliminated by the use of the dummies, allowing the marginal propensity to consume to be more precisely estimated. All the dummies are significant, implying that the fourth quarter (the base period) is different from the other three.

Index

moving average method, 232–5
multicollinearity, 225
multiplication rule, 68–70
multistage sampling, 163
mutually exclusive events, 64

non-linear transformations, 212–16
non-parametric methods, 119
Normal distribution, 86–9
null hypothesis, 135

ogive, 13
omitted variable bias, 224–5
outcome of an experiment,
    64

Paasche index
    price, 38–9
    quantity, 44
percentiles, 26
permutations, 71
point estimate, 107–8
Poisson distribution, 99–100
pooled variance, 122
population parameter,
    in estimation, 107
    in regression, 203
posterior probability, 74
power, 134
precision, 109–110
prediction, 210–12
prior probabilities, 74
probability of an event
    frequentist view, 62–3
    subjective view, 63–4

quantity indices
    Laspeyres, 43
    Paasche, 44
quartiles, 26
quintiles, 26
quota sampling, 163–4

R^2, 204–9
random component,
    in time series, 232
random sampling
    cluster, 162
    defined, 157
    multistage, 163
    quota, 163

simple, 159–60
    stratified, 160–2
random variables, 81–2
range, 26
rank correlation coefficient, 196–8
reference year, 34
rejection region, 137
relative frequency distribution, 13
residual, in regression, 199
retail price index, 49–50
rounding, 26

sample size, 124
sample space, 64
sampling, see random sampling
sampling frame, 164–5
seasonal adjustment, 239
seasonal component, 232
seasonal factors, 235–8
semi-interquartile range, 26
semolina, 1
sigma notation, 30–2
significance level, 136–7
simultaneity, in regression, 225–6
standard deviation
    of sample, 24
standard error,
    of sample mean, 95, 115
    of sample proportion, 115
    of regression coefficients, 208
standard Normal distribution, 89–92
Student's distribution, see *t* distribution

t distribution, 119–120
tree diagrams, 70–1
trend, in time series, 232
trial, 65
type I error, 130
type II error, 130

units of measurement
    in price indices, 40
    in regression, 216–17

value indices, 46
variance, 23
variance operator, 102–3

z-score,
    defined, 25
    in hypothesis tests, 137